Thinking about change

D1289765

Thinking about change

ESSAYS EDITED BY DAVID P. SHUGARMAN
for the University League for Social Reform

UNIVERSITY OF TORONTO PRESS
Toronto / Buffalo

© University of Toronto Press 1974
Toronto and Buffalo
Printed in Canada
ISBN 0-8020-2169-7 (cloth)
ISBN 0-8020-6251-2 (paper)
LC 74-82285

Publication of this work
has been assisted by the block grant program
of the Canada Council.

Contents

Preface

This book grew out of a series of seminars prepared under the direction of the editor as a project of the University League for Social Reform. All but two of these essays were written specifically for the project. 'Marx on human emancipation,' by Bentley Le Baron, was first published in the *Canadian Journal of Political Science* in 1971. 'The false imperatives of technology,' by William Leiss, is a revised version of his article published as 'The social consequences of technological progress: critical comments on recent theories' in *Canadian Public Administration* in 1970.

Though this collection may differ somewhat in style, temper, and substance from previous ULSR volumes, it is, nevertheless, in many ways complementary to its predecessors. It aims to carry forward what Northrop Frye in his foreword to *The Prospect of Change* characterized as an attempt 'to re-examine the myths which make up our customary vision of life.'

Over the three-year gestation of this book, many of the authors contributed to strengthening each other's presentations. In addition, a number of others were kind enough to devote time and attention to criticism of various papers. In this regard I want to thank Harold Kaplan, Michael Goldrick, David Bell, Dale Posgate, Michael Stevenson, Robert Drummond, and George Szablowski, all of York University, and Gad Horowitz of the University of Toronto.

The executive of the ULSR encouraged the project from start to finish. Thanks here go to Abraham Rotstein, Stephen Clarkson, Eilert Frerichs, Larry Higgins, James St John, and Alan Powell. Professors Rotstein and

Clarkson were particularly generous in offering suggestions based on their experiences as past editors of ULSR volumes.

Jack Layton served as a first-rate editorial assistant when things got particularly hectic. Gloria Hiscock and Kathy Wilson were especially helpful in typing various portions of the manuscript.

A special acknowledgement is due Alkis Kontos, Michael Stevenson, and Laurel Douglas Shugarman, three close friends who refused to let their affection for me prevent them from subjecting an earlier draft of my introduction to substantial criticism. I am also grateful to my friend Kenneth Gibson for drawing my attention to some infelicitous phraseology.

Thanks to Patricia Lagacé and Rik Davidson of University of Toronto Press, I am now in a position to appreciate the talents of a demanding and excellent Editorial Department.

DAVID P. SHUGARMAN

Thinking about change

David P. Shugarman

Introduction: changing our assumptions about change

There are big changes for you but you will be happy.

CHINESE FORTUNE COOKIE

DEFICIENCIES IN THE STUDY OF CHANGE

By the use of a simple negative conjunction – but – the message in the fortune cookie challenges one of the central assumptions of our modern society: that things continually change and, willy nilly, they change for the better. The notion that the world is in a perpetual state of flux goes back at least as far as Heraclitus (500 BC). The notion that that flux is, *ipso facto*, good for man is less ancient.

It has become all too common to identify change, especially technological change, with social progress. Too often, what it is that is or needs changing is left unspecified. In such circumstances almost every 'new' feature of modern industrial society, from the yearly introduction of new models off the automobile assembly lines to fancy packaging and more sophisticated and scientific methods of social manipulation, is treated as falling under the rubric of social change.

The messages in this book are that we ought to be a good deal more cautious about using the term 'social change'; that many so-called changes have little or no impact on existing social relationships and practices; that not all social change is good; that certain changes that *would* contribute beneficially and materially to social life are not easy to bring about, given the prevailing framework of power and ideology; furthermore, that efforts to incorporate new designs, techniques, and programs ostensibly justified in so far as they are to bring about a re-ordering of social priorities – exemplified by phrases like, the just society, the technological society, participatory democracy, or simply, social change – often conceal the machinations of the established order.[1]

There is certainly no dearth of material on social change. Books and studies abound. But contemporary analysis of social change has for the most part been sociological. This is not to denigrate sociology. It is rather to acknowledge that the sociological study of change – particularly as it has been propagated in American academia and influenced by its American practitioners – has tended to adopt an anti-historical bias[2] along with a mistrust of philosophy.[3] Indeed, contemporary social science in general has tended to either shy away from epistemological questions or treat philosophical problems as methodological problems.[4]

IDEOLOGICAL ORIENTATIONS

Contemporary perspectives on social change have retained considerable affinities with mid-nineteenth century English thought. Englishmen at that time 'were acutely conscious of living in an age of transition. They were always talking about it as such.'[5] 'Even,' notes Phyllis Deane, 'those who criticized the horrors of industrialism took an optimistic view of the transition. They were immensely impressed by the sheer magnitude of their achievement — bigger populations, longer lines of railway, more tons of coal, more blast-furnaces, more exports, etc. It was an industrial achievement which compared favourably with that of any other nation in the contemporary world and it is perhaps not surprising that they overrated the significance of their material progress. Some of them saw the railways as an instrument of moral and intellectual progress, and associated industrial progress with the end of war.'[6] Now it may well be understandable that the Victorians overrated the significance of material progress, but it is surely curious that so many of our social scientists and leaders should continue to do so. And yet, if for railways we substitute, say, space travel or cybernetics, that is precisely what is done. It requires no quantum leap to follow the line of thought that runs from John Stuart Mill to Pierre Elliott Trudeau. For Mill the achievements of the industrial revolution provided for a new environment such 'that human beings are no longer born to their place in life ... but are free to employ their faculties and such favourable chances as offer, to achieve the lot which may appear to them most desirable.'[7] In Trudeau's estimation, 'the many techniques of cybernetics, by transforming the control function and the manipulation of information, will transform our whole society. With this knowledge, we are wide awake, alert, capable of action; no longer are we blind, inert pawns of fate.'[8] Mill's was the voice of industrial liberalism, Trudeau's is the voice of technological liberalism.

It is sometimes difficult to fully appreciate the extent to which contemporary analysis and expectations of social change are seen through liberal spectacles. However much our understanding of modern society has changed over the past two centuries that understanding has largely been enveloped by the parameters of liberalism. Indeed, with exceptions here and there, modern social science has largely consisted in the modification and development of liberal perspectives: the concept of rational man as a calculating, maximizing consumer and appropriator who submits decisions about how to invest his time to cost-benefit analysis, the ideal of freedom *in* the marketplace, the belief in the benevolent, if sometimes latent, social consequences of self-interest and competition, the view that what is good for the economy is good for society, the belief in material progress through the domination of nature.

I earlier referred to certain nineteenth-century tendencies and assumptions that have dominated the contemporary study of social change. In some respects, however, the study of change has moved away from its earlier moorings. As Wayne Hield puts it, 'One of the most significant changes in the social sciences today is the way the subject of "social change" [has been] redefined for investigation.'[9] Whereas social scientists in the eighteenth and nineteenth centuries conceived of 'social change' as inextricably bound up with the 'problem of how to mould a society characterized by rational order and progress for all,' contemporary social scientists have tended to focus their attention on "the reverse emphasis of how to help man successfully adjust to the existing social and political order.'[10] In short, analyses of change have regressed to an obsessional interest in a Hobbesian research program: delineating the attributes of a stable order, ascertaining the institutional and socio-psychological requisites of social control. Given this kind of perspective, 'it becomes the task of the social scientist to investigate means of maintaining control or reducing tensions or conflicts to restore a condition of harmony and equilibrium.'[11] This change in emphasis is important and perfectly understandable. The dominant concerns of liberal society and liberal social theory in the last century were to see removed the last remnants of the older, pre-industrial, order. In the twentieth century, liberals, at least since 1917 and certainly since the Second World War, have been concerned with consolidating their gains and maintaining the central features of their society. The philosophical radicalism of the nineteenth century has become the ideological pragmatism of the twentieth. Neither has proved benign.

Even when there is no apparent bias in favour of maintaining the status quo there has been an overemphasis on 'adjustment.' Here is a good example: 'The rate of change is unlikely to slow down in the near future, and so people have to find a way of adjusting themselves to what is happening ... government will have to do more and more to make adjustment to change possible.'[12] 'Adjustment' denotes regulation, arrangement, harmonization, and conformity. It connotes reactivity on the part of decision-makers; and with respect to the dynamics of change itself, passivity on the part of man.

If change is generally viewed as coming about in a 'gradual, adjustive fashion, and not in a revolutionary way'[13] this may have considerable implications for practical social policy. For how we perceive reality – and the place of change as a constituent of that reality – affects our estimation of what it makes sense to do. In sum, our conception of reality influences our conception of rationality, just as our conception of what constitutes the rational influences our ideas as to what constitutes reality. For instance, Robert Dahl and Charles Lindblom refer to the process of change as a 'patching' job: 'The ultimate result of "patching" is a transformation of the social system. Capitalism was only a series of patches on feudalism.'[14] Thus, for Dahl and Lindblom, 'patching up an old system is the most rational way to change it, for the patch constitutes about as big a change as one can comprehend at a time.' (The question of who that 'one' is who is doing the comprehending is of no small importance, I submit.) Given this 'patching' perspective it is not at all surprising that Dahl and Lindblom should recommend a pragmatic, incrementalist approach to planning and social change.

As another example, if one is persuaded by Daniel Bell's view that 'perhaps the most important social change of our time is the emergence of a process of direct and deliberate contrivance of change itself' and that 'men now seek to anticipate change, measure the course of its direction and its impact, control it, and even shape it for predetermined ends,' then it makes sense to focus attention on the process of political decision-making. If one is also a liberal technocrat, as Bell is, then the recommended procedure for implementing change is to have technocrats and politicians 'interplay with each other.'[15]

There are a number of difficulties associated with the perspectives outlined above. For one thing, 'patching' up an old system may not be the most rational way to change it for the very good reason that the patch may not change anything. It may rather hide those things that require change. Or it may simply cover superficial problems by 'trying to patch up symptoms without touching the causes.'[16] In addition, this piecemeal social engineering approach to change may betray a lack of imagination or conviction, or both, in dealing with the removal of social ills. This approach also assumes what is most certainly a moot issue in the analysis of social change, namely, that it is possible to change one significant feature of a society without changing others at the same time.

Bell's reference to 'the deliberate contrivance of change' begs the question of who is to do the contriving in whose interests? His view that technologists and politicians will together function as the leading lights is hardly encouraging since, at present, the functioning of these roles represents an important part of the problem of modern society. Bell's belief in the benevolent and rational orientation of the technologically oriented intellectual too easily passes over the objection that these may be 'the least suitable people for redirecting Technology because their thinking has been more corrupted by the concept of Technology as Power than the thinking of other people.'[17]

The emphasis on rational decision-making obscures the fact that 'social change is not only a matter of the taking of a series of discrete and distinguishable decisions'[18] — or patches. It is just as important to recognize that there is such a thing as 'slow, non-deliberate, unforeseen, and unintended change.'[19] And this sort of change may often entail the domination and social control of the majority by those who are at the top of the structure of power. That structure of power may very well be 'invisible' or at least hidden from view amidst a web of social and economic relationships. Certain decisions may not even arise if it is in the interests of those with power to render particular issues outside the pale of legitimacy. Such 'non-decisions' might be 'taken' habitually or unconsciously.[20]

The ubiquitous nature of social control and conformity to certain norms and patterns of behaviour is one of the features of present-day society. This is what Marcuse has called one-dimensionality.[21] What appear at first glance to be instances of a radical change in life styles are, on reflection, examples of the way in which established norms, in the sense of overriding values and habits, subsume, redirect, and co-opt unconventional behaviour. Much has been made, for instance, of the new sexual permissiveness. Undoubtedly there has been a liberalization in sexual attitudes and practices. But so far this has been generally a liberalization of the bourgeoisie for the bourgeoisie by the bourgeoisie. The recent phenomenon of mate-swapping by middle-class American suburbanites 'resembles,' says Paul Delaney, 'America's other great weekend sport, football, in being a display of instinctual physicality confined by formal and compulsive rules.'[22] The swappers go to great lengths to prevent their promiscuity from interfering with normal routine at home and at work. And sex is separated from intimacy. As Delaney puts it, this activity 'represent[s] capitalist values carried to their logical extreme.' The swappers

non-sexual life is not eroticised, but rather the contrary, for in their obsession with secrecy they do their best to blend inconspicuously into a conventional and conservative suburban milieu. By requiring that their sexual partners be as numerous and as homogeneous as possible they create a system devoted to the ultimate consumption fetish: each weekend you trade in your old lover, in exchange for a new model that differs in no significant way from the old one. Their avoidance of intimacy guarantees that none need suffer jealousy or other tensions; but it ensures, also, that they need make no real change in traditional sex roles or in other styles of relationship. In fact, organized swapping seems positively to reinforce the status quo in both the lesser system of the nuclear family, and the larger one of post-industrial capitalism.[23]

Far from transforming ideas and social relations then, certain types of behavioural change may leave the material and ideological foundations of social order not only intact but strengthened, at least in the short run.

By focusing attention on only certain aspects of society we may misperceive, assume too much about, the extent to which particular changes affect other aspects. We know for example, that political changes – even of the most dramatic kind – may not always give rise to social change. C.E. Black has made the point abundantly clear in his discussion of *The Dynamics of Modernization:*

If the consolidation of modernizing leadership is a period of dramatic political change – of coups, revolutions, and wars of national liberation and unification – it is nevertheless one of relatively superficial developments that affect the nationality, citizenship, and legal status of the average person more than they affect his daily life. Empires have come and gone for centuries with relatively little effect on the personal affairs of the great majority of their peoples ... Economic and social transformation, on the other hand, is less dramatic but much more profound. The change in values and way of life of the average person in the more advanced countries has been greater between the mid-nineteenth and mid-twentieth centuries than between ancient Mesopotamia, Egypt, or China and the early modern period. This has been a period of transformation in all realms of human activity that is unprecedented in history.[24]

We also know that even when there is a correspondence between political and socio-economic change the relationship may involve a time lag of varying proportions. It took over ten years and three elections in Quebec before the social and economic repercussions of the Asbestos strikes were translated into political change. It took slightly more than twenty years before the Quebec party system was transformed in a way that began to reflect the social and economic transformations that were involved in a move from an agrarian, traditional, politically quiescent society to a liberal, increasingly bureaucratic and industrial, actively nationalistic society. Clearly, if we consider the number of years it took before liberal societies turned into liberal democracies the time lag between socio-economic change and political change appears to be getting considerably shorter.

How then, can we see change? And furthermore, how can we distinguish among different kinds of change? At the most basic level social change implies a substantial alteration in the way people live. It means that sets of habits, practices, social relationships, attitudes, and beliefs are replaced by other sets. These new sets do not fall out of the sky. They are always in some sense modifications, or developments of pre-existing ideas and practices. Such developments or modifications are not necessarily linear, irreversible, or inevitable.

Two polar types of change can be conceptualized. What is involved is a distinction between changes *within* a given structure, framework, or pattern of behaviour and change *of* the structure. In the language of systems analysis we are herein drawing a dichotomy between systemic change and changes in sub-systems or within sub-systems. We are talking about total change and partial change.[25] An attempt to wrestle with these different conceptualizations is thematic in a number of the papers in this volume, although by no means are all the contributors at one in subscribing to it.[26]

For Robert Nisbet, distinguishing between these two types of change 'must be the beginning of any valid theory of social change.'[27] And S.D. Clark, as well, holds that these two categories of change 'should be kept clearly distinct.'[28] But Clark also notes that choosing to study these different changes is not a matter of tossing coins. For our analytic procedures reflect a prior ontological commitment. 'The structure of a society ... can be analyzed as a social system or social order. But so as well can it be analyzed as a society undergoing change ... However, the moment interest shifts from the analysis of the society as a social order to its analysis as a society changing in character, what comes to be talked about is not "change within the system" but "change of the system." '[29] Nisbet implies that the type of change that is taking place is an empirical question. I think Nisbet is quite wrong about this; for as Clark notes, 'with reference to any particular situation of change, it is simply not possible to make any valid empirical distinction between change of the system and change within the system. The same order of facts can be taken care of within the one framework as the other.'[30] Whether we concentrate on the parts, that is, the subsystems, or the whole, is not ultimately an empirical question. It is a question that rests on philosophical judgment. And − not to extend the *petitio principii* too much further − this entails, at the least, conceptual clarification and re-examination, an understanding of the relation between history and theory, and an appreciation of the empirical − all tempered with a vision of the ideal.

So long as power is unevenly distributed, not every member of a society will experience the same sets of change nor will everyone be equally affected by the same changes. Students of the industrial revolution have recently been reminded of what Marx and Engels documented over a hundred years ago: the sweep of events had profoundly different implications for different people, depending upon their place in the English class structure. The aristocracy and gentry were 'little affected by industrialization, except for the better.' Their social importance and political power remained largely intact. For the merchants and financiers associated with overseas trade, 'which was the basis of British eighteenth century power,' E.J. Hobsbawm notes, 'the Industrial Revolution brought no major transformations.' Most of the middle class did experience a fundamental change in their lives. But unlike the labouring poor, that is, the majority of Britons, the bourgeoisie did not suffer a fundamental *disorganization* of their lives. The industrial city, the factory, and the new bourgeois determination of work destroyed the traditional way of life of the majority.[31]

It would seem redundant to call attention to the importance of an analysis of classes for an understanding of social change. And yet if we turn, for instance, to Canadian social history it is apparent that historians have been remiss in their duties. With a few exceptions, 'Canadian history has tended to be written as if social classes were something almost which did not exist.' This is one of the reasons why our new 'revisionists' have begun to fill a lacuna in Canadian studies. One of the hallmarks of this new history consists in the elaboration of the significance of contradictions within the development of Canadian capitalism: contradictions between the industrial and mercantile (or commercial) sectors of business. It is these contradictions, according to Naylor and Teeple, which help explain Canada's colonial dependence on the United States on the one hand and retardation in the development of the Canadian working class on the other.[32]

CONTRADICTIONS, HUMAN NATURE, AND SOCIETY

The notion of 'contradictions' has been a major conceptual component of critical theory since Marx. Put simply, and crudely, the theory is that the loci of social dynamics are found in contradictions in social life and man's attempts to resolve them. The analysis of contradictions is an important feature in several of the papers in this volume, though, as will become obvious, there is a good deal of disagreement among our authors as to the utility of the Marxian use of the term. According to Marx the requirements of capitalist production were at odds with and undermined – contradicted – the requirements of a humane and rational social order. Man's attempt to express his social being, his humanity, was blunted; he was enchained by a nexus of power relationships. It was Marx's view that capitalism would not be able to withstand man's claim to freedom.

The Marxian analysis of change is interesting and provocative, for Marx believed that change of the structure of society could take place through reform or revolutionary measures. The basic possibility of social emancipation lay 'in the formation of a class with *radical chains,* a class in civil society that is not of civil society, a class that is the dissolution of all classes ...'[33] That dissolution, according to Marx, 'will take a form more brutal or more humane, according to the degree of development of the working-class itself.'[34] Furthermore, said Marx, 'we know that institutions, manners and customs of the various countries must be considered, and we do not deny that there are countries, like England and America ... where the worker may attain his object by peaceful means.'[35]

In short, the Marxian view seems to entertain contradictory strategies. In fact, socialists never have been able to agree on strategies. If one theorizes that significant change – and here the criterion and measure of significance become crucial – can be brought about only by a change of the total system, then the strategy of change prescribed may be radically different from a strategy that is consistent with attempting change within the given system.

Reformers tend to play by the rules of the system in order to bring about changes in sub-systems. If the reformer is ultimately concerned with bringing about radical changes he has to assume both an organic and functional view of change: (1) any social system has immanent potentialities for change, (2) the 'parts,' sub-systems of a society are interrelated: a change in one part affects the others.

Revolutionaires tend to challenge the rules. The rules (laws, norms, conventions) of a system *are* functional – they maintain the system. Thus, from a revolutionary perspective it may be argued that if you play by the rules you will either lose, since the rules are stacked against change on the side of those with vested interests, or if successful you will merely *improve* the functioning of the system. Ergo, the following strategy: to bring about systemic change it is necessary to play by rules which negate and contradict those in practice.

Ultimately, however, the question of strategy was irrelevant to Marx's view of change. One way or another, capitalism was doomed. Capitalist society would 'burst asunder' as a result of the contradictions of its own making, the claim to freedom would be realized, and the history of man as a fully social being could then begin.

It is precisely the end result of this scenario that Sigmund Freud's theory of human nature appears to deny. According to Freud, if the claim to freedom were ever completely satisfied there would be no new social history to write, because no society could exist in such circumstances. Man was a creature whose instinctual endowments included 'a powerful share of aggressiveness.' Freud's view of human nature was summed up in a phrase: *Homo homini lupus* – Man is a wolf to man. From this point of view there is indeed a contradiction between man's search for freedom (and happiness) and the requirements of society – any society. But the contradiction can never be resolved; at best there is a frustrated trade-off: a portion of security in society for a portion of the possibilities of happiness.[36]

Obviously, then, the question of what constitutes man's humanity is a major ingredient of any theory of social change. The positions of Marx and Freud in this respect have often been taken as essentially antithetical to each other. It is appropriate, therefore, that the first two chapters of our book are devoted to an elaboration of Freudian and Marxian categories. The third chapter offers the reader a clear exposition of the major attempt to synthesize the insights of Freud and Marx.

The reader at this point may well wonder what all this has to do with social change in Canada. It is worth pointing out that Canada is a society driven by the performance principle, where the liberation of sensual gratification is suppressed, repressed, and subordinated to the production of more and more goods and services for profit; a society which still adheres to the mythology of possessive individualism, where the essence of freedom is construed to be the individual right to infinite appropriation and where the social consequences of the marketplace, at times anarchic, at times manipulated, are perceived as constituting the best approximation to justice. These features are hardly *unique* to Canadian society. While one should never dismiss the omnipresent reality of Canada's colonial status, it would be a mistake to become parochially obsessed with Canadian uniqueness. In such circumstances the legacies of Marx and Freud are as relevant to Canada as 'relevant' can be.

Mildred Bakan's opening chapter consists of an exploration in philosophical social biology. She suggests that a re-interpretation of a key feature of Freud's thought is in order. Bakan is concerned with the implications for social change that may stem from the contradictions between thought and body. It is her view that there is a disjunction between our publicly accepted verbal language and our body language; between words and feelings, behaviour and action, criticality and sensuality, with the result that the full flowering of humanity is unnecessarily frustrated.

Bentley Le Baron's exegesis of Marx focuses attention on the necessary relation between transformation of human nature and transformation of society. An excellent feature of Le Baron's argument is his admonition to the left to beware of adopting a 'holier than thou' stance. There has been a misplaced tendency, notes Le Baron, to categorize the class struggle 'too narrowly as violent confrontation between "us and them," ' whereas the Marxian notion of human emancipation also involves 'us versus ourselves ... of beginning to be new people, creating new kinds of social relations.'

Alkis Kontos then goes on to examine the contradictions inherent in the prevailing mental and material dimensions of life, between consciousness and social activity, between the realm of necessity and the realm of freedom, between 'poetic vision' and the all-too-real, between memory and dream. In his attention to the crucial significance of human essence and imagination in social philosophy Kontos contributes to our understanding of social change. His most important contribution may lie in providing us with an authoritative appreciation of Herbert Marcuse, perhaps the most important thinker of the twentieth century. Partly due to ideological reasons (left, right, and centre), and partly due to the complexities of his own formulations, Marcuse has been subjected to distortion and misunderstanding. Through an unorthodox fusion of Marx and Freud he has hypothesized the desirability and feasibility of a civilization without surplus repression, especially one without capitalism and the work ethic. That hypothesis has been met with incomprehension and hostility by those who are incapable of envisioning any satisfactory society other than the one we now have. Marcuse has also argued that modern industrial societies have become so totally pervasive in terms of domination and socialization that change of the system from within the system through the traditional Marxian vehicle of the proletariat is improbable in the short run and by no means inevitable in the long run. Given the convictions of 'orthodox' Marxian social science this is tantamount to pointing out that the Emperor's pants have fallen off.

From a perspective which holds that the 'ultimate presuppositions' upon which modern philosophy bases its notion of the goodness of society are tenụous,[37] Barry Cooper offers an analysis of the FLQ crisis of October 1970. His analysis rests on a particular appreciation of classical presuppositions. In Cooper's judgment, 'classical political science provides not only a non-modern view of politics, but ... a more intelligible one.' According to Cooper, an understanding of the crisis through the categories of classical thought indicates that *both* the FLQ and the government displayed an unconscionable ignorance of the requirements of political action; for both parties to the crisis, Cooper maintains, operated on 'distinctly non-political premises.' Given such premises, he argues, it is impossible to distinguish between persuasion based on reason and persuasion based on force; and equally impossible to locate a ground for the condemnation of violence in the pursuit of social change.

Melvyn Hill's paper, in contrast, presupposes the modern distinction between civil society and the state. It is Hill's contention that we can learn much from the contradictory interpretations of revolution and society offered by Burke, de Tocqueville, Rousseau and Marx. In this sense, of course, Hill's use of 'contradiction' follows the conventional meaning, rather than the usage adopted in critical theory. In fact, Hill argues that Marx's theory of change — whereby contradictions account for an inevitable transformation of society and politics throughout history — is inferior to de Tocqueville's 'theory of institutional viability.' In the assessment of revolutionary potential it is, according to Hill, de Tocqueville's analysis that offers the better paradigm of change. In the process, Hill presents a strong case that ideological movements are not likely to represent a very solid base for social change.

The next two papers by Leiss and Adelman direct attention to some of the problems associated with technological determinism. There has been a marked tendency in contemporary social theory to treat technology as an independent variable of change, the determining cause, or, as one writer has put it, 'the exogenous prime mover of social change.'[38] Even some of the most sensitive critics of technological development, those least sanguine about technological 'progress,' seem to fall into the trap of technological determinism.[39]

Leiss exposes a number of serious difficulties in the outlook of technological determinists. He notes that theories of change embedded in such a perspective fail to account for the possible contradictions that may ensue from a conception of the rationality of the whole of society as against a conception of the rationality of a part of society. Explanations of change which take technological determinism as their point of departure assume too much on the one hand and leave too much unanswered on the other, with the result that, in Leiss' words, 'both the general dynamic of advanced societies and the specific role of technology in that dynamic' remain obscure.

Adelman's debunking of the idea of youth as a revolutionary new social class reveals the extent to which technological explanations can lead us astray. 'It is,' says Adelman, 'as if the concept "technology" has become for our contemporary North American thinkers what the concept "nature" was for seventeenth century Europeans. Technology has become divine ... the key to the root of all good and all evil.'

The last group of essays deals more specifically with 'the particular' in our study of change. The particular is Canada.

A good deal has changed in Canada – at least in the climate of opinion – since the first University League for Social Reform publication in 1965, wherein Mel Watkins argued that Canada should 'abandon economic national-ism as a policy,' an 'irrelevant and outmoded' policy.[40] The same year saw the publication of George Grant's lament for a nation, which, with the blessings of its elites, appeared destined to be absorbed by the United States.[41] Today most Canadians have become sensitized to the Americanization issue and are of the opinion that some form of economic nationalism is necessary to resist further American control of the economy. That sensitivity has been extended to the political and cultural areas of social life and has been reflected in numerous reports and task forces at both levels of government. There have been some other changes as well. For instance, since 1965, the year John Porter's *Vertical Mosaic*[42] documented the extent of inequalities in wealth and power in Canada, Canada has become an even more unequal nation. People at the top end of the income scales (when measured in quintiles and whether or not the measure is of families or individuals) have increased their share of the national income at the expense of those at the bottom end of the scales. In short, from 1965 to 1971 the rich got richer while the poor got poorer. But that's not the sort of tune one feels like humming; nor is it the song most of our politicians are wont to sing. As one editorial writer put it, Canada's income distribution tables 'look more appropriate to a feudal oil sheikdom than to a progressive democracy.' Other features of Canadian society have been pretty well unaltered. We are still very much an economic-ally dependent, class-based, corporate, work-oriented, capitalist, elitist society. Frank Underhill once remarked that Canadian public policy developing out of Confederation was based 'on a triple alliance of federal government, Conservative party, and big-business interests: government of the people, by lawyers, for big business.'[43] Parties, it would seem, come and go, while the structure of power retains a certain identity.[44] Such are the quandaries for those who seek not only to interpret Canadian society but to change it.

Donald Willmott adopts a radical humanist perspective in his analysis of interest groups and their impact on Canadian society. Radical humanism, as expressed by Christian Bay, has a 'normative emphasis' which points in the direction of the achievement of 'optimal human rights as the legitimate aim of politics.'[45] In Canada the radical humanist, argues Willmott, has little reason to be overly optimistic about short-run probabilities, and is continually faced with the dilemmas involved in setting priorities that can mesh with practical politics. Willmott notes, for instance, that 'the predominant role of existing voluntary associations in the political process is to protect the interests of the already privileged groups and therefore to prevent basic change.' He suggests that a partial answer to effecting social change in Canada lies in supporting the 'citizen participation' movement.

James St John attempts to provide the notion of participation with a concrete application to a coherent strategy on the left. St John challenges the conventional wisdom that the dilemmas of leftist attempts to bring about social change are inevitably beset by the contradictions of movement and party. It is St John's view that such contradictions are not insoluble. To the extent that there are difficulties associated with leftist strategy in Canada they can, he argues, be reasonably resolved in the form of a movement party. He holds that electoral activity must go hand-in-hand with extra-parliamentary activity. In a sense, St John's emphasis on a movement party which would provide practical opportunity to 'live the revolution' has parallels with Le Baron's earlier discussion.

Joan Williams turns our attention to an analysis of change at the local level. Williams shows that there are some large obstacles in the path of reorienting legal services to an advocacy on behalf of the less privileged. Here the issue is a sense of legal professionalism which is held to be contradictory to the attempt to alter community power relations. It is, I think, worth pointing out in this respect that just prior to the 1973 academic term a proposed radical law program at l'Université du Québec à Montréal was refused implementation by the University's Board of Directors. The Board was supported by the ministry of education and the Quebec Bar Association.[46] The program was designed 'Former des avocats qui soient au service de toute la population et non seulement au service de la classe dirigeante.' According to the Quebec minister of education the proposed program was too 'revolutionary' and 'Marxist in tone,' and was not in keeping with the general objectives of a legal education.

Gerry Hunnius' chapter provides a summary of the way the game of parliamentary democracy is played in Canada. He comes to the conclusion that the rules appropriate to that game are in contradiction to the rules necessary to make a thoroughgoing participatory democracy function. His essay presents a trenchant critique of liberal democracy and electoral politics which includes a discussion of the strategies required to overcome barriers to 'a politics of self-government,' a politics which, says Hunnius, 'must permeate every institution and organization in society.'

BEYOND LIBERALISM

In one of his less optimistic moments Mill reflected that although there seemed to be all kinds of gradual improvements in his generation's approach to problems, 'as to the means of curing or even alleviating great social evils people are as much at sea as they were before.'[47] What Mill and the dominant class of his time could not do was extricate themselves from the sea of liberalism. Over a hundred years later our society is still floundering in that sea.

Sensitive liberals have always been a bit schizophrenic. In entertaining the notion of a stationary state Mill had to 'confess' that he was 'not charmed with the ideal of life held out by those who think that the normal state of human beings is that of struggling to get on; that the trampling, crushing, elbowing, and treading on each others' heels, which form the existing type of social life, are the most desirable lot of human kind, or anything but the disagreable symptoms of one of the phases of industrial progress ... But the best state for human nature is that in which, while no one is poor, no one desires to be richer, nor has any reason to fear being thrust back by the efforts of others to push themselves forward.'[48] And Keynes some eighty years later echoed the same sentiments when he spoke of some day being able 'to discard' capitalist principles in order 'once more' to 'value ends above means and prefer the good to the useful ... to honour those who can teach us how to pluck the hour and the day virtuously and well, the delightful people who are capable of taking direct enjoyment in things, the lilies of the field who toil not, neither do they spin.'[49] And occasionally today we can hear Trudeau speak of the end of the work ethic and the coming of a leisure society.[50] But the time to reckon with the twisted values and practices of our brutalizing social system is always set somewhere off in the future. Surely, as C.B. Macpherson has argued, the time has come to scrap our inherited bourgeois concepts of freedom and man and our institutions of greed.[51]

It is, I think, obvious that we require a new self-definition that will be compatible with the evolution of 'a different foundation for technological society.'[52] The crunch comes, of course, when we try to ascertain what that new foundation entails. Taylor has speculated that we might move to something like 'a dialogue society,' or perhaps a society 'dominated by ... a contemplative aspiration.'[53] Marcuse has envisioned the possibility of a society of play. However other-worldly such speculative futures may appear they seem a good deal more attractive and practical than the notion of, say, twenty million Canadians laboriously cooperating according to the thoughts of Chairman Mao. The Soviet Union's Stalinist mode of repression and intolerance also provides no model.

How we are to achieve a new society raises yet another complicated issue. There was a time when this issue could only be discussed after weighing sides in the philosophical controversy over idealism versus materialism and entering the lists on behalf of either Marx or Weber. That debate has largely been a false one. Neither was the vulgarizer his disciples have made him out to be. It is not necessary to agree with either the view that ideas are precursory to advances in a material civilization, or the view that our thoughts are simply rationalizations of material conditions in order to appreciate the truth that changes in consciousness are integral to changes in society. We have a good deal to learn from the dictum that when our concepts change, 'our concept of the world has changed too.'[54] Perhaps most pertinent of all in this respect is the claim that repressive structures '... can be brought down only by those who still sustain the established work process, who constitute its human base, who reproduce its profits and its power ... To prepare the ground for this development makes the emancipation of *consciousness* still the primary task. Without it, all emancipation of the senses, all radical activism, remains blind, self-defeating. Political practice still depends on theory (only the Establishment can dispense with it!): on education, persuasion – on Reason.'[55] And not just anybody's. Today what passes for political education is frequently elitist propaganda, or at best training and socialization in the dominant norms of the dominant social class. Our teachings should be aimed 'to encourage dissatisfaction about rights poorly achieved, not satisfaction with largely illusory qualities of a political system.'[56] It is not just education, but a *radical* political education that is necessary (which is not to say, sufficient). Naturally this raises the question of who will educate the educators. Here Le Baron's reminder that revolutionary self-change must accompany revolutionary social change – there must be a praxis – is crucial. Social change is not the prerogative of any one class or group or individual. It involves all of us. And if we are concerned to move in the direction of a more humane and rational society it is worth emphasizing that, as Peter Winch puts it: 'We must, if you like, be open to new possibilities of what could be invoked and accepted under the rubric of "rationality" — possibilities which are perhaps suggested and limited by what we have hitherto so accepted, but not uniquely determined thereby.'[57]

Failing an alteration of the essential features of present liberal industrial societies it is entirely possible that the future will bring more of the same: a fifth of the population living in poverty, 5 to 10 per cent unemployed, two cars and a three-bedroom condominium for the rest, violence in the streets, larger insane asylums, bigger escape-proof penitentiaries, and, of course, better colour on TV. Which is to say that continual accretions — in terms of quantitative change — may not yield qualitative change. On the other hand it may well be the case that as technological factors become more and more crucial to the corporate state certain qualitative changes may ensue; we may be headed for a technological tyranny where most people respond like robots to the command of computer programs and where major decisions are made by a few highly skilled scientist administrators in the employ of giant corporations.[58] It is also not unthinkable that unless the privileged — whether we speak of nations or classes — are capable of properly responding to the demands of the exploited a new era of barbarism could erupt.

To help us understand where we have been, where we are, and where we might be going, the essays in this book raise important questions about how such things as public policy, social communication, technological development, elections, structures of authority and ideas relate to the issues of total or partial change, reform or revolutionary strategies. Not all of our contributors are in agreement as to how to provide the best answers. Practically all of them do share the beliefs that our society is in need of some rather fundamental re-structuring and that discovering the right path for social change is not a simple task. There are no predictions of imminent revolution or collapse and no defeatist resignations to fate. There is also no unbridled faith in the march of progress; no promises of liberation through technological breakthroughs and better business management; no advocacy of mediation, LSD, group therapy, personal gurus, or charismatic leaders as the way to social change. A spate of other books has already performed these functions well enough. What this book should do is provide the reader with some sober second thoughts. It is clearly an attempt to educate — by re-examining and, it is hoped, by changing some all-too-common ideas about social change.

NOTES

1 Lester Milbrath in *Political Participation* (Chicago, 1965), at p. 152 has suggested that the idea of democratic participation is more a functional myth than a reality: '... It is important to continue moral admonishment for citizens to become active in politics, *not because we want or expect great masses of them to become active,* but rather because

the admonishment helps keep the system open and sustains the belief in the right of all to participate, which is an important norm governing the behavior of political elites ... It is a curious social fact that a norm, such as that which says citizens should be interested and active in politics, which is violated wholesale, still can be an important ingredient in the functioning of the political system ... Perhaps one of the reasons the norm remains viable is that elites realize a decline of the norm could spell their own doom as they compete for the power to govern' (emphasis added).

2 S.D. Clark, *The Developing Canadian Community* (Toronto, 2nd ed., 1968), 271-85. In addition to Clark's work there have been some good recent Canadian efforts to combine theory and historical analysis in sociological writing. See, for instance, *Social and Cultural Change,* ed. W.E. Mann (Toronto, 1970), and *Canadian Society: Pluralism, Change, and Conflict,* ed. Richard Ossenberg (Scarborough, Ont., 1971).

3 Karl Mannheim, 'American Sociology,' *Sociology on Trial,* ed. Maurice Stein and Arthur Vidich (Engelwood Cliffs, 1963), 7

4 For a brilliant elaboration and exposure of this confusion see Peter Winch, *The Idea of a Social Science* (London, 1958), passim, and especially sections 1 and 5 of chap. 1. Winch is concerned to argue for a philosophical sociology, that is, that a philosophical dimension is part and parcel of any social science. In this connection also, see John O'Neill, *Sociology as a Skin Trade: Essays Towards a Reflexive Sociology* (New York, 1972).

5 Phyllis Deane, *The First Industrial Revolution* (Cambridge, 1967), 259-60

6 Ibid., 260

7 J.S. Mill, in *The Subjection of Women,* as cited by Deane, *First Industrial Revolution.*

8 Office of the Prime Minister, 'Notes for Remarks by the Prime Minister at the Harrison Liberal Conference,' Harrison Hot Springs, British Columbia, 21 November 1969, 3-4. See also the almost identical sentiments expressed in *Federalism and the French Canadians* (Toronto, 1968), 203.

9 'The Study of Change in Social Science,' *System, Change, and Conflict,* ed. N.J. Demerath and Richard A. Peterson (New York, 1967), 253

10 Ibid., 253-4

11 Ibid. '... In much sociological work, so great has been the concern with how society is made into a functioning social system that how it undergoes change and is made into a different society becomes completely ignored,' Clark, *Developing Canadian Community,* 295.

12 Trevor Lloyd, 'Introduction: Our Ideological Tradition,' *Agenda 1970: Proposals for a Creative Politics,* ed. Trevor Lloyd and Jack McLeod (Toronto, 1968), 14

13 This is how Pierre L. van den Berghe characterizes the functionalist approach to change, 'Dialectic and Functionalism: Toward a Synthesis,' in Demerath and Peterson, *System, Change,* 295

14 *Politics, Economics, and Welfare* (New York, 1953), 86

15 Daniel Bell, 'Notes on the Post-Industrial Society,' *The Public Interest* (Winter 1967), 25

16 Eric Fromm, *The Sane Society* (New York, 1967), 239

17 Henryk Skolimowski, 'Technology. The Myth Behind the Reality,' *Architectural Association Quarterly* (July 1970), 31

18 P.H. Partridge, 'Some Notes on the Concept of Power,' *Contemporary Political Theory,* ed. Anthony de Crespigny and Alan Wertheimer (London, 1971), 31

19 Ibid.

20 See Peter Bachrach and Morton S. Baratz, 'Two Faces of Power,' *American Political Science Review,* 56 (December, 1962).

21 *One Dimensional Man* (Boston, 1964)

22 See Paul Delany's review of Gilbert Bartel, *Group Sex* (New York, 1971), in *Canadian Dimension,* 9 (January 1973), 51-2.

23 Ibid., 52

24 (New York, 1967), 76

25 This conceptualization of dichotomies owes a good deal to the formulations of S.D. Clark, A.R. Radcliffe-Brown, and Karl Marx.
26 I am here explicitly seeking to avoid committing Robert Nisbet's error of attributing too much complementarity to the editor's own position in the selected articles. In his reader, *Social Change* (Oxford, 1972), Nisbet includes a selection from T.S. Kuhn. Two of Nisbet's principal claims are that change is not 'directional,' and that the biological metaphor is inappropriate in the study of social change. But Kuhn argues that 'scientific development is, like biological, a unidirectional and irreversible process,' *The Structure of Scientific Revolutions* (Chicago, 2nd ed., 1970), 206
27 Nisbet, *Social Change,* 15
28 *Developing Canadian Community,* 299
29 Ibid., 298-299
30 Ibid., 311
31 *Industry and Empire* (London, 1969), 80-2, 83ff
32 Clark, *Developing Canadian Community,* 288; R.T. Naylor, 'The Rise and Fall of the Third Commercial Empire of the St Lawrence,' and Gary Teeple, 'Land, Labour, and Capital in pre-Confederation Canada,' *Capitalism and the National Question in Canada,* ed. Gary Teeple (Toronto, 1972).
33 *Writings of the Young Marx on Philosophy and Society,* ed. Lloyd Easton and Kurt Guddat (New York, 1967), 263
34 *Capital, Volume I* (Modern Library edition), 9-10
35 As quoted in Hans Kelsen, *The Political Theory of Bolshevism* (Berkeley, 1948), 41; cf. Shlomo Avineri, *The Social and Political Thought of Karl Marx* (Cambridge, 1970), chap. 8
36 *Civilization and Its Discontents* (London, 1963), 48-52
37 George Grant, *Technology and Empire* (Toronto, 1969); and Grant's *Philosophy in the Mass Age* (Toronto, 2nd ed., 1966), esp. vii and viii
38 Otis Dudley Duncan, 'Social Forecasting – The State of the Art,' *The Public Interest* (Fall 1967), 106
39 Conservatives such as Jacques Ellul and Robert Nisbet speak of technology as 'itself a social system,' as an autonomous, self-generating force or system; and Grant uses the term 'fate' to describe the direction of modern society geared to technological progress. The neo-Malthusian approaches of ecodoomsters like Jay Forrester and Dennis Meadows are not strictly technological determinist. But their profoundly pessimistic predictions, based on a computerized model of analysis which assumes an exponential growth rate in the consumption of physical resources and a linear growth rate of technology, do have a fundamental characteristic in common with the determinists: the omission of a consideration of man as a purposeful agent of change. See Marie Jahoda, 'Postscript on Social Change,' *Futures,* 5 (April 1973).
40 'Canadian Economic Policy: A Proposal,' in *The Prospect of Change,* ed. Abraham Rotstein (Toronto, 1965), 79
41 *Lament for a Nation* (Toronto, 1965)
42 Toronto, 1965
43 *The Image of Confederation* (Toronto, 1964), 25
44 This is by no means to deny that the federal distribution of power, reflected in the relations of the two levels of government, has not changed dramatically over the years. It is rather to emphasize that the structure of power as reflected in class and elite distributions has generally remained the same. Excellent analyses of the former changes are contained in Paul Fox, 'Regionalism and Confederation,' *Regionalism in the Canadian Community,* ed. Mason Wade (Toronto, 1969), and D.V. Smiley, *Canada in Question: Federalism in the Seventies* (Toronto, 1972).
45 'Beyond Liberalism: The Priorities of Political Humanism,' in L. LaPierre et al., *Essays on the Left* (Toronto, 1971), 277
46 Israel Cinman, ' "Revolutionary" Law Course Shelved,' *Bulletin of the Canadian Association of University Teachers* (September 1973), 8

47 John Stuart Mill, *Earlier Letters,* vol. XIII of the *Collected Works* (Toronto, 1963), 544

48 From *The Principles of Political Economy,* as cited in *Views on Capitalism,* ed.
    R. Romano and M. Leiman (Beverly Hills, 1970), 114

49 As cited in *Views on Capitalism,* 131-3

50 As this book was going to press, Trudeau, in return for an honourary degree, delivered an
    address at Duke University wherein he attacked 'the 20th century devotion to material
    gain ... Prosperity is the rallying cry of politicians everywhere. But what of happiness?
    What of contentment? What of satisfaction?' As cited in the *Toronto Star,* 13 May 1974

51 *The Real World of Democracy* (Toronto, 1965) especially 62-5; *Democratic Theory:
    Essays in Retrieval* (Oxford, 1973), especially 139-140

52 Charles Taylor, 'The Agony of Economic Man,' in LaPierre, *Essays on the Left,* 221-35

53 The notion of a dialogue society is explored in Taylor's *The Pattern of Politics* (Toronto,
    1970), 123ff. The more recent formulation of a contemplative civilization is sketched in
    'The Agony of Economic Man.' For another interesting formulation see John Wilson,
    'Towards a Society of Friends: Some Reflections on the Meaning of Democratic Social-
    ism,' *Canadian Journal of Political Science* 3 (4), December (1970), 628-54; also Victor
    Ferkiss, *Technological Man: The Myth and the Reality* (New York, 1969).

54 Winch, *The Idea of a Social Science,* 15

55 Herbert Marcuse, *Counterrevolution and Revolt* (Boston, 1972), 132

56 Bay, 'Beyond Liberalism,' 278

57 'Understanding a Primitive Society,' in *Rationality,* ed. B. Wilson (Oxford, 1970), 100

58 *Freedom and Tyranny: Social Problems in a Technological Society,* ed. Jack D. Douglas
    (New York, 1970); and *The Technological Threat,* ed. Jack D. Douglas (Englewood
    Cliffs, 1971)

Mildred Bakan

Between body and thought

The framework within which one interprets the world is complicated by its
internal divisions: divisions that are rooted in the relations between the biological dimension of self and the thinking dimension of self and between
these dimensions and the external world. The development of Western civilization has exacerbated these divisions to such an extent that the public sector
is now characterized by an incomprehensible instability. In this paper, the
search for the potential basis for social change leads to an analysis of the interpretative framework. The analysis suggests that the separation of concrete intersubjective meaning from publicly accepted language is, at once, a primary
source of malaise and a foundation for concerted remedial action. The first
part of the paper provides a basis for interpreting the unconscious as a bodily
based species of communication or intersubjective communication. The second
part explores the relation of the unconscious to consciousness in terms of this
framework and sketches some implications of this relation for social change.

Freud's concept of the unconscious is often taken to refer to a storehouse
of instinctual biological drives, which in the absence of anxiety and guilt
would find bodily expression. It is true that, according to Freud, such in-
stincts repressed, can lead to devious gratification through consciously
accepted routes.[1] In the most simplistic interpretation, it is simply ignored
that for Freud even the devious behavioural route has a symbolic aspect, a
meaning. Something is being *said* through the neurotic, or psychotic, symptom. The psychoanalyst's task is to decipher that meaning; and the basis of
psychoanalytic cure is the individual's conscious acceptance of at least some
aspects of that meaning – that is, the integration of this unconscious meaning
with his conscious life. Therapy takes place through an expansion of consciousness, not simply through physiological expression. Indeed, some sorts
of physiological expression – such as promiscuity – are taken to be distorted,
substitute gratifications. Accessibility of the unconscious to consciousness
indicates that the unconscious itself, in Freud's use of the concept, has something to do with meaning. What Freud seems to be struggling for is a concept
of the biological which is not alien to the dimension of meaning. His lifelong
work indicates a concern with the biological as Telos – as Nature infused
with Mind – in the tradition of German classical idealism.[2]

We can recognize an arena of mutual influence among entities, any whatsoever, that takes place through direct physical contact, an arena of influence
we participate in when, for example, we cut meat, chop wood, push a table,
or strike another person. But there is another arena of mutual influence to
which the human order, social and solitary, bears testimony: communicative
influence through language. The first arena of influence is that of physical
force; the second we can call the arena of meaning. Language transmits meaning, and the influence of language – and it is important to recognize that

language is influential – is effected by the transmission (to use a term heavily laden with overtones of the model of physical influence) of *meaning*. This is not to say that the transmission of meaning does not use a physical medium, or that human violence is not infused with meaning. Nevertheless, a distinction can be drawn between influence by force and influence through the communication of meaning. The dimension of meaning is, of course, the dimension of mind, and wherever there is something like the effective influence of meaning, there we have something like mind.

In short, the banal interpretation of Freud fails to recognize that Freud is concerned with a biology which is somehow mind-infused. The interpretation of dreams is a way of deciphering the mind of the body. To speak in this way of the mind of the body seems, at first sight, to be reminiscent of Maurice Merleau-Ponty's concept of the lived body.[3] The lived body is the body as intentional. Indeed, intentionality is a term that was first used by philosophers to delineate meaning as a referential relation to objects. The lived body, in Merleau-Ponty's perspective, is the body as meaningfully related to entities (including other lived bodies) in the world; sentience itself being taken as such a meaningful relation. However, for Merleau-Ponty, the lived body is not contrasted to consciousness as Freud's unconscious is to conscious levels of the ego and superego. For Merleau-Ponty, the basic dimension of the self is the lived body. The body, so to speak, pulls itself together as a self, thought being continuous with the body as lived. Moreover, Merleau-Ponty explicated the lived body as the pre-objective world, and the pre-objective world was for the most part interpreted, as his language indicates, as developing along the way to objectivity.[4] One of Merleau-Ponty's primary concerns was the epistemological grounding of the known object in a pre-objective intentional context.

Something very much like the concept of the lived body, divorced from this epistemological concern, is developed by Adolph Portmann, the German biologist and others of his school.[5] This concept was worked out in a biological context to characterize a living body. Central to Portmann's concept are two key expressions: (1) 'Selbstdarstellung,' 'self-presentation' or 'display,' and (2) 'Weltbeziehung durch Innerlichkeit,' usually rendered as 'centredness' but literally 'world relation through inwardness.' 'Display' refers to the appearance of a living body to other living bodies; 'centredness' refers to the regulation of the body's relation to its environment by its internal organization, which must be maintained if the organism is to remain alive. Portmann, along with Plessner and Buitendyck, emphasizes the role of the body boundary in maintaining the separation of the organism from its environment. The body boundary controls the access of the environment to the internal organization of the organism. Its body boundary is also the way an organism is presented – displayed – in its environment. Biologists of this school point to ethologically gathered evidence that among some animals, at least, highly specific patterned sequences of behaviour, which are invariant within a species, are indispensable for such vital relations among members of a species as mating. (Interestingly enough, the colour and scent of flowers enter into mating also as essential components of cross-pollination by insects.) The significant point is that the appearance of the body of one member of a species to another plays an apparently indispensable role in the survival of the species. Beyond that, there is evidence that the appearance of the body plays an indispensable role in the social organization of some animals. As one example, Portmann cites the role of the appearance of antlers in maintaining dominance relations among the members of a species of reindeer. Though this sort of body presentation is hardly voluntary, we can recognize it as communicative. The body of one living entity influences other living bodies not simply by physical force – though the body belongs to the physical order of things – but by its *appearance* to other living bodies.

Portmann and other biologists of this school take the position that the genetically controlled appearance of the animal is involved in its life in an irreducible way, the appearance of the animal playing a communicative role between animals. Thus animal display – self-presentation – may be placed with human language on the dimension of communication. Correlatively, animal centredness, 'world relation through inwardness,' is to be understood as something like our human self-experience, without, however, any experienced distinction of self from its body. To attribute centredness to animals is to suppose that something like experience plays a role in their relation to their environment. This sort of experience may be taken as inseparable from a bodily context, perhaps as something like pain or hunger. It is as centred that one living body experiences the display of another living body.

Thus, centredness can be taken as inwardly showing the body and its environment (which includes other living bodies) in terms of the promise – or threat – of that environment to the body's continuation as a living entity. Such experiences as a frightening landscape, threatening thunder, beckoning grass, or an inviting potential mate are experiences of aspects of the environment in terms of threat or promise. This showing is a disclosure of the body in its relation to other entities, in terms of the future well-being of the body, and it may also become a disclosure of other entities as analogously centred. This sort of experience, as disclosure of either itself or other entities in terms of the future well-being of its own body is recognizably a locus of meaning. Such experience can be taken as a primary affectivity. As a disclosure of the body in its relation to other entities, such experience admits of no separability of body, environment, and others. It is important to note, however, that this sort of experience, as disclosure, is constitutive of a dimension other than the bare materiality of the body. In effect, a dimension of identity as well as meaning is introduced, an identity which has to do with prospects for endurance and development of the body in the surrounding environment.

According to this school of biology, every living entity is centred[6] and every living entity has a body boundary. As centred, every living entity obviously takes some account of its body boundary. However, this in no way implies that every – or indeed any – living body takes account of its body boundary in the same way as other living (or non-living) bodies do. Indeed, we can analyse evolutionary development in terms of the interrelation of centredness and display. In lower animals display is, by and large, genetically controlled, with some leeway for adjustment to the environment and other entities through centred behaviour. In human beings, display has cultural and even voluntary – in short, non-genetically controlled – aspects, with reverse effects on centredness of the display of its own body boundary. Such display takes on communicative aspects which are clearly akin to language.

There is no question here of a separation of conscious and unconscious. However, with the human development of consciousness this dimension of body disclosure can be shown to take on aspects of the unconscious. Thus, the development of the unconscious takes place in the context of the development of consciousness. Furthermore, depending on the social context for the development of consciousness, the relation of the unconscious to consciousness will differ.

In lower animals we were able to use the concepts of centredness and display to delineate communication through the vehicle of genetically controlled parts of the body. It is important to note that if the body boundary is communicative, this communicative aspect is inseparable from its particular context. The communication is context specific. On the other hand, the pattern of display, being genetically controlled, repeats itself from context to context.

In the case of the human being, centredness, and with that self-hood, is complicated by a change in communicative style. A human being communicates not entirely in terms of body boundary – genetically controlled appearance – but through sign and symbol. The specific structure of language is not genetically controlled, though there may be a genetic disposition to the use of language, or a genetic disposition to the use of language in suitable social contexts. Clothes, manners, forms of government, religions, myths, etc., are not genetically controlled either. Human beings are centred in terms of a world disclosed as a structure of possible objects distinct from the human beings themselves. The question of the validity of the disclosure of objects is irrelevant here. Indeed, our criteria for the validity of disclosure are aspects of the way in which the world is disclosed. It is hardly a startling position, today, to tie the human disclosure of world to language. A language can be understood as structuring possible world experience. In his book, *The Idea of a Social Science,* Peter Winch points out, interpreting Wittgenstein: "Our idea of what belongs to reality is given for us in the language that we use. The concepts we have settle for us the form of the experience we have of the world ... The world is for us what is presented through these concepts. That is not to say that our concepts may not change, but when they do, that means that our concept of the world has changed too."[7] The accepted grammatical structure of a language and its accepted vocabulary set limits to what can be meaningfully communicated in the language by the speakers of that language. But being centred in terms of a language, human beings communicate in terms of a structure which is, in so far as it is linguistic, invariant across specific contexts. Whereas genetically controlled appearance is context specific, non-genetically controlled language is supra-contextual.

It is fascinating to note that both Wittgenstein and Husserl tied cognition to 'seeing' something as the same, and that both related this 'seeing' to language, however different their emphasis and interests were otherwise. Wittgenstein stressed the rule-regulated aspect of language and argued that rules to be rules must be social institutions. Husserl, in his later writing, stressed the intersubjective dimension of concepts of reality, and as early as his *Logical Investigations*[8] analysed reference as the identification of an object as the same, tying the process to both perception and language. Words, Husserl notes, serve as pointers, referring to objects as identical across varied experiential contexts. Berger and Luckmann, whose sociology is phenomenologically oriented, write of language:

Its foundation is, of course, in the intrinsic capacity of the human organism for vocal expressivity but we can begin to speak of language only when vocal expressions have become capable of detachment from the immediate 'here and now' ... It is not yet language if I snarl, grunt, howl or hiss, although these vocal expressions are capable of becoming linguistic insofar as they are integrated into an objectively available sign system ...

Language has its origins in the face-to-face situation, but can be readily detached from it.

... I can speak about innumerable matters that are not present at all in the face-to-face situation, including matters that I never have and never will experience directly ...

Language also typifies experiences allowing one to subsume them under the broad categories in terms of which they have meaning not only to myself but also to my fellow man. As it typifies it also anonymizes experiences, for the typified experience can in principle be duplicated by anyone under the category in question.

They cite the following example:

For instance, I have a quarrel with my mother-in-law. This concrete and subjectively unique experience is typified linguistically under the category 'mother-in-law trouble.' In this typification it makes sense to myself, to others and presumably to my mother-in-law. The same typification however entails anonymity. Not only I but anyone (more accurately, anyone in the category of son-in-law) can have 'mother-in-law trouble.' In this way my biographical experiences are ongoingly subsumed under general orders of meaning that are both objectively and subjectively real.[9]

Let us take this view of language for granted. I am not proposing we stop with it as mysterious. We can show its profound relevance to the human self by relating the self to action. By action I mean any body movement regulated by its possible outcome in a disclosed world. Body movements regulated by possible, or unknown outcomes, qualify as actions in this sense as well as movements regulated by expected outcomes. All such actions have an intentional dimension. Whether or not full-blown voluntary action, in the sense of deliberate choice based upon knowledge of what leads to what, can develop on the basis of such action is not central here. What is more to the point is that action, intentional in the sense that it is regulated by a possible outcome, can be taken as the basis for the development of linguistic communication. For action which awaits a possible outcome allows, generally, for the identification of objects and, particularly, for the development of dialogue in suitable social contexts. An awaited possible outcome opens the future as a bounded indeterminacy, a locus of unspecified alternatives[10] which may be determined or specified, in general, by the object awaited and, specifically, by a heard sound.

The occurrence of a dialogical situation is particularly significant for the development of language. Indeed it is reasonable to suppose that it is essential. That the word uttered is heard, or in some way perceived, not only by the person addressed, but reflexively, by the speaker as well, allows sounds, or gestures, to become the physical medium of language.[11] However, the barking of dogs does not develop into language. We might speculate that dogs do not develop language because their actions are not sufficiently open-ended as to outcome. In order that a child develop linguistically, something like crying for food must be constituted as an anticipation of food as possible rather than an expression – a display – of pain. Anticipating food as possible introduces into the here and now a possibility that may be realized. The child is then asking for something which is not now present. And the food provided can then be named as excluding some alternate possible outcome: not food, or some other kind of food. However, a hungry child, given food, will devour it, not name it, or listen to its name. Awaiting has ended. It is the period of waiting that allows an absent object to be present as possible. The child can ask for awaited food by gesture and a good parent will understand. In this way the child is encouraged to ask and rudimentary language development has begun. Bion,[12] a psychoanalyst with Kleinian roots, speculates that the child's positive relation to his absent mother marks beginning of thought and the birth of the ego. According to Bion, if the child makes his absent mother present through rudimentary thought (in the form of projective identification), frustration tolerance is increased and the basis is laid for future ego strength. Furthermore, 'An infant capable of tolerating frustration can permit itself to be dominated by the reality principle.'[13] Whatever the conditions of its development, the occurrence of anticipation as a relation to possible absent objects may be uniquely human (though restricted to a suitable social context).

A learned language structures anticipation, maps its possible satisfaction in the world. Language thus co-ordinaly discloses the world by mapping the world as an arena in which anticipation may be fulfilled. It should be noted that a language maps the world *as a totality*, as all that there is, by structuring *possibility*, delineating alternatives, hence structuring the very questions that can be asked. Indeed, it is only in terms of language in this sense that voluntary action emerges full blown and, with it, human being, as self in the world. For only in terms of the linguistic constitution of a world as a domain of possibilities can action emerge which is guided by anticipated alternate possibilities. At this level of action, anticipated, formulated, or formulable possibility is itself the basis on which an action is undertaken. Such anticipated possibility is either realizeable through my action or another's, if action is taken broadly enough to include such body movements as looking or listening. Realizing such possibility through my action (anticipation is involved in the realization of possibility by another, if or when another is allowed, or awaited, to realize some possible outcome), its non-realization is excluded, and self-awareness as awareness of my doing emerges, which is also awareness of my not-doing. We have reached a level of disclosure of personal being as excluding personal non-being. Personal being as self-being involves, then, two components:

(1) language as a map of totality and (2) action guided by that map. Voluntary action is, at this level, critically undertaken and centred, not in feeling as
the disclosure of body intertwined with the world, but in thought as the
disclosure of a world as world, in which one's body is itself found as an
object. In short the human self is not simply body-centred; it is thought-
centred and language-mediated. Feeling, in the broadest sense, fulfils thought
under certain conditions, and, in so far as it does, is intelligible.[14] But thought
also has the capacity to stay in its own domain. Thought can refer to thought.
It is this aspect of thought that is reflected in the structural or grammatical
dimensions of language.

This sketch of language learning is enough to indicate that with the learning of language the limits of reality are mapped for the individuals sharing this
language. At the same time, a field of possible consciousness is mapped. We
recognize here Freud's concept of the ego. In *Beyond the Pleasure Principle*,[15]
for example, Freud speaks of the ego as unifying conscious experience and, in
the maintenance of this unity, repressing unacceptable feelings. The ego is, in
effect, the unifying force of conscious experience, which, as unifying force,
excludes disruptive possible experience. In terms of our model of language
learning, what the individual can achieve in the world shared by a group of
language users defines that individual's identity as his self-concept. In learning
a language, the individual learns not merely what he may anticipate, but how
to publicly communicate what he may anticipate, and to think about what he
may anticipate. In so doing he learns the limits of what he may be in that
group and in the world shared by that group.[16] What is not realizable in the
world defined by that language is simply unreal. It may be dreamed or
imagined. But even the fantasy will be informed by the language used, at least
with respect to its manifest content.[17]

However, selves have bodies. Not even a thought-centred self is bodiless.
The self as the Freudian ego is correlated with a world as the realm of what
the individual is conscious of and prepared to be conscious of. This world
structures his anticipations, and so his voluntary actions, his reasonable or his
realistically achievable goals. This world also structures the goals he is expected to have by others sharing his world and his society and the goals he
expects to have if he is to be like the others and belong to that society and to
its world. Clearly, whatever inclinations, impulses, wishes the individual has
which, as possible actions, take him off the map of the real world will come
into conflict with that map. Indeed, such inclinations may not even be
formulable – speakable – in that language. If they are expressible or realizable, even imaginatively, such inclinations must threaten his self-concept as
the correlate of the publicly acknowledged world[18] and be felt as challenging
his personal reality, because the expression of these wishes – the realization

of these actions – has no place on his map of reality. But what impulses, wishes, imaginations could deviate from the map of reality to the extent that their realization is destructive of the very identity of the individual? Wishes, inclinations, impulses which are in no way under voluntary control, and are totally body- rather than thought-centred. Wishes that are body-centred are the possible actions of a body-centred self. These actions are communicative; they have a dimension of meaning, but the meaning is context specific, as we saw. This meaning is in terms of the concrete experience of oneself and others (including other entities), and relates to a body-centred identity which obliterates distinctions between self and other.

Wishes and inclinations are themselves moulded in childhood, in the family setting, in concretely specific face-to-face situations, through a communicated language. If the child's development of personal being is integrated with the family language, then the child's thought-centred self becomes integrated with its body-centred self. The child becomes aware of himself as a doer – as, at least, to some degree, self-determining – in the world defined by the family context.[19] However, in so far as the family language is discontinuous with the public language of the society in which the family is embedded, discontinuites between the inclinations appropriate to the childhood-family setting and those appropriate to the adult-social setting, can and do emerge. Moreover, these inclinations and wishes having developed in the intimate face-to-face family setting, are not always formulable in terms of language as supra-contextual, and even when so formulable have an irreducible component which is as context specific as one's body. The wishes, inclinations, impulses which belong to my body in its concrete social context as communicating bodily, as looked at and looking, as embraced and embracing, as acknowledged and acknowledging, as physically violated or physically violating, may not, as meaning, be at all integrated with the public language – the language of the society in which I make my way as an adult. In other words, intersubjective relations in their highly particularized aspects are, at best problematically related to the public map. These impulses and wishes are concretely intersubjectively communicative, and to the extent that they cannot be integrated with any sort of publicly accepted language become unconscious, repressed to maintain the integrity of the ego. Such wishes would display themselves as meaningless behaviour, alien feeling, irrational and ununderstandable, unintegrated with the thought-centred self, whose correlate is the world – symptoms in the Freudian sense, threatening the supportive map of reality. In so far as such wishes are accessible to personal consciousness, they would be masked, distorted, so as to admit of integration with the publicly accepted language.[20] Generally speaking, then, the

body-centred self which relates to others and to objects context-specifically
is problematically related to a public language.

We can now ask: what sort of languages entail such dissociation? Do all
languages dissociate in this way? Primitive societies engage in periodic public
rituals which allow for the integration of intersubjective bodily communication with the public language, the context-invariant language of the society as
a historic entity. Diamond writes of primitive societies:

There is a very high degree of integration among the various major modalities
of culture ... These correlations ... integrate a whole series of emotions and
attitudes around a given activity, rather than isolating or abstracting the
activity from its human contexts. The ... effect is exemplified in the valida-
tion of practical activities by magico-religious means, as in the classic case
of the expert Trobriand canoe maker, who confirms the step-by-step construction of his craft with spell and incantation ...

Primitive modes of thinking are substantially concrete, existential, and
nominalistic within a personalistic context. This does not suggest a lack of abstract capacity (*all* language, *all* culture and convention flow from this phylo-
genetic human endowment), but it does indicate an emphasis functional with
the kinship structure of primitive society, and a lack of concern with the specific
type of abstraction that may be called, in the western civilized world, platonic ...

In primitive society, the ritual drama is a culturally comprehensive vehicle for
group and individual expression at critical junctures in the social round or
personal life cycle, as these crises are enjoined by the natural environment or
defined by culture. In such ceremonies, art, religion and daily life fuse, and
cultural meanings are renewed and re-created on a stage as wide as society
itself.

In a sequence from archaic to modern civilization, we can trace the process
through which religion, drama, and daily life split apart. The drama, the
primary form of art, retreats to the theater, and religion escapes into the
church. The sacraments, those formalized remnants of the primitive crisis
rites, and the 'theatre, the play' develop into carefully culturated and narrowly bounded conventions. Civilized participation in culture becomes increasingly passive, as culture becomes increasingly secularized.

Among primitives, rituals are cathartic and creative. They are cathartic in that
they serve as occasions for open, if culturally molded expressions of

ambivalent feelings about sacred traditions, constituted authority, animal and human nature, and nature at large ...

These rituals are also creative in the dramatic revelations of symbols, and the anticipation and elaboration of new roles for individuals; they make meanings explicit and renew the vitality of the group.[21]

We can recognize it as a peculiarly modern problem that our public language is not integrated with shared bodily intersubjectivity. In short, we have a framework to deal with the relation of public language, which is supra-contextual, and affective communication, which is context-specific. If this relation is problematic in every society it is peculiarly problematic in Western industrialized society with its high mobility, its disruption of kinship patterns, its emphasis on productivity and work schedules which render concrete experience trivial, and its increasing reliance on highly formalized languages such as mathematics and scientific theory. Whatever in our society militates against the unity of meaning as context-specific experience and meaning as supra-contextual structure contributes to the problem.

Primitive societies, it should be noted, show a characteristic cultural stability, which seems to be unattainable in Western industrialized society.[22] As industrialization and language formalization proceed, as mobility increases, and kinship patterns are increasingly stretched, we can expect the problem to become more acute. The central role of ritualized national drama in the Chinese cultural scene, the particular penchant of our own young to experiment with new sorts of communal togetherness, the resurgence of the political importance of ethnic ties, the push to community involvement in urban living, the current vogue of encounter groups, can all be understood as attempts to restore concrete intersubjectivity to the public sector. In so far as the problem cannot be solved at the rational level in terms of our thought-world, we can expect not understandable social change, but instability.

If this analysis has any point, our current public order is unstable because of very deep-seated factors. I see no merit in stability for the sake of stability. Indeed, the lack of integration of concretely intersubjective meaning with the publicly accepted language can be a powerful potential force for constructive social change. Marcuse's work can be understood as informed by the exploration of just this potentiality. According to Marcuse, the emphasis on productivity in Western industrialized societies has encouraged dominance as a mode of concrete experience and has, in this way, achieved the repression and diminution of unconscious impulses which are binding (expressive of *eros*, rather than *thanatos*, in the Freudian sense). Marcuse recognizes that the societal emphasis on productivity (and competition) in contemporary industrialized society has influenced our prevalent concepts of reality, though he fails to develop any significant implications in terms of the relation of our use of language to personal experience. As Marcuse points out, fantasy – whether imaginal, musical or literary – can escape this repression. However it is important to note that the interpretation of the cognitive import of phantasy does not escape repression. Only a change in our thought-world – which would amount to a change in our concept of reality – can effect a change in the interpretation of fantasy. And Marcuse does indeed call for a change in our interpretation of reality.[23] Such a change in our thought world would entail a change in our legitimation of social roles, and as legitimation of social roles changes, even institutionalized modes of productivity must change. As evidence in this connection, witness the widespread contemporary dissatisfaction of young workers in Western industrialized societies, and the great attention being given in Canada and the United States and Europe to modes of alleviating the dissatisfaction through profit-sharing and participation in decision-making. However, if the unconscious loses its integration with the thought-world, and breaks out – as indeed it does in our society – as erratic adventure, sometimes suicidal or murderous, and sometimes, simply fun,[24] the publicly accepted language which conveys the publicly accepted view of the real is in no way altered. The interpretation of the unconscious is dominated by the publicly accepted language. We have then instability, but no other significant social change. Significant change necessitates a change in the interpretative framework so as to accommodate the disclosure of the world which is body- as well as thought-centred. Only a body-centred self can disclose the world as concretely threatening or promising. Only a body-centred self can disclose as sensuous experience the evaluative dimension of our environment. That is why a body-centred self which is integrated with a thought-centred self might serve as a basis for the development of a critical social theory oriented to social change which is life-supportive. The whole question of the development of sensuous meaning and its relation to cognitive meaning is just emerging from years of ideological taboo. Marcuse, Sartre, and Merleau-Ponty have been contemporary pioneers in this area. But Freud's work – and in a certain sense Husserl's – also must be recognized as belonging to this domain of investigation. The integration of sensory meaning and cognitive meaning was richly explored by the German classical idealists of the nineteenth century with the advent of industrialization, as Marcuse astutely points out,[25] and then virtually tabooed as industrialization proceeded.

As a matter of fact, the body-centred self, which is open to sensuous meaning, develops biographically in tandem with the thought-centred self. Would Œdipal development occur outside the family setting and independently of the child's cognitive development? (In this connection it would, incidentally, prove very fruitful to correlate the child's stages of libidinal development, as outlined by Freud and his followers, with the child's stages of cognitive development, as outlined by Piaget.) It is important to note however, that the body-centred self lacks words to talk about itself. The body-centred self *feels*. If it is no stranger to love, it is also no stranger to hate.[26] The body-centred self does not choose; it is strictly speaking not capable of voluntary action. If the body-centred self behaves in an environment, it does not act in a world (aspects of which are not, and cannot be, immediately present). In short, the body-centred self is incapable of self-determination in the sense of full deliberate choice. The body-centred self is bound by its body in a way that the thought-centred self is not. For the thought-centred self to abdicate to the body-centred self, is in effect, to abdicate criticality. The social dimension itself as a dimension in which dialogue and concerted action can take place would disappear. Actions reduced to behaviour are responsive only to the immediate environment. Behaviour, so understood, is subject to manipulation or, at least, to causal determination by the de facto power relations of the society at large, without any possibility of critical recovery. Only if the body-centred self is integrated with the thought-centred self, can criticality be maintained as self-determinating in the light of possible consequences. It is thought in particular, that renders absent objects present in such a way that they are not merely sensuously present. If, for example, I see the front of a chair, I expect a back to be there as well, and this expectation is an aspect of my seeing the front of the chair as its front. I would not see the front as front, unless I expected to be able to see its back if I changed my bodily relation to the chair. In perception, expected experience is sensuously present as an implicit (Husserl's term is 'horizonal') aspect of what is seen. Only thought allows expected experience to be present here and now as possibly so, and therefore also as possibly otherwise. Analogously, only thought allows the presence of what is not the case as not the case. Language allows the formulation of what is *not* the case, the negation of what is real, and what is expected to be real. That is why thought and language are inseparable.[27] If we did not speak, we could not hope to transform our environment, we could not anticipate personal death, we could not stand outside our lives to question our conduct. In short, the risk of a splintered self is inherent in the very possibility of criticality.

However, the thought-centred self can remain open to the body-centred self without surrendering to it. Is this not the meaning of Freud's dictum: 'Where Id was, there shall ego be.'? That is the way of *critical* integration as a self, not as an isolated entity, but as exercising choice and active self-determination in a disclosed world, in concerted action with others.

NOTES

1 Thus, for example, Freud writes, in *The Problem of Anxiety* (New York 1963): 'If by means of a signal of distress the ego attains its object of completely suppressing the instinctual impulse, we have no estimation as to how this happens. We learn something about it only from the cases in which repression is more or less unsuccessful. Then it appears, in general, that the instinctual impulse despite repression has found a substitute satisfaction, but one which is greatly crippled, displaced, or inhibited. If a substitute satisfaction is achieved, pleasure is not experienced but instead the achieving of this substitute satisfaction has acquired the character of a compulsion.'
2 Consider the following description of the relation of instinct to repression. 'The ego controls the *entrance into consciousness* as well as the *passage into activity* directed to the environment; in repression it exerts its power at both places. The *instinct representative* experiences to one, the *instinctual impulse* itself the other side of the ego's manifestation of authority' (italics mine), ibid., 22. The point is that instinct, as Freud understands it, has two aspects: *experiential* and *motoric*.
3 See *Phenomenology of Perception* (London, 1962). Especially, in relation to this paper, chapter 6, 'The Body as Expression and Speech,' 174-99.
4 I say 'for the most part' because Merleau-Ponty is concerned to show the primordial reality of the pre-objective world.
5 See, in this connection, Marjorie Grene, *Approaches to a Philosophical Biology* (New York, 1965). Excerpts from the work of Buitendyk, Plessner, Erwin Strauss, and Kurt Goldstein are reproduced in the book. The work of Konrad Lorenz and other ethologists has some affinities with this school as well. See also Adolf Portmann, *Animals as Social Beings* (London, 1962).
6 Hans Jonas takes the most general characteristic of *every* living entity to be the metabolic maintenance of an *identity of form in time*. He argues that the metabolism of both plants and animals is to be understood as achieving an identity of form. He traces the difference between plant irritability, whose range of response is presumably limited to what is contiguous, and animal sentience, which can experience what is distant, to the difference between plant and animal modes of mobility. Plants remain relatively stationary, whereas animals move and their relation to their food supply is accordingly different. [*The Phenomenon of Life* (New York, 1966), third essay, 'Is God a Mathematician,' 64-98 and fourth essay, 'To Move and to Feel: On the Animal Soul,' 99-107.] His concept of self-maintenance is at least close to Portmann's concept of centredness. It is interesting to note that Marjorie Grene interprets Portmann's concept of centredness in the case of plants as the 'achievement and preservation' by the plant of its 'being' (itself as a living individual), a concept of self-maintenance which is virtually that of Jonas. See Grene, *Philosophical Biology,* 33.
7 Peter Winch, *The Idea of a Social Science* (London, 1958), 15
8 Edmund Husserl, *Logical Investigations* (New York, 1970), Investigation VI, chapter 1, 675-705
9 Peter L. Berger, and Thomas Luckmann, *The Social Construction of Reality* (Garden City, NY, 1966), 34-7
10 For a development of this aspect of awareness see my article 'Awareness and Possibility,' *The Review of Metaphysics, 1960 XIV,* no. 2, 230-42. See also Merleau-Ponty, *Phenomenology of Perception,* 28.
11 Berger and Luckmann stress this aspect of the development of language in *Social Construction of Reality,* 36.
12 W.R. Bion, *Learning from Experience* (London, 1962), 28-37
13 Ibid., 37
14 Husserl explored this aspect of the relation of thought to feeling in detail in *Logical Investigations.* See in particular Investigation I, chapter 2, 299-311, and Investigation VI, Section I, chapters 1, 2, and 3, pp. 675-747.

15 (New York, 1950), 5-6, 20-1, and chapter IV, especially 34-8
16 See in this connection the excerpt from Berger and Luckmann, *Social Construction of Reality,* 29 beginning with 'Language also typifies experiences ...'
17 The term 'manifest' is used here in the strict Freudian sense.
18 There is a sense in which every world, as a map of reality, has an irreducible, intersubjective public aspect. *My world* is a perspectival view of the world; otherwise the concept of a world as *mine* would have no meaning. The same arguments holding for a conception of language as a social institution hold for a conception of world as irreducibly intersubjective. However, language, structuring anticipation, allows for criticality regarding *what* is anticipated. If such criticality were not possible, language itself would not be possible. To structure anticipation is to structure *possibility* as *possibility.* Concepts of reality implicitly *refer to what is possible.* As criticism of possibility proceeds, so does criticism of our concepts of reality and of our language. However, this criticism is *thought-centred.* This point is taken up again on p. 36.
19 If the family setting does not allow for the integration of body and thought as self-awareness, then a basis is laid for those anomalies of personality development that R.D. Laing speaks of in *The Divided Self* (Baltimore, Maryland: 1965).
20 Indeed, the publicly accepted language, to maintain its structure, can stretch to include the masked formulation of forbidden unconscious wishes. See pp. 34-5.
21 Stanley Diamond, 'The Search for the Primitive,' in Ashley Montagu, *The Concept of the Primitive* (New York, 1968), 120, 128, 131-2
22 Ibid., 119-20
23 Herbert Marcuse, *Eros and Civilization,* (New York, 1955), 127-202. Also, 'Nature and Revolution,' in *Counter-Revolution and Revolt* (Boston, 1972), 59-78
24 A development encouraged by the contemporary explosion of the mass media. I can do no more here than raise the very interesting question of the relation of the mass media to the unconscious. To what extent do the mass media contribute to 'one dimensionality' and to 'liberation' in Marcuse's sense of the terms? See Marcuse, *One Dimensional Man,* (Boston, 1968), and *Essay on Liberation,* (Boston, 1969).
25 Marcuse, *Eros and Civilization,* 164-76
26 It is one of Marcuse's basic themes throughout his work that our competitive, productivity-oriented society *develops* hatred. See, for example, *Eros and Civilization,* 77-92.
27 It was Merleau-Ponty's mistake to have attributed too much to the body-centred self. In the end, he had to introduce language as the 'body of thought,' but he nowhere took account of the reverse, 'feedback,' effect of the development of language on body-centred disclosure. It is absurd to suppose that the sensuous experience of the non-linguistic ape approaches ours.

Bentley Le Baron

Marx on human emancipation

A crucial problem for all revolutionaries, Marxist and non-Marxist, is to know how to prevent the exigencies of struggle from corrupting that for which they struggle: namely freedom, community, 'human emancipation.'

I assume that the concept of revolution, as it has been developed in thought and practice since 1776 and 1789, does imply effort towards human emancipation. That is, I assume that the concept implies far-reaching social change, rather than just another (unusually rough) round of musical chairs at the top of the political pile. Revolution, in other words, is to be sharply distinguished from coups, palace revolts, and other forms of political change which, often as not, change nothing. It is also to be distinguished from counter-revolution, which serves to reverse the gains of freedom and equality. These distinctions might seem so obvious as to be hardly worth making, were it not that contemporary academic discussions of 'revolution' typically use the term as a catch-all for any more or less sudden change of regime or government, provided it is violent and/or extra-constitutional.[1] So completely has preoccupation with violence and illegality dominated our discussions in recent years that there came to be, during the 1960s, a considerable vogue for replacement of the term 'revolution' with the term 'internal war,' a usage which effectively de-rails the crucial question of what the revolution is about.

As against these contemporary and greatly impoverished discussions — concerned primarily with the form of change and hardly at all with its content — a re-reading of Marx comes as something of a restorative of richness, complexity, and 'human' substance. Marx means by revolution a thorough-going change in modes of production, *together with* a thorough-going change of *men:* their ideas and relationships, their habits and pleasures, their institutions. In his work, revolution is defined not in terms of violence, nor of illegality, but primarily in terms of the direction and content of change. I do not imply that analysis of violence and illegality is neglected, but only that they are not allowed to present themselves as the essence of the revolutionary endeavour.

Similarly, Hannah Arendt, in her recent study of revolutions, reminds us that change is revolutionary only in so far as it serves to create something new — a beginning — and that the significant new beginnings which we call revolutions in fact have been pointed towards greater freedom, greater equality, greater material and spiritual well-being not for the few but for the many.[2]

Let me summarize these introductory remarks about the concept of revolution by suggesting that those theorists who dwell entirely on 'internal war,' and on analyses of forcible, violent, or illegal seizures of power, are effectively stymied at just that point. Unlike Arendt and Marx, they lack conceptual tools to get on with examination of the social transformations, the momentous changes in human conditions and consciousness, which constitute the real stuff of revolution.

In this paper I shall look at the transformation or praxis which Marx called, among other things, 'human emancipation,' showing how this transformation is central to his concept of revolution. What follows does not purport to be a complete summary of Marx on revolution: it is a reminder of a particular aspect of his thought which is too often and too easily neglected, both by contemporary social scientists and by makers of revolutions.

To begin, let us recall what is meant by the term 'praxis.' It is well known that this concept finds no footing where head work is divorced from hand work, or vice versa. What is perhaps not as fully appreciated, and deserves some attention here, is that praxis is also a transcending of the all too common disjunction between goals and methods. By defining revolution in terms of violence and illegality – means divorced from ends – contemporary theorists of revolution tend to solidify and perpetuate this disjunction.[3] Over-fascination with vanguard parties and seizures of power – whether on the part of Bolsheviks or of behavioralists – has a similar tendency. Thus, the revolution is itself split in two, and division of labour works its poison once again. '*Now* our task is to create an instrument for seizing power; *later* our task, or that of another generation, will be to create a new society, to become new men. Violent *methods* now; gentle *goals* bye and bye.' From the standpoint of Marx's own thinking this way of proceeding is profoundly wrong, for it perpetuates a disjunction which functions to maintain bondage, albeit perhaps in a new form. It perpetuates social activity which is un-whole and therefore un-free.

For Marx the making of revolution cannot be separated from that which is made, namely 'communism,' or emancipation, or freedom. Revolution is not merely a struggle now for emancipation after the battle; it is, at the same time, a beginning to be emancipated here, now. It is beginning to think differently, act differently, live differently, here, now. It is the activity of appropriating our world in a distinctively human way, which is to say sensously, socially, and in a rich all-sided manner. To put it crudely, revolution is not merely, or even primarily, a matter of eliminating our oppressors, the evil bourgeoisie, after which the millennium.

Revolution implies class struggle, class struggle implies guns and blood, and these effectively command our attention; hence the tendency (for both activists and academics) to concentrate almost exclusively on the violent, dramatic aspects of the struggle, to the detriment of other aspects. But revolutionaries should beware of categorizing class struggle too narrowly as violent confrontation between 'us' and 'them,' because it is also, in a very deep sense, us versus ourselves, as Lenin and Mao have so often reminded us. It is the self-activity of becoming other than we are, the activity of surpassing the given (which is ourselves), and of beginning to be new people, creating new kinds of social relations. For those of us who have always taken the capitalist ethic for granted, this is likely to be particularly difficult. Capitalism, like religion, is at once external and internal, so that, as Marx said of the 'layman's struggle': it is not just a 'struggle against the priest outside himself, but ... [also] against his *own internal priest,* against his own *priestly nature.*'[4] Like religious men, we have priestly attachments to alien gods (for example, Profit) before whom we regularly prostrate ourselves. Hence, unless major self-change is simultaneously in process, it will avail us little or nothing to 'expropriate the expropriators,' and replace private with public ownership. If our mentality, habits, and social relations (our conditions of work and leisure, the things we produce and consume, including ideas and values), if all of these continuously recreate old patterns of egoism and advantage and division, not to mention triviality, then the removal of particular bosses, or a proclamation of socialism, will avail little. In such a case, new bosses step into the shoes of the old, and the same ponderous machine continues to gobble up its victims under a different label. Revolution is then no praxis; it is empty, fake. Disjunction of goals from methods ensures that methods belong to and perpetuate the old, the limited, while goals degenerate into mirages, always just beyond our grasp. In Gajo Petrovic's pithy summation, 'the atomic bomb will not start producing edible mushrooms the moment we affix a socialist label to it.'[5]

In dwelling so long on the ideas of revolution and of praxis, I have not been avoiding discussion of 'human emancipation,' for these three are one. It is important to see that Marx's 'revolution,' which is also his 'human emancipation,' must be a praxis. That is, it is not a destination – the station at the end of the line, the 'good society' – where we hope to arrive someday. Nor is it a locomotive, an external mechanism, the vehicle which would carry us to freedomland if only we could get the engine started. It is neither destination nor vehicle, but the journey itself, the continuous *effort* of enlarging freedom and community.

These generalities, admittedly, are somewhat abstract. To give them content, let us look at a few passages from Marx. Let us begin in 1843, with his comments 'On the Jewish Question,' where he contrasts 'human emancipation' with a more limited 'political emancipation.'[6] The latter he refers to as 'the splitting of man into *public* and *private* ... the *disintegration* of man into Jew and citizen, Protestant and citizen,' or, we might add, into owner and citizen, worker and citizen, French (or English) Canadian and citizen, black and citizen, woman and citizen, and so on through a long list of particularities which come to have precedence over our universal interests, our humanity in common, which Marx sometimes calls our 'species being.' When each particularistic group struggles for its own interests, each private individual for his own emancipation, the community shrivels. Or, more to the point, our capacities for 'citizenship,' by which Marx means our capacities for social creation and enjoyment, remain shrivelled and stunted. From the perspective of (merely) 'political' emancipation, not just one but every man is to be taken as '*sovereign* and sumpreme.' 'But this means in his uncivilized and unsocial aspect, in his fortuitous existence and just as he is, corrupted by the entire organization of our society, lost and alienated from himself, oppressed by inhuman relations and elements – in a word, man who is not yet an actual species being.'[7] For Marx, man is 'uncivilized,' and also unfree, just in so far as he is 'unsocial.' He is 'lost and alienated from himself' just in so far as he stands in an antagonistic relation to his fellows, for there can be no 'human' self apart from them. Atomistic relations of advantage and privilege *are* 'inhuman relations.'

I think it is evident that the above is precisely a description of our own society in its dominant aspect, the society which we so pridefully describe as pluralistic and individualistic, but which Marx less flatteringly describes as egoistic. Political emancipation we have, or, at least, where we do not have it yet, we know how to fight for it. Jews have fought and, to some extent, won. Blacks and French Canadians are well launched into their struggles. Women, North American Indians, homosexuals, and other repressed groups begin to stir. And, says Marx, let us not underestimate the importance of these particularistic struggles. '*Political* emancipation is indeed a great step forward.'[8] Nevertheless, it is not yet 'human emancipation'; it is as far from human emancipation as 'separation and withdrawal of man from man' are from what Marx calls the 'human world.'[9] If any of us are to be free, as Marx understands freedom, it will be only in so far as the emancipation of blacks, of women, or of native Canadians comes to be understood as the emancipation of all of us; otherwise we remain in the bondage of private, divisive attainments and satisfactions. The best spokesmen of the Panthers, and of Women's Liberation, have clearly recognized this.

Marx's argument reaches still further: it holds that our emancipation, here in wealthy Canada, ultimately requires the emancipation (which is to say well-being) of many hungry millions elsewhere. Obviously this is a staggering expectation, but this, and nothing less, is entailed in what Marx means by human emancipation, or revolution. Just as obviously, it is not soon to be accomplished. But it is at least a step forward to become clear about what revolution means, and what is at stake.

Marx takes it as evident that emancipation from 'necessity' – that is, crude physical need – is the primary emancipation upon which political and human emancipation must rest. There is no sense pretending that we can achieve 'community' and 'species being' with a man who is hungry, cold, or mutilated by napalm, for he is necessarily ruled by private need (which Marx calls 'practical' need). Such a person cannot yet attain to 'human' needs, such as beauty, excellence, creativity, conversation, and love. Obviously the most fundamental level of revolution is the overcoming of crude exigency. Nevertheless, while we struggle for the obvious, we must not lose sight of that which is less obvious, namely, that physical well-being alone is but a fragment of the revolution of which Marx spoke, which is a revolution of man as a total being. That means fundamental changes in consciousness and culture, in social relations and in productive labour. It is not merely a matter of political institutions, or of redistributing wealth. Hence my opening statement, that revolutionaries face the crucial problem of learning to struggle for several levels of emancipation at once, and of preventing this struggle from degenerating. Let me put this concretely: the struggle at its most basic level must be divisive, harsh, because it is *against* those human beings, ideologies, and institutions which defend privilege, with its dark underbelly of oppression and misery; yet the struggle at the same time must be *towards* 'human' community, 'human' need, 'human' emancipation, which means among other things that it must be *for* all of us, oppressed and oppressors alike.

A revolutionary must not seek to evade this paradox: that he struggles for a 'human' world, with all the richness which Marx gives to that concept, yet he must do so, in the first instance, in an 'inhuman' way. He wants to humanize the natural and social world, that is, to recreate them – and himself–'in a form adequate to the *human* being.'[10] He wants to move from crude 'sense' to 'sensitivity,' and ultimately to 'sensibility,' He wants to become the creator, the man who is consciously, socially, 'self-transcending.'[11] How can he do any of this when the first order of business seems to be destruction, violation, deepened divisions – force against force and violence against violence? What if the struggle effectively negates the very community and communication which is essential to species being?

I do not want to try to answer these questions on behalf of those who have fought and still must fight in a context of appalling deprivation, whether of material necessities or of political liberties. Specifically (for example) I do not presume to instruct Vietnamese peasants, South Africans, American blacks, Canadian Indians and Eskimos, or those among us who are desperately poor. I direct my remarks specifically to those of us whose lot is privilege and security, even affluence, and who therefore can afford the luxury of imagining what revolution might mean in its fullest dimensions. I am recalling that Marx was *primarily* interested in precisely those countries where capitalism had already created great material and cultural wealth, sufficient for 'universal' emancipation. In this context, the question arises: what did Marx mean by revolution, beyond mere negation? I want to re-identify those ends which must be contained within the revolutionary struggle, if it is to fulfil its potential.

In a famous passage from the 1844 manuscripts, Marx speaks of the 'crude and unreflective communism' which is *not* human emancipation, which is merely the old bondage under a new banner, because the old relation of 'private property' (of having and possessing material objects) still rules, and because egoism still rules.[12] It is the communism of 'envy' and 'levelling,' of 'the desire to reduce everything to a common level.' This is the legacy of an unhumanized struggle, a revolution scarcely deserving of the name, since it fails to transcend the given. It is mere negation with no surpassing. 'How little this abolition of private property represents a genuine appropriation is shown by the abstract negation of the whole world of culture and civilization, and the regression to the *unnatural* simplicity of the poor and wantless individual who has not only not surpassed private property but has not yet even attained to it.'[13]

There is, of course, a different praxis which *is* the revolution and the emancipation which we need. It is characterized by wholeness, or integrity. *First,* the wholeness of the individual 'for himself.' Just as 'private property' is fundamentally the shrinkage of whole, sensuous, creative man into 'the sense of having' so the otherness of private property is our emancipation from having into being and doing. We must come to find our humanity not in what we can grab and hold, but in what we can perform, create, and become. 'Private property has made us so stupid and partial that an object is only *ours* when we have it, when it exists for us as capital or when it is directly eaten, drunk, worn, inhabited, etc., in short, utilized in some way ... The supression of private property is ... the complete *emancipation* of all the human qualities and senses ... The human eye appreciates things in a different way from the crude, non-human eye, the human *ear* differently from the crude ear ... Man's musical sense is awakened only by music. The most beautiful music has no meaning for a non-musical ear, is not an object for it, because my object can only be the confirmation of one of my own faculties.'[14] It is sometimes argued – apparently by those who have not bothered to read him – that Marx cared little or nothing for the uniqueness and value of individual development. Here we see that the opposite is true, for Marx is passionately committed to that rich sensuous way of being in which a person 'appropriates his manifold being in an all-inclusive way, and thus as a whole man.'[15]

Second, the praxis which we must practise is characterized by the wholeness of an individual with other individuals, with his history, his culture, his community. 'Though man is a unique individual – and it is just his particularity which makes him an individual, a really *individual* communal being – he is

equally the *whole* ... the subjective existence of society as thought and experienced. He exists in reality as the representation and the real mind of
social existence, and as the sum of human manifestations of life.'[16] It is
sometimes ignorantly argued that Marx has no care for anything but
'material' values. The truth is that in his view material and cultural values are
inseparable, cannot be taken apart. 'Positive' abolition of private property,
according to Marx, 'assimilates all the wealth of previous development.'[17] It is
essential to see that this wealth is the humanization of the senses already
discussed, and the capacity to share in the rich inheritance of experience of
other men, in other times and places. 'Just as society at its beginnings finds,
through the development of *private property* with its wealth and poverty
(both intellectual and material), the materials necessary for this *cultural
development,* so the fully constituted society produces man in all the plenitude of his being, the wealthy man endowed with all the senses as an enduring
reality.'[18] The above, from the 1844 manuscripts; and two years later, in *The
German Ideology,* another formulation of the same dialectic between individual, culture, and community, 'Only in community with others has each
individual the means of cultivating his gifts in all directions; only in the
community, therefore, is personal freedom possible.'[19] Too often we have
formulated our perceptions of individual *versus* community in a way which
militates against their unity. Marx is reminding us, as did Aristotle so long
before, how false and pernicious must be the disjunction of individual and
community. The fact is that if there could be an 'ideal' isolated individual he
would not be a 'human' being at all, let alone a free or wealthy being. 'The
real intellectual wealth of the individual depends entirely on the wealth of his
real connections ... [He must] be liberated from the various national and local
barriers, be brought into practical connection with the material and intellectual production of the ... whole earth (the creations of man).'[20]

   Earlier I spoke of our need for self-change, but we need to see that self-
change is also, necessarily, social change, since we are not self-contained
monads, Jeremy Bentham notwithstanding. Self-change abstracted from
world-change is no praxis, no revolution; it is another egoism. Ultimately it is
an illusion. We are suckled on egoism, but egoistic behaviour is inherently
self-contradictory and self-defeating, for its aim is freedom and plenitude,
which its practice effectively negates. More to the immediate point, it is a
mistake to imagine that revolutionary self-change can be undertaken apart
from social change, because it will be curtailed and crushed, or at least
rendered trivial and impotent, in isolation. Certain kinds of self-change can be
tolerated within a capitalistic structure, but this structure is far from permitting what Marx called human emancipation, precisely because human

emancipation is a move beyond private property and the profit motive. Jewish emancipation our 'given' can tolerate – and perhaps black emancipation, women's emancipation, and many other particularisms (witness our indulgence towards hippie-dom). But can our 'given' surpass the cash nexus, the commodity fetish, which thus far it has held sacred? And can my self-change or yours amount to human emancipation so long as 'huckstering' is the hinge on which our social system swings?

De-alienations of society and of individuals are interdependent, such that neither can be completed without the other, nor can one be reduced to the other. This brings us back to the question of the kinds of class struggle which are commonly taken as the essence of Marx's revolutionary theory, the rough and bloody forms of struggle which Marx thought would be necessary,[21] which Lenin and Mao found necessary, and which I greatly fear because they are grossly inadequate to accomplish 'communism' or emancipation, in the sense discussed here. The problem is that far from 'assimilating all the wealth of previous development,' crude struggle may do much to destroy it. Instead of creating 'human' community, the barricades create at best a partial and particularistic community. Too often, instead of 'real connections' the struggle has issued in the tragic silence of dogmatism and death.

Again, I am far from denying that class struggle in the crude sense – that is, finding ways to physically expropriate the expropriators, who cling to privilege as if it were their own – I am far from denying that this kind of struggle, harsh and violent as it is, may sometimes be appropriate and justifiable, as well as inevitable. But, clearly it falls far short of the total revolution of which Marx spoke. Necessary it may be in some contexts, but it is far from sufficient. And there is always danger that it will prove counter-productive, that it will create new barriers to human emancipation.[22]

Much depends on the specific historical circumstances in which struggle is undertaken. Forms of struggle which are liberating in one time and place may be less than helpful in another. The question arises, what form – if any – revolutionary struggle should take in Canada, in 1971. It is a question which I cannot answer, for, unfortunately, I have no happy solution to the puzzle I have posed: how to make revolution without corrupting it; how to fight for freedom without destroying it. I could exhort my fellow academics to work within academia towards a new consciousness, transcending habits of egoism, competition, and possessing, but I am all too conscious of Marx's biting attacks on such 'idealistic' and 'utopian' methods. And, indeed, it would be naive to imagine that the effects of exhortation in the face of 'Commodity' and 'Profit' are likely to be anything but miniscule. Alternately, I could advise working towards non-revolutionary ('reformist') socialism, but I am all too conscious of its limitations. If it is true that human emancipation has not yet been ushered in by violence, it is equally true that it has nowhere been achieved through trade unions and parliaments.

In the works of Lenin, Mao, and others, much attention has been paid to the techniques of organizing vanguard parties, seizing and holding power, waging civil war, eliminating the opposition, establishing the 'correct line.' To what extent should revolutionary praxis in Canada, in the 1970s, move in these familiar patterns? I think marginally, if at all, for I am not convinced that these methods, in this context, will succeed in furthering social justice, let alone freedom and community.[23] I am not convinced that by these means we would even 'preserve the wealth of previous development,' let alone enhance or universalize it. For one thing, I do not see how, by these methods, we will create the man to whom Marcuse assigns the task of social construction: 'man with a different sensitivity as well as consciousness: men who would speak a different language, have different gestures, follow different impulses; men who have developed an instinctual barrier against cruelty, brutality, ugliness.'[24]

For another thing, I do not see that the oppressing class, in Canada, is going to be eliminated by 1917 methods. Class demarcation here is not sufficiently straightforward; oppression is too diffuse.[25] I have said that it is not just a question of identifying a few corrupt or brutal government officials and a few factory owners with greedy pockets, who are sitting on the rest of us. If my earlier argument is correct, *most of us,* certainly a large majority, are involved in the oppression, if only in the alienating affluence and the mentality which support it.[26] Our struggle, therefore, cannot be simplified into us against the enemy because the enemy is also us. Our lives are permeated with privilege. Our habits are those of private profit and possession. And, unfortunately, our profits, privileges, and superfluity of possessions are the reverse side of the poverty and oppression of others: for example, the oppression of the Canadian Indian whose land we have appropriated and whose culture we have destroyed. Unless we are ready to recognize the extent to which we are part of the enemy there is little point in assaults on Bay Street, Parliament Hill, or even the Pentagon.

My intention here is not to universalize guilt, or to argue that all of us are responsible (or *equally* responsible) for demonstrable social evils. On the contrary, where vast material resources today are commanded and defended by overwhelming concentrations of power and violence, there we would have to examine guilt and responsibility. But my present purpose is not to raise questions of guilt, or to assign responsibility. My purpose is simply to examine a problem, which is that in Canada most of us participate in, benefit from, and actively or tacitly support the capitalist system, even while we are being manipulated and debased by it. Therefore, in Canada today 'the enemy' cannot be got rid of by getting rid of a few particular oppressors. Therefore classical models of communist revolution give us little guidance, for they presuppose a context where class lines are relatively clear, and where there is a readily identifiable enemy in the form of a small exploitative elite, for whom legitimacy has obviously ebbed away, from whom power can be captured, with large-scale public support.

In rejecting these revolutionary models as unhelpful, I must take note of at least three difficulties. First, there is a danger of misconstruing Marx. Here let me say that in rejecting a Leninist model of revolution I do not claim to be speaking in Marx's name; I do not know what assessment he would make of our situation.

Second, there is the danger that we might de-fuse and trivialize the concept of revolution, turning it into another exhortation or incantation, without any dimension of real social struggle. Here let me acknowledge that revolutionary change is unlikely to be easy or painless. Though I have not discussed them here, I take it for granted that political and economic institutions too must be changed, together with the changes in consciousness and life style which I have mentioned, and I know that resistance to such changes is formidable. This any Marxist would take as self-evident. A Marxist typically argues that at some point revolutionary violence will prove necessary, and will be justified, against the established violence of the old order; and this too I have conceded, with respect to some times and places. The problem is that I cannot see any clear prospect for emancipation by violence in our own historical context.

Third, and most important, one who rejects well-known revolutionary models will be asked to produce a viable alternative. And here I can offer little, for I do not have in my head a new, up-to-date, well-articulated 'what is to be done?' — nor do I know of anyone who has. In fact, I suspect that our revolution (if there is to be one) will not have a Lenin, for its complexity requires the imagination and creativity of many, not one.

I have no brave new ideas which would lead out of this impasse: that in crucial areas our immense potential for freedom and creativity is blocked by social relations which are obviously stupifying to all of us and desperately repressive to some of us; yet there is no obvious revolutionary praxis which would move towards new liberating social relations. Still, a couple of modestly hopeful things might be said. We should remember that a large part of what Lenin and Mao had to accomplish is already accomplished for us, namely material abundance. They had to learn how to create it; we only have to humanize it: to learn how to use it towards freedom. Lenin and Mao had to deal very long and painfully with 'practical need,' whereas we, if we will, can quickly get beyond that to 'human need,' and to a serious struggle against the hosts of 'false needs' which we have accumulated. These considerations should give us some guidance towards out collective 'what is to be done?'

Further, we should not imagine that nothing significant can be done within a capitalist framework. Some change, both of consciousness and of social relations, is possible within what Marcuse has called the 'interstices' of the capitalist order. In his words, 'it is necessary to feel out every possibility of a crack in the enormously concentrated power structure of existing society.'[27] 'In established societies there are still gaps and interstices in which heretical methods can be practiced without meaningless sacrifice, and still help the cause ... One of the most important tasks is to make use of them to the full.'[28] He gives, as examples, radical psychoanalysis and radical law practice. To these examples we might want to add radical teaching and writing.

I know this is not much; it will hardly be a comfort to those who are burning with indignation, or to those whose sufferings are immediate and cruel. Nevertheless, it may be worth more than revolutionary efforts of meagre conception and crude execution.

In summary, a two-part reminder, to revolutionaries on one hand, and to my fellow academics on the other.

To revolutionaries, in Canada, in 1971, the still pertinent question which Marx posed in 1843: 'It is by no means sufficient to ask: Who should emancipate and who should be emancipated? Criticism had to be concerned with a third question. It must ask: *What kind of emancipation ... ?*'[29] I should think that a revolutionary endeavour today must take more seriously than ever the challenge posed by what Marx called 'human emancipation,' and must be judged by its success in actualizing that promise.

To my fellow teachers and students who, in numerous learned treatises on revolution, have failed to appreciate the full range and content of the praxis which Marx articulated, and have too often concentrated their attention exclusively on seizures of power and 'internal war,' I suggest that an important concept has been truncated and an important subject matter neglected.

Both revolutionaries and students of revolutions must concern themselves more carefully with Marx's question 'What kind of emancipation?' and must remind themselves that emancipation which deserves to be called 'human' must begin to be actualized within the revolutionary process, in the praxis of the revolutionaries. Men must somehow begin to be free and 'communal' even in the process of getting rid of institutions, habits, dogmas, and privileges which will not permit community and freedom. 'The struggle for a free society is not a struggle for a free society unless through it an ever greater ... personal freedom is created.'[30] Those are the words of Petrovic, from Yugoslavia, 1964. Here are the words of Marx, from Brussels, 1846: 'Both for the production on a mass scale of this communist consciousness, and for the success of the cause itself, the alteration of men on a mass scale is necessary, an alteration which can only take place in a practical movement, a *revolution;* this revolution is necessary, therefore, not only because the ruling class cannot be overthrown in any other way, but also because the class *overthrowing* it can only in a revolution succeed in ridding itself of all the muck of ages and become fitted to found society anew.'[31]

A problem with both crude class struggle and crude theory of revolution, in the past, is that they have separated goal from method instead of incorporating goal into method and beginning to actualize it there. But revolution must begin to be emancipation in the full, rich, 'human' sense discussed above. It must not push the goal off into a 'good society' of the future. Communism is no such 'good society,' nor is it just passive deliverance from that which was oppressive. It is social-individual *activity,* an 'alteration of men,' a getting rid of accumulated mucky prejudices, habits, institutions, and social relations, and the creation of new ones. Turning that around, we might say that to the extent that we achieve a revolutionary praxis, mediating goal with method and vice versa, we already begin to actualize our freedom. Whatever form our class struggle takes, therefore, it will be a snare and a delusion, a kind of monster, unless it begins now to make of us a new kind of 'human' being.

NOTES

1 See, for example, Peter Calvert, *Revolution* (London 1970), 15 and passim; James C. Davies, 'Toward a Theory of Revolution,' *American Sociological Review,* XXVII (Feb 1962), 6n3 and passim; Harry Eckstein, ed., *Internal War* (New York 1964), 1 and passim; Chalmers Johnson, *Revolutionary Change* (Boston 1966), 1, 7, 11, 12, and passim; Carl Leiden and Karl M. Schmitt, *The Politics of Violence: Revolution in the Modern World* (Englewood Cliffs, NJ 1968), chap. 1; Lawrence Stone, 'Theories of Revolution,' *World Politics,* XVIII (1966), 159ff.
2 *On Revolution* (New York 1965), chaps. 1 and 2, and passim. See also Herbert Marcuse, 'Ethics and Revolution,' *Ethics and Society,* ed. R.T. DeGeorge (New York 1966). Marcuse assumes what I am arguing: that revolution must aim at 'altering the social as well as the political structure' (134). Like Arendt, he holds that the function of revolutions in history has been 'demonstrable enlargement of the range of human freedom' (143). There are, of course, other exceptions to my generalization about the impoverishment of contemporary academic discussions of revolution. For example, see the excellent article by Eugene Kamenka, 'The Concept of a Political Revolution,' *Revolution,* ed. Carl J. Friedrich (New York 1966), reprinted in *Struggles in the State,* ed. George A. Kelly and Clifford W. Brown, Jr (New York 1970).
3 An exception to this is Marcuse, who clearly sees that the relation between means and ends must be 'dialectical.' 'The end must be operative in the repressive means for attaining the end.' Ibid., 147.

4 'Contribution to the Critique of Hegel's *Philosophy of Right,* Introduction,' *Karl Marx: Early Writings,* ed. and trans. T.B. Bottomore (New York 1963), 53

5 *Marx in the Mid-Twentieth Century* (Anchor ed., Garden City, NY 1967), 134

6 'On the Jewish Question,' *Writings of the Young Marx on Philosophy and Society,* ed. and trans. L.D. Easton and K.H. Guddat (Anchor ed., Garden City, NY 1967), 226, 227

7 Ibid., 231

8 Ibid., 227

9 Ibid., 231, 247

10 'Critique of Hegel's Dialectic and General Philosophy,' Bottomore, *Early Writings,* 208

11 Ibid.

12 'Private Property and Communism,' ibid., 152ff

13 Ibid., 153

14 Ibid., 159-61

15 Ibid., 159

16 Ibid., 158

17 Ibid., 155

18 Ibid., 162

19 Karl Marx and Frederick Engels, *The German Ideology,* ed. R. Pascal (New York 1968), 74

20 Ibid., 27

21 At various times Marx acknowledged the possibility that in exceptional cases there might be a peaceful transition to socialism, perhaps via party politics and parliaments, as in England, Holland, or the United States of America, perhaps via traditional socialistic institutions, such as the 'mir' in Russia. As Lenin put it, in one of his un-dogmatic moods:
   'Marx did not commit himself, or the future leaders of the socialist revolution, to matters of form, to ways and means of bringing about the revolution ...
   'Marx taught that (as an exception, and Britain was then an exception) the idea was conceivable of *paying the capitalists well,* of buying them off, if the circumstances were such as to compel the capitalists to submit peacefully and to come over to socialism in a cultured and organized fashion, provided they were bought off.' V.I. Lenin, 'The Tax in Kind,' *Lenin on Politics and Revolution: Selected Writings,* ed. James E. Connor (New York 1968), 330-1
   Nevertheless, Marx and Lenin both argued that as a general rule violent struggle would be required to overthrow the entrenched violence of the bourgeois order.

22 Marcuse argues that 'no matter how rational, how necessary, how liberating – revolution involves violence.' But he also notices that 'there are forms of violence and suppression which no revolutionary situation can justify because they negate the very end for which the revolution is a means.' 'Ethics and Revolution,' 147, 141

23 'A revolutionary movement must be able to give rational grounds for its chances to grasp real possibilities of human freedom and happiness, and it must be able to demonstrate the adequacy of its means for obtaining this end.' Ibid., 135

24 *An Essay on Liberation* (Boston 1969), 21

25 According to Marcuse we are at a stage 'where the people cannot reject the system of domination without rejecting themselves, their own repressive instinctual needs and values.' At this stage, 'liberation would mean subversion *against the will* and against the prevailing interests *of the great majority* of the people.' Ibid., 17, my emphasis

26 Marcuse remarks on 'cruel affluence' and on 'the affluent monster.' Ibid., 6, 7

27 'The End of Utopia,' *Five Lectures* (Boston 1970), 74

28 Ibid., 76, 77

29 'On the Jewish Question,' 220

30 Petrovic, *Marx in the Mid-Twentieth Century,* 130

31 Marx and Engels, *The German Ideology,* 69

Alkis Kontos

Between memory and dream

When History sleeps, it speaks in dreams: on the forehead of the sleeping people, the poem is a constellation of blood. When History wakes, image becomes act, the poem happens: poetry gets into the action.

Deserve your dream.

OCTAVIO PAZ

The terror and magic of the human journey through time is best captured by the imagination. The articulation of imaginative vision reveals the limitation and the necessity of language and renders poetry inevitable. Imaginative vision, both a discovery and a creation, grants the human drama its inexhaustible meaning through its poetic articulation.

Plato was the first great philosopher to realize and employ this unique relation between philosophy and poetry. He embedded his philosophy in the poetry of the dramatic form, making content and mode of expression inseparable. Any attempt to dissociate them fully would only impoverish and distort the meaning achieved by their unity.

Aristotle was the first great philosopher to ignore this unity. He neglected the most essential feature of Plato's achievement. Aristotle's critique of Plato's political philosophy is rooted in his unwillingness to appreciate the poetic dimension of Plato's philosophic totalization. The cosmological scope of Plato's endeavour was transformed into cosmogony by the poetry of its expression. Aristotle, by replacing the poetic word with categories, silenced the inner eloquence of the philosophic vision. But the vision itself has not been obliterated. The intimate connection between philosophy and the imagination has survived. Philosophy did not lose its strength to dream, to create a cosmos as yet unseen and contra the world as such, to illuminate the enduring, and to defy the mundane. Philosophy, prevented from embracing poetry, sought refuge in the realm of the imagination and found some relief in conceptual clarity and precision of expression.

Much of the current writing on social change lacks both vision and conceptual clarity. Rhetoric and obscurantism replace vision, enslavement to sterile definitions replaces conceptual clarity. The difficulties and dangers endemic to any abstract discourse about social change are many and serious.[1] A fruitful exploration of the phenomenon of social change requires lucid thinking and a refusal to succumb to either intellectual despair or activist euphoria. The study of social change must begin with certain indispensable distinctions regarding society and change.

This essay attempts to stress some distinctions necessary for the study of the phenomenon of social change, which are too frequently ignored, and to suggest that theoretical totalizations about social transformation are imaginative exercises stretching beyond the practico-political: they are not without practical significance, but their value is much more than practical. The work of Marcuse is referred to as an example of this type of social philosophy.

A society is not a mere group of individuals sharing space in the flux of time. Individuals encounter one another in specific relations which define actual human lives. Social relations veil all individuals and condition how they live and die; dreams and fears are confined by such relations. No one is completely determined; no one is fully autonomous.

The analysis of the quality of human life in society warrants more than the systematic dissection of how the members of a society live. Even the most elaborate and insightful anatomy of this kind must be seen as inadequate, for it does not touch upon the forces that generate and sustain a specific mode of social existence. To understand a society we must comprehend not only *how* but also *why* a particular mode of social existence prevails. The analyst must penetrate the very core of social structure and activity, beyond all appearance, in order to discover the dynamics of society and the universality of the human condition and potential.

To understand a society, therefore, we must go far beyond description, beyond a detailed portrayal of social life. The strictly empirical, phenomenological encounter with the myriad of situational actualities of society does not in itself allow us to grasp the totality. The empirical does not yield meaning spontaneously; meaning is never self-evident. A situation always invites and demands interpretation, understanding. To interpret is to express a specific understanding, to advance a certain definition; it is an activity of inclusion and exclusion, of establishing relations, of assigning significance. Interpretation entails a perspective, explicit or implicit, through which coherence and meaning are imposed on the empirical and our experience of it. But the empirical sets the boundaries within which meaningfulness unfolds. Discovery and creation can never be fully dissociated; they constantly overlap. The empirical limits are uncovered through discovery of the objective reality. Meaning, however, is creatively founded. That is why the objective must always be established from a subjective perspective which de-objectifies the former without necessarily destroying its objective status. It is not the essence of the objective that eludes us, but its precise demarcation.

To judge the quality of human life prevalent in a society one must have not only an understanding of the inner workings of that society but also a criterion not inherent in the factual and empirical aspects of the society. To evaluate what a society does and does not do to its members, a concept of human essence[2] is needed as the external criterion. It is against such a concept that the quality of social existence can be measured. Only in the light of such a concept can a social critique be developed and social inadequacies be made visible.

Obviously not just any concept of human essence will do. Postulates about human essence cannot be either totally a priori or totally empirical. They must be a combination of both, moderated and strengthened under the aegis of the imagination. Such postulates need not be explicit. Their implicit presence suffices. The most imperative aspect of any attempt to establish a valid perspective on human essence is the need to distinguish ontology from history. The mere pronouncement and acknowledgment of such need does not overcome the problematics of the issue. It is only the beginning, for the paradox and the challenge remain: to differentiate ontology from history within the flow of history itself.

The difficulties inherent in any attempt to extricate ontology from the web of history are enormous,[3] but because they are not permanently fixed they are not insurmountable. Different historical epochs render ontology more or less discernible. Much depends on the degree of disjuncture between ontology and the historically prevailing social mode of life. The social negation of the human potential could become sufficiently visible under certain circumstances.

My intention here is not to resolve the philosophical issue of human essence, but to point out that such a concept is imperative in evaluating social life and that the distinction between ontology and history is necessary for the achievement of a valid notion of humanity. It is what we understand humanity to be that leads us to the acceptance or rejection of what we see around us. Without such a point of reference social life becomes a qualitatively undifferentiated variation of life styles. From the premise of human essence, life styles are not compared and contrasted, scrutinized and explained on a comparative social science scale; they are judged.

The prevailing form of social life can then be seen as conducive or detrimental to the fulfilment of the potential of the members of a society. Desires, needs, whole lives are no longer arbitrary, whimsical elements. Nor are they accidents. They are teleological, purposive, and, hence, meaningful. The empirical and the normative are joined reciprocally. The normative seeks its realization and in doing so exposes and condemns the inadequacies of the empirical. The latter restrains the demands of the normative when faithful to its historical capability. The *is* and the *ought* are not juxtaposed in a vacuum but in historical time and space.

The adamant demand of the normative is that the structure of society ought to promote what is essentially human. To promote does not mean to realize. The intransigence of a moral absolute applies only in terms of the intention of social organization. Such organization must always seek the advancement of humanizing institutions and practices and avoid the negation of human potentiality. This remains an absolute guiding principle. But the realization of what is posited as the human essence must occur within historical circumstances. Therefore, the measure of the quality of human life in society cannot be exclusively the concept of human essence and the intention of social organization but must include the material-technological capabilities

of the society. All the willingness to achieve the realization of human fulfilment will not suffice in the face of severe material inadequacy. The stage of
development of a society becomes the objective context in which we can
judge social life in its historical movement towards the deliberate realization
or negation of the human essence. The imperative scheme of social organization is the mobilization of the material potential of society towards the
creation of the circumstances which are necessary for the uninhibited realization of humanity. Discrepancy between capability and organization is the
vital socio-political issue as opposed to discrepancy between willingness and
inability, which is a technical-scientific issue.

The material-technological development of a society is evaluated not in
abstraction but in the context of its purpose in relation to the postulated
concept of human essence. The ontological and the historical, the moral and the
political are inexorably bound together so that neither relativism nor unhistori-
cal absolute moralism are viable. It is the specificity of the historical moment in
the light of our vision of humanity that must be coordinated and *humanly*
compromised. Neither divine purity nor political immorality would suffice.

A society is an agglomeration of human relations overt and covert: legal,
political, economic, psychological. These relations correspond to specific
activities from which ensue organizational, institutional structures. The
fundamental organizational aspects of a society constitute its identifying
characteristics. It is these characteristics which condition and reveal the
actuality of human life in the social space. Social life as actual, lived experience rather than as an abstract systemic pattern, discloses what binds men
as social beings. Only when we have discovered that bond can we begin to
grasp the context and subject of social change, society itself.

In any society over a period of time, a variation, a difference would
inevitably occur. Life cannot exist without change. However, not just any
array of differences in time, be it sudden or protracted, qualifies as social
change. The phenomenon of social change occurs either as change *in* society
or as change *of* society. Change *in* society suggests a significant variation of
important aspects of social life. Such change does not have any effect on the
essential character of the society; the prevailing style of life, its quality,
remains unchanged. The social bond, the very core of social structure,
remains untouched. Neither the scope nor the degree of this type of change
alter the fact that its goal is never the transformation of the society itself. It is
always confined within the basic and substantive boundaries of the existing
social order. This is its ultimate limit in scope and degree. Change *of* society
seeks the transformation of the essentials of society – of society itself.

Change could be deliberate or accidental. It could be the unintended result
of other intended actions. Not all change is consciously sought. It has been

claimed that some monumental changes were not deliberate.[4] Furthermore, change, deliberate or not, extensive or minor, should not automatically be presumed to be good and positive. Unless we evaluate the intention and results of change in reference to the human essence and the quality of life no verdict is possible. The Nazi rule was a deliberate, drastic change. Its atrocious intention was only intensified by its actual magnitude.

Describing the degree and mode of change does not determine whether such change is positive or negative. The final and most reliable criterion remains the degree to which change improves the quality of social life in accordance with the precepts of human essence and the historical capabilities of a given society.

The political dimension of social change concerns only deliberate change. When we deal with change *in* society politically we deal with reform. When we deal with change *of* society, change which seeks the transformation of society *in order to actualize* the human essence, we deal with revolution.[5] Change that does not disturb the basic structure of society, that honours the essentials of the status quo, irrespective of improvements, is reform and not revolution. If the term revolutionary change is used to indicate extensive reforms rather than social transformation, it only obscures the central difference between reform and revolution. Equally, not any transformation of society irrespective of whether it dehumanizes or humanizes can be termed a revolution. Neither the method nor the scope but the goal renders reform and revolution distinct and irreconcilable.[6] The sole determinant must be the principle which informs the revolutionary purpose.

The shrewd conservative Edmund Burke understood well the profound difference between reform and revolution, but he misread the intention of revolution, for the status quo was more than acceptable to him.[7] By comparison to Alexis de Tocqueville, Burke failed to grasp the prolonged institutional erosion which brought about the French revolution. But it was Burke who perceived the lasting and perhaps irreversible philosophical and political implication of this historical event: the conviction that a new society can be created on preconceived theoretical grounds. He grasped the novelty of the situation. But he saw the spirit of the events as disruptive and pernicious.[8] Burke's hostility towards revolutionary thinking is best modified and rectified by Albert Camus who renounced both revolutionary excess and ossified conservatism. He wished to tame revolution by ostracizing its nihilistic proclivity. The taming force is the muted principle of rebellion, a principle of moderation, and mediation between ends and means.[9]

We live in a time of acute crisis, moral and material, but not in a revolutionary situation. Politically, the French revolution is the origin of our life-scenario; and it has remained a catalyst. It did not achieve the promise of its naïve lyricism: it closed the curtain on a past era; it did not give birth to something new. We remain suspended between the obsolete past and the unborn future. And there is no reasonable ground to believe that this crisis would inevitably find a happy resolution. Deterioration is infinite. It has its limit in death. There is no inherent force demanding reversibility. There is no inexorable march towards emancipation marred only by mere regressions. Renouncing inevitability as simplistic does not mean that our social universe is either incomprehensible or acceptable. As Collingwood put it, we should not be carried away with 'opium-dreams of coming felicity.'[10]

The awareness of the fact of dehumanization is neither the privilege of some nor the unerring product of specific objective conditions. Objective negative changes in society need not be experienced uniformly. Human consciousness need not appropriate the truth of an objective situation in a single, unified, and accurate manner. The contradictions between actuality and potentiality need not be obscured indefinitely. Yet a diversified response to that contradiction cannot be precluded. It was perhaps Max Weber's seminal and sobering contribution to social thought to point out that men as actors are never determined as objects of an iron law. An altered situation demands a response, but the range of response can vary.[11] Neither miracles nor mechanical formulas can perform the task of liberation destined only for human action founded on a consciousness for the need of such liberation, a consciousness which defies any metaphysical guarantees regarding its emergence. This consciousness cannot be forced upon anyone. That it cannot be forced is a testament to human dignity, its historical fragility and vulnerability.

The intimate and complex relation between the mental and material dimensions of life, between consciousness and social activity, warrants a more dynamic and imaginative schematization.[12] The Marxian insight into human activity and consciousness must find its philosophical equilibration: Marx's thought has not been completely immune to the intrusion of historicity.[13] Its purification does not imply a return to a rigid and supposedly orthodox doctrine. A re-orientation of our thinking is in order. Further progression, revitalization, and expression should be considered. The belief that a particular body of thought has all the truth we need or that a sophisticated eclecticism would lead us to a happy synthesis ought to be discarded.

The de-petrification of the Marxian perspective would reveal the *social* orientation of the reconstruction of collective life. The transformation of society cannot be a private affair. It is a political, collective issue. Personal, individual change without a corresponding change of society is inadequate. Drastic personal transformation so frequently described in world literature and occasionally witnessed in real life does not suffice. Moral rebirth of this kind, profound as it may be, remains insulated and ultimately impotent vis-à-vis the massive inhumanity of social life. Its exemplary and cathartic effects constitute the essence of classical Greek tragedy. Such change remains elliptical, for the individual is still denied the fundamentally necessary social context in order to be fully humanized. A reciprocal change involving individual and society is necessary. There can be no solace either in the complete renunciation of the self, the extinction of individualism (there is such a thing as healthy individualism), or in the total withdrawal of one's fidelity to and concern with others and the fate of the world. Either way impoverishes, destroys the balance, fragments and empties the world of any possible reasonable meaning.

Social change aiming at the humanization of the world must presuppose and demand the possibility of a dimension where the individual and the collective are so joined together in common destiny and impenetrable solidarity as to safeguard them without the one asphyxiating the other. The articulation of this dimension is primarily the work of the imagination.

It is the poetic licence of philosophy to dream of a distant future, of a dignified style of life without immediate concern for the strategy of the actualization of this vision. Poets and philosophers evoke the most primordial and human symbols by liberating their divine madness, by breaking the silence of the universe with the voice of the imagination in the name of humanity. This visionary activity can never be the subject of science or be fully translated into a program of action. The poetic totalization is the best expression of human rebellion against the inadequacy of reality. But it is a creative rebellion. It awakens the human spirit, it mobilizes, it orients, it promises a new life. It does not, or rather it ought not, reject all known human existence. Creative imagination differs from both delusion and the insistence to alter the world as such. In totalizing, the philosopher includes an aspect of imagination which is by nature beyond action. Poetic vision parts ways with ideological programs and doctrines. Until and unless we realize this necessary utopian aspect of totalization we can only struggle against the impossible in utter futility and quite ignorant of the Archemedian point of the aesthetics of the imagination from which life and the world are interpreted, castigated, and loved.

A visionary philosophy of social transformation cannot be oblivious to reality; nor can it be fully immersed in reality. The theorist provides the vision; the strategist must find the way. This is the demand for the division of labour in the creative process, for the continuity and innovation of human life in time and space, our inescapable perspectival boundaries.

Marcuse is one of the very few contemporary social philosophers who engages in visionary totalization and who reaffirms its meaning and validity. This is especially so now that he appears to be resigned to the fact that no revolutionary situation exists. The counter-revolution has arrived before the revolution.[14] Marcuse's articulation of the possibility of a free society restores the imaginative premise of social philosophy initiated by Plato. The absence of programmatic strategy in Marcuse's thought is its strength, not its weakness.

Marcuse's notion of a non-repressive civilisation, a free human society, is intended as a 'hypothesis.'[15] His whole thesis suggests and elucidates a future possibility,[16] not an inevitability. Any existing positive tendencies are interpreted with caution.[17] Marcuse suggests that we live in an ambiguous historical situation which forces him to 'vacillate ... between two contradictory hypotheses: (1) that advanced industrial society is capable of containing qualitative change for the foreseeable future; (2) that forces and tendencies exist which may break this containment and explode the society.'[18] Such vacillation concerns only the chance of liberation. Marcuse has no theoretical reservation regarding society's capability of being transformed into a free society. 'Critical theory' unveils such potential; it cannot materialize it.[19] It is in this context of sheer possibility and the chances for its realization that he distinguishes between freedom and liberation.

Freedom is a specific condition of human life which Marcuse regards both desirable and possible. Liberation refers to a state of consciousness that ultimately manifests itself in the political act of the rejection, and, it is hoped, the defeat of unfree society.[20] For Marcuse, freedom is a future possibility. Freedom 'is nowhere already in existence.'[21] Marcuse's notion of freedom insists on the rejection of both Freud's identification of civilization with repression and Marx's dichotomy between necessity and freedom. Marcuse, unlike Marx, believes in 'the possibility of freedom *within* the realm of necessity.'[22] This double rejection centres on a creative synthesis of two perspectives on the individual and society: Marxian and Freudian.

According to Marx, man 'only truly produces in freedom' from physical need.[23] Free activity cannot be a means to survival.[24] Regarding freedom and necessity, Marx states: 'In fact, the realm of freedom actually begins only where labour which is determined by necessity and mundane considerations ceases; thus in the very nature of things it lies beyond the sphere of actual material production.'[25] Human activity under the dominion of necessity is not compatible with genuine freedom. In distinguishing freedom from necessity he says: 'Beyond it [the realm of necessity] begins that development of human energy which is an end in itself, the true realm of freedom ...'[26]

Marx does not believe that men can ever liberate themselves from the sway of necessity. 'Just as the savage must wrestle with Nature to satisfy his wants, to maintain and reproduce life, so must civilized man, and he must do so in all social formations and under all possible modes of production.'[27] Because of the ineradicable character of necessity and its omnipresence in all socio-political organizations, Marx, deeply concerned with man's fate within the realm of necessity, sought to ameliorate it. He wished to render the realm of necessity rational and less inhuman.[28] But whatever the improvements within the realm of necessity 'it nonetheless still remains a realm of necessity.'[29] Marx somberly curtails any excessive optimism by reminding us that freedom and necessity always remain distinct. Improvements within the realm of necessity cannot transform it into a realm of freedom. Such improvements are themselves seriously limited.[30]

The two realms, though distinct, relate in a specific way in Marx's view. He states: '... the true realm of freedom ... can blossom forth only with this [rational] realm of necessity as its basis. The shortening of the working-day is its basic prerequisite.'[31] The foundation of freedom is for Marx a rationally technologically structured realm of necessity in the context of a humanized society.[32]

Marcuse's philosophical inquiry into Freud is his most comprehensive statement on the theme of a non-repressive civilization. Marcuse's central theme is that repression is an historical phenomenon which Freud takes to be an inherent, eternal aspect of civilization. The historicity of repression renders it dispensable at a certain point in time, according to Marcuse.

Marcuse's essential claim is that Freud does not maintain a distinction between historical contingencies and biological necessities. 'Precisely because all civilization has been organized domination, the historical development assumes the dignity and necessity of a universal biological development.'[33] It is this mystification of historical processes that Marcuse intends to expose. He proposes to extrapolate the historical dimension contained in Freud's un-historical concepts. He wants to put the conflict between the pleasure principle and the reality principle back into an historical context. In order to do so, to extricate the biological from the socio-historical, Marcuse introduces two basic concepts: surplus-repression and performance principle.

Surplus-repression refers to repression emanating from social domination. It differs from basic repression which is necessary 'for the perpetuation of the human race in civilization.'[34] Surplus-repression is imposed over and above the degree of repression objectively warranted. It is excess repression in the service of domination. Marcuse clearly subscribes to the idea that not all repression can or ought to be removed. His target is only surplus-repression, domination, and not repression per se. Performance principle denotes the prevailing historical form of the reality principle in contemporary civiliza-tion.[35] Historically, the reality principle differs in form at different stages of civilization. Performance principle corresponds to only one historical reality principle exemplified in a society 'stratified according to the competitive economic performances of its members.'[36] It is imperative to realize that for Marcuse all historical forms of the reality principle are different modes of domination. Surplus-repression is the common denominator of all such forms manifested through specific historical institutional structures.

As the historical reality principle changes, so do the institutions of domination. But domination remains. The performance principle then, according to Marcuse's terminology, determines the specific institutional and ideological forms through which surplus-repression is exercised in contemporary society.

Marcuse claims that Freud assigned to the fact of scarcity 'what actually is the consequence of a specific *organization* of scarcity, and of a specific existential attitude enforced by this organization.'[37] Not distinguishing the distribution of scarcity from the fact of scarcity itself forces Freud to view the struggle for existence in a non-historical context and to believe in the eternal antagonism between the pleasure principle and the reality principle. Marcuse does not deny the fact of scarcity. He sees it, however, as an historical phenomenon.

Marcuse's social critique is founded on his assertion that freedom is now possible to the extent that the conquest of scarcity is possible. Such conquest amounts to the 'rational mastery of nature and society.'[38] Rationally guided technological advancement eradicates scarcity not in some absolute quantitative manner but in a rationally determined qualitative mode. Scarcity is seen from the perspective of *real* human needs. The conquest of scarcity is tantamount to the satisfaction of such true human needs. This satisfaction 'does not depend on the existence of abundance for all.'[39] Neither is the lowering of the standard of living that would result from the redirection of social productivity towards the universal gratification of human needs something regrettable for Marcuse.[40] Men lose their humanity not only in ruthless poverty but also in the loneliness and boredom of opulence. We should not forget that for Marx neither proletarians nor capitalists achieve true humanity. We should be able by now to differentiate opulence, poverty, frugality, sufficiency. Mastery of nature does not imply the ability of men to force nature to yield miraculous amounts of material wealth. It is not abundance as such that is the goal; it is the qualitative distinction between the truly human and the false that determines the issue.

The liberation of technological advancements from 'productive' irrationality would not eliminate necessity. For 'the elimination of surplus-repression would *per se* tend to eliminate, not labor, but the organization of human existence into an instrument of labor.'[41] Put differently, mature industrial society rationally realizing its technological capabilities recaptures Marx's distinction between the rationally structured realm of necessity and freedom.

Marcuse claims that progressive advancement towards automation creates possibilities beyond those Marx had visualized.[42] Automation would minimize 'the time necessary for the production of the necessities of life.'[43] Drastic reduction of the working day is the natural consequence of automation. But the 'quantitative reduction of necessary labor could turn into quality (freedom), not in proportion to the reduction but rather to the transformation of the working day, a transformation in which the stupefying, enervating, pseudo-automatic jobs of capitalist progress would be abolished.'[44]

It is in this context that Marcuse argues the possibility of freedom within necessity. Socially necessary work cannot be abolished, but it can be transformed. Work and freedom are not inherently irreconcilable; freedom and alienated labour are.[45] Work, socially useful activity, rational and non-alienated, can, according to Marcuse, become play, that is, free activity. Marcuse distinguishes work from play, free activity, according to purpose. Work has a purpose outside itself; it serves 'the ends of self-preservation.'[46] Play is purposeless; it is an end in itself. Precisely because 'it is the purpose and not the content which marks an activity as play or work' the latter can be transformed into play 'without losing its *work* content.'[47] It should be remembered that Marcuse speaks of such transformation only in relation to socially necessary, non-alienated work in the presence of a fully developed industrial civilization. This transformation does not apply to alienated labour.

The all-pervasive freedom that Marcuse envisages finds no ground in history. Its support and strength are from that aspect of human personality which remains undefeated by the historical reality principle: fantasy. The public expression of fantasy is art. Imagination longs for and dreams of a world free from the fetters of existing historical reality. But imagination confined in the form of art suffers, for ultimately art through its own form reconciles itself to the existing reality.[48] 'Art survives only where it cancels itself, where it saves its substance by denying its traditional form and thereby denying reconciliation: where it becomes surrealistic and atonal.'[49] And even then its fate is doomed.[50] Even surrealistic art cannot be an instrument of liberation. 'It seems that the poems and the songs of protest and liberation are always too late or too early: memory or dream. Their time is not the present; they preserve their truth in their hope, in their refusal of the actual.'[51]

This refusal, perennial and primordial as it is, testifies to the desire for a totally free existence. The free society of the future, in the womb of the present, must create its own cultural order.[52] Marcuse, by resorting to the mythological images of Orpheus and Narcissus, clearly indicates that no detailed elaboration can be given of such new order.[53] He prudently abstains from describing the structure of the future free society in strictly empirical terms. It is intimated in poetic and mythic metaphor.

Marcuse's free society is not one with *no* order. A totally new, rational order would prevail.[54] Freedom is incompatible with domination, but not with rational authority.[55] Rationality safeguards harmony between the individual and society, the individual and nature.[56] Human activity would become 'the free manifestation of potentialities.'[57] The collective cannot absorb the individual if the latter is to be free. But neither should the individual encounter the whole as an antagonistic, hostile force. The two can relate freely on the basis of the satisfaction of human, individual needs. Freedom cannot be wholly a private or wholly a social affair. Unless it is both, it is not freedom.[58] The free cooperative society would allow men for the first time to think freely and express their wants.[59] To determine this expression in its specificity beforehand is to pre-empt and obliterate freedom itself.

What motivates Marcuse to employ the language of psychology is the breakdown of the traditional boundaries between psychology and political and social philosophy; psychological categories have been transformed into political ones.[60] The vicissitudes of the modern psyche mirror the individual's public, political existence and its problems. The total absorption of the individual by the collective does testify to the absence of individual autonomy. Freudian theory is not just a convenient means of re-opening the philosophic issue of individual authenticity and social existence. It also presents the individual psychic dynamics in a way most acceptable to Marcuse. It is this presentation that when reinterpreted is not fully transubstantiated. Marcuse, through extrapolation and textual analysis, denies Freud's dialectic of civilization its finality.[61] Through Freud, more accurately through the reinterpreted Freud, Marcuse can speak more precisely and more concretely about the free individual. Sensuality, eros, pleasure, and happiness are referred to as specific, vital attributes of the free individual.

Marcuse claims that the ultimate form of freedom must be freedom from anxiety.[62] His idea of a fully free human society must finally come to terms with the fact of mortality.[63] Marcuse suggests that death can be confined to its 'natural' dimension.[64] But this implies the conquest of disease on a scale that transcends technology – it has to do with scientific knowledge. Marcuse's brief reference to such an eventuality warrants on his part a more serious and extensive elaboration.[65] Here the resolution is not as fortunate as the one between freedom and necessity. Though the fulfilled present would allow men to render death rational, this would not be adequate because 'even the ultimate advent of freedom cannot redeem those who died in pain. It is the remembrance of them, and the accumulated guilt of mankind against its victims, that darken the prospect of a civilization without repression.'[66] Marcuse does not pursue the impact of the guilt ensuing from the memory of the inhuman past on the actual behaviour of the free individual.

Ultimately, men as creatures of time cannot fully escape their past. Memory anchors history to prehistory and tarnishes the most rational achievements of a mature industrial civilization. The memory of what has been does not vanish; but neither does the dream of what can be.

Marcuse's future earth must be seen as both a claim to freedom from unnecessary, manmade suffering and domination, and a creative vision that rebels against and negates historical existence. For Marcuse, if we are to be eternally bound to the guilt wrought by the memory of past inhumanities, it does not mean that we should also remain living witnesses to the perpetuation of such inhumanities. If we cannot erase the past, we can drastically alter the future. Between memory and dream the individual must chart his voyage. The courage to dream about the future resides in the imagination. This courage alone does not change society, but a society without the courage and strength to dream neither can change nor is worth changing. The dialectic of the imaginative vision and reality, the contra reality poetic totalization, can never be translated and thus be exhausted into a program for social change, a systematic remedy for our social inadequacies. But neither can we ever drastically change the quality of our life without the expression of this trans-realization image of the world. It motivates and enriches; without it we have the sound and fury of mindless action or a barren, bureaucratic process – institutionalized mediocrity. Neither can salvage human destiny for neither knows the humanistic purpose of social change and its boundless horizon which can never be reduced to a concrete reality though its utterance is and must always be a vital and intrinsic dimension of all human reality.

NOTES

1 Robert A. Nisbet, *Social Change and History: Aspects of the Western Theory of Development* (New York 1969); *The Social Bond: An Introduction to the Study of Society* (New York 1970), part III. In both works Nisbet warns of and indicates the possible dangers in attempts to conceptualize change. However, here his contribution ends; neither society nor change are made comprehensible.
2 Marx's view of human essence as free creative activity provides a sound starting point. It also holds the promise of the resolution of the social conflict between the individual and the collective. Marx's image of man is not free from ambivalence and ambiguity. Its problematic character is exemplified in the fact that Marx underscored the existential dimension. But Marx ontologized aesthetics, something that only Marcuse has had the courage to pursue further. For Marx on human essence see *Economic and Philosophic Manuscripts of 1844* (Moscow 1961), 75-6.
3 Herbert Marcuse, *Eros and Civilization: A Philosophical Inquiry into Freud* (New York

1962), 120. This book is predicated upon and devoted to the differentiation of ontology from history.

4 See Max Weber, *The Protestant Ethic and the Spirit of Capitalism,* trans. Talcott Parsons (New York 1958); Emile Durkheim, *The Division of Labor in Society,* trans. George Simpson (New York 1968), bk. 2, chap. 2; Mircea Eliade, *Myth and Reality,* trans. Willard R. Trask (New York 1968); Hannah Arendt, *The Human Condition* (Chicago 1958), chap. VI; also her *Between Past and Future: Eight Exercises in Political Thought* (New York 1968), chaps. 2, 8. It should be borne in mind that for Marx alienation does not result from a deliberate policy.

5 Rosa Luxemburg, 'Social Reform or Revolution,' in *Selected Political Writings of Rosa Luxemburg,* ed. Dick Howard (New York 1971), esp. 113-23. For the history of the concept of revolution see Sigmund Newmann, 'The International Civil War,' *World Politics,* 1 (1948-9), 333-50; Vernon F. Snow, 'The Concept of Revolution in Seventeenth-Century England,' *The Historical Journal,* 5 (1962), 167-74; Arthur Hatto, ' "Revolution": An Enquiry into the Usefulness of an Historical Term,' *Mind,* 58 (1949), 495-517. To my knowledge the only person who denies the astronomical origin of the term is R.G. Collingwood, *The New Leviathan: Or Man, Society, Civilization and Barbarism* (Oxford 1942, 1958), 199. He states: 'The word "revolution" was borrowed towards the end of the seventeenth century by the vocabulary of politics from the vocabulary of literary criticism. In literary criticism it meant what Aristotle in his *Poetics* has called a "peripety," of which "revolution" was a literal translation.' See further 199-202.

6 Current literature on the topic of revolution and social change is, with few exceptions, hopeless in its abysmal linguistic confusion. Emphasis on method rather than purpose, particularly excessive concern with violence, as well as unwillingness to distinguish between sweeping reforms *in* society and transformation of society itself, establish the premise for a shallow, pseudo-intellectual analysis. As examples of the exceptions I have in mind, see Hannah Arendt, *On Revolution* (New York 1963); Eugene Kamenka, 'The Concept of a Political Revolution,' in *Revolution,* ed., Carl J. Friedrich (New York 1966), 122-35; Herbert Marcuse, 'Ethics and Revolution,' in *Ethics and Society,* ed. R.T. DeGeorge (New York 1966), 133-147; Maurice Merleau-Ponty, *Humanism and Terror: An Essay on the Communist Problem,* trans. John O'Neill (Boston 1969), part II; Jean-Paul Sartre, *Search for a Method,* trans. Hazel E. Barnes (New York 1963).

7 *Reflections on the Revolution in France* (Indianapolis 1955).

8 The following terminology indicates what Burke took to be the dangerous evil: 'metaphysical abstraction,' 'speculations,' 'political metaphysics,' 'abstract rule,' 'metaphysic rights,' 'loose theories.' Ibid., 8, 39, 66, 69, 70, 193. Burke states: 'Political reason is a computing principle: adding, subtracting, multiplying, and dividing, morally and not metaphysically, or mathematically, true moral denominations,' 71.

9 Camus is adamant on the need for continuity between present and revolutionary future. Revolution must not only destroy but also create. Men should not be reduced to either objects or 'to simple historical terms.' Albert Camus, *The Rebel: An Essay on Man in Revolt,* trans. Anthony Bower (New York 1956), 250. On the need for continuity see also Herbert Marcuse, *Counter-Revolution and Revolt* (Boston 1972), chap. 3. Whereas Camus emphasizes men, Marcuse stresses the enduring value and meaning of art. But see Camus, *The Rebel,* 276. 'Beauty, no doubt, does not make revolutions. But a day will come when revolutions will have need of beauty.' Also see his *The Myth of Sisyphus and Other Essays,* trans. Justin O'Brien (New York 1959). Camus states: 'Yes, there is beauty and there are the humiliated. Whatever may be the difficulties of the undertaking I should like never to be unfaithful either to one or to the other,' 145.

10 *The New Leviathan,* 201

11 Reasonableness is not an inevitable factor in perceptions of reality, especially in cases of religiously guided responses. See Norman Cohn, *The Pursuit of the Millennium: Revolutionary Millenarians and Mystical Anarchists of the Middle Ages* (London rev. ed. 1970);

Sylvia L. Thrupp, ed., *Millennial Dreams in Action: Essays in Comparative Study* (The Hague 1962).

12 For Marx's insistence on the primacy, not the exclusivity, of economic activity see 'Letters on Historical Materialism' in Karl Marx and Frederick Engels, *Basic Writings on Politics and Philosophy,* ed. Lewis S. Feuer (New York 1959), esp. 397-400. According to Max Weber, 'Not ideas, but material and ideal interests, directly govern men's conduct. Yet very frequently the "world images" that have been created by "ideas" have, like switchmen, determined the tracks along which action has been pushed by the dynamic of interest.' 'The Social Psychology of the World Religions,' in *From Max Weber: Essays in Sociology,* ed. H.H. Gerth and C. Wright Mills (New York 1958), 280.

13 Merleau-Ponty, *Humanism and Terror,* 153, 155-6; Marcuse, *Eros and Civilization; Five Lectures: Psychoanalysis, Politics and Utopia* (Boston 1970), chap. 4; 'Re-examination of the Concept of Revolution,' *New Left Review* (July-August 1969), 27-34; Sartre, *Search for a Method;* Arthur Koestler, *The Yogi and the Commissar: and Other Essays* (London 1945, 1964), 19-20. 'The swinging of this pendulum from rationalistic to romantic periods and back is not contradictory to the conception of a basic dialectic movement of History. It is like the tidal waves on a river which yet flows into the sea. One of the fatal lacunae in the Marxist interpretation of history is that it was only concerned with the course of the river, not with the waves. The mass-psychological aspect of Nazism is not describable in Marxist terms, in terms of the river's course ...' Also Frantz Fanon, *The Wretched of the Earth,* trans. Constance Farrington (New York 1966), 32-3.

14 Marcuse, *Counter-Revolution and Revolt,* chap. 1

15 *Eros and Civilization,* viii

16 *One-Dimensional Man: Studies in the Ideology of Advanced Industrial Society* (Boston 1968), xv

17 *An Essay on Liberation* (Boston 1969), viii; *One Dimensional Man,* 257; *Five Lectures,* 69

18 *One-Dimensional Man,* xv; but see, *Counter-Revolution and Revolt,* chap 1

19 *One-Dimensional Man,* 257

20 *Eros and Civilization,* viii, xi, chaps. 7-8 passim; *One-Dimensional Man,* 41; *An Essay on Liberation,* x. This whole book deals with the manifestations of a new awareness, a 'new sensibility.' But these manifestations though they 'herald a total break with the dominant needs of repressive society,' do not constitute a 'revolutionary force.' *Five Lectures,* 69

21 *Five Lectures,* 69

22 *An Essay on Liberation,* 21. *Five Lectures,* 62-3, 68

23 *Economic and Philosophic Manuscripts,* 75

24 Ibid., 76

25 *Capital* (Moscow 1962), III, 799

26 Ibid., 800

27 Ibid., 799. On this see Shlomo Avineri, *The Social and Political Thought of Karl Marx* (Cambridge 1968), 237, 232-5

28 *Capital,* III, 800. For Marx's more programmatic ideas regarding the combination of education and production see *Capital,* I, 483, 484, 488; *The Communist Manifesto,* 54; *Critique of the Gotha Programme,* 24, 36 in Karl Marx and Frederick Engels, *Selected Works* (Moscow 1962), I and II respectively. Marx does not glorify work in these passages. Since non-alienated but necessary work cannot be done away with, his task is to minimize the fragmentation of human personality through the improvement of the working conditions, particularly through the unity of the mental and physical energies of the workers.

29 *Capital,* III, 800

30 Ibid., I, 530

31 Ibid., III, 800

32 Ibid.

33 *Eros and Civilization*, 32
34 Ibid., 32. Also '... While any form of the reality principle demands a considerable degree
    and scope of repressive control over the instincts, the specific historical institutions of
    the reality principle and the specific interests of domination introduce *additional* con-
    trols over and above those indispensable for civilized human association. These addi-
    tional controls arising from the specific institutions of domination are what we denote as
    surplus-repression,' 34.
35 Ibid., 32
36 Ibid., 41
37 Ibid., 33
38 Ibid., 80
39 Ibid., 137
40 Ibid., 137-9; *One-Dimensional Man*, 241ff. Regarding the satisfaction of human needs
    and the technological conquest of scarcity see the lucid, perceptive and engaging argu-
    ments of C.B. Macpherson in his 'Democratic Theory: Ontology and Technology,' in
    Political Theory and Social Change, ed. David Spitz (New York 1967); 'The Maximiza-
    tion of Democracy,' in *Philosophy, Politics and Society*, ed. Peter Laslett and W.C.
    Runciman (Oxford Third Series, 1967); *The Real World of Democracy* (Oxford 1966),
    61-5. Also Christian Bay, 'Needs, Wants, and Political Legitimacy,' in *Canadian Journal
    of Political Science*, 1 (1968), 241-60. On technology and nature see the comprehensive
    work of William Leiss, *The Domination of Nature* (New York 1973).
41 *Eros and Civilization*, 140
42 *One-Dimensional Man*, 22-37; *Five Lectures*, 64-6; *Eros and Civilization*, viii, 84-5, 138,
    142. Marx in the *Grundrisse* is primarily concerned with the cataclysmic impact of auto-
    mation on the capitalist mode of production, the intensification of the internal contra-
    dictions. His few utopian suggestions do not approximate Marcuse's vision. Marcuse ack-
    nowledges the utopian passages in the *Grundrisse;* see *An Essay on Liberation*, 21, n7.
43 *Eros and Civilization*, 84-5
44 *An Essay on Liberation*, 21
45 *Eros and Civilization*, 43, n45
46 Ibid., 196
47 Ibid. For Marcuse societal conditions when altered set the basis for the transformation of
    the instinctual structure of men. Marcuse's total vision demands external and internal
    changes; it is a socio-psychological revolution. See *Eros and Civilization*, chap. 10.
48 'Aristotle's proposition on the cathartic effect of art epitomizes the dual function of art:
    both to oppose and to reconcile; both to indict and to acquit; both to recall the re-
    pressed and to repress it again – "purified." ' Ibid., 131. See also *One-Dimensional Man*,
    60ff; *An Essay on Liberation*, 38ff. esp. 44. On art see Marcuse's changed, but more
    profound, statements in his *Counter-Revolution and Revolt*, chap. 3.
49 *Eros and Civilization*, 132
50 *One-Dimensional Man*, 70
51 *An Essay on Liberation*, 33-4
52 *Eros and Civilization*, 198-9
53 Ibid., 150
54 Ibid., 156
55 *Five Lectures*, 81; *Eros and Civilization*, 33
56 *Eros and Civilization*, 177
57 Ibid., 173; also, 'The expanding realm of freedom becomes truly a realm of play – of the
    free play of individual faculties,' 204
58 Ibid., 205
59 *An Essay on Liberation*, 91, 20
60 Ibid., xvii
61 On Marcuse's optimistic reinterpretation of Freud see Philip Rieff, *Freud: The Mind of
    the Moralist* (New York 1961), 256.

62 *Eros and Civilization,* 122
63 Ibid., 216
64 *Eros and Civilization,* 215
65 On mortality Marx says: 'Death seems to be a harsh victory of the species over the definite individual and to contradict their unity. But the determinate individual is only a determinate species being, and as such mortal.' *Economic and Philosophic Manuscripts,* 105
66 *Eros and Civilization,* 216

Barry Cooper

Rhetoric and violence:

some considerations of the events of October 1970*

We were all surprised at the violence of October 1970. Whether we were numbed at the deeds of the FLQ or astonished at the support which English Canadians gave to the government, the effect was the same; what we thought a problem of other times and other places had become, it seemed, our own. Our recent and indeed our continuing history make imperative the need to get a view of events of which we are still a part so as to begin to comprehend the significance of violence as a government response and as a political strategy. The complexity and delicacy of the October crisis dictate caution and a certain tentativeness in judgment. Yet, the importance of these events requires a response from all of us. Some insight may be gained with the aid of certain theoretical distinctions taken from the tradition of political philosophy.

This essay begins with a consideration of the place of rhetoric in politics and its relation to dialectic.[1] Rhetoric is broadly defined as the art of persuasion: it seeks to change attitude or behaviour, or both, and consequently is never innocent of intention. Rhetoric, moreover, deals with the immediate, the concrete, the particular. Like poetry it affects the passions, it moves men by appealing, in Richard Weaver's words, to 'the whole man.'[2] The importance of rhetoric for politics lies not only in the seemingly uncontroversial observation that politics requires persuasion but also in the matter of wholeness. One recalls that Plato said that the public representatives of the city reflected the type of citizens who composed it,[3] and that is to say that politics is the public expression of the characteristically whole man.

The whole man, however, is not necessarily the highest representative of human being. If I may employ the terms of Platonic anthropology, the whole man is a compound of three forces, the appetitive, the spirited, and the rational, which in turn are ordered by the virtues of wisdom, courage, moderation, and justice.[4] Forces and virtues do not simply form a homogeneous catalogue of attributes but are hierarchically related in terms of the real characters that embody them; thus, the philosopher is the representative of true order, the sophist of disorder. This point may need stressing today when the philosopher and the sophist are both considered as mere 'intellectuals,' and when all argument is conceived as opinion beyond which there is no appeal. The Platonic-Aristotelean understanding of the representative truth of human existence is not a matter of opinion; nor is it a doctrine which presumes to provide an objective and timeless truth. It is simply the rational exploration of the structure of existence or, as it appeared in the Socratic dialogues, the practice of dialectic. The dialectical elaboration of the true order of being is philosophical existence, the standard by which both human character and the empirical, political representatives of human character are to be judged. Dialectic, therefore, can serve as the instrument of political criticism; but what is the relationship between rhetoric and dialectic?

This has always been a puzzling question. Aristotle, for example, began his treatise on the subject with an observation that prior writers had concerned themselves only with 'non-essential' aspects of rhetoric, 'the arousing of prejudice, pity, anger and similar passions.'[5] He allowed that this was a faithful enough account of current practice, but also that the essence of rhetoric was not simply persuasion, but a particular kind of persuasion, namely demonstration, 'since we are most fully persuaded when we consider something to have been demonstrated.' Rhetorical demonstration, Aristotle calls an enthymeme: 'The enthymeme is a kind of syllogism, and the consideration of all kinds of syllogisms is the task of dialectic.'[6] The enthymeme deals with what is probable rather than what is rationally necessary; its truth is established by dialectic. One can judge the nobility or baseness of rhetoric not simply by whether it proceeds by enthymeme or prejudice but also by a dialectical examination of the major premise of the orator, which serves to characterize the user.[7]

These brief hints will have to serve as a preliminary for this analysis of the rhetoric of the Quebec crisis. In addition, one must always remember to distinguish between the understanding of violence in prospect and the rhetoric that accompanied it, as with someone such as Pierre Vallières, and violence in retrospect and the rhetoric that accompanied it, as with someone such as Pierre Trudeau. Finally, one must distinguish between the rhetoric and the actual intentions and actions of the FLQ and the government.

Vallières view of violence as a magic wand was set forth in *Nègres blancs d'Amérique* and is well enough known that only a summary comment is required. Whatever the truth that his 'premature autobiography' revealed of the misery of life in a Montreal slum, and despite Vallières' ambiguous repudiation[8] of some of his earlier dreams, two things must be said of this work. First, it envisaged violence as constitutive of liberation much as Fanon in his more excessive moments, and certainly as Sartre in his introduction to *The Wretched of the Earth,* conceived of violence as the act whereby man 'creates' himself.[9] Second, despite Vallières' apparent change of heart, *Nègres blancs* remains a source of inspiration for the more enthusiastic intellectuals of Quebec, as the outbursts of Charles Gagnon testify.[10]

My interest, however, is not in the bizzare dreams of Vallières and Gagnon but in the men of government.[11] During the days following the abduction of James Cross, the men of government were haunted by a series of spectres which revealed the 'deeper significance' of the FLQ action. The kidnapping was linked to anti-poverty work in the Gaspé, drugs, Algerian, Cuban, and Palestinian guerilla movements, and to prostitution.[12] Jean Marchand saw the

FLQ as 'racists' who communicated with each other through coded messages 'broadcast free of charge by our radio stations,' who 'have infiltrated every strategic place in the province,' and who threaten 'to blow up the core of downtown Montreal.'[13] The minister of justice divined the presence of men 'who undoubtedly envisage themselves as totalitarian masters in Quebec and perhaps even further afield,' men who have the 'ultimate goal' of 'a totalitarian state.'[14] Moreover, government spokesmen broadened the self-declared mandate of the FLQ so that the Front stood simply for separatism and violence. David MacDonald brought the whole matter into public when he raised the question, introduced by Marchand, as to whether 'what we are really out to deal with here by these measures is not just acts of terrorism by one relatively small group of people, who are seeking through anarchic means to destroy society, but a much larger group of people, 25 per cent if we can go by the last provincial election results, who believe there is a realistic option in considering some form of independence for the province of Quebec.'[15] Indeed, a day earlier, the prime minister replied to David Lewis' observation 'that the best way to stop people turning to violence is to remove the root causes which make them frustrated with the democratic process' with a rhetorical question: 'And let Quebec separate? That is what they want.'[16] Here at least was something one could come to grips with. Perhaps that is why the government refused to discuss it again.

It is clear that the October crisis was a constitutional crisis. But what is the constitution? There exists, obviously, the law of the constitution; but supporting it is the collection of people who constitute or articulate themselves into a community with a potential for historical action. Government, as the representative of the community, must be both the legal representative and the real or existential representative. When there exists a disjunction between the empirical support for the government, when the government is no longer the real representative of the community but simply the legal representative, it is fair to say that a constitutional crisis exists.

Constitutional crises are not unintelligible disasters that drop devilishly from the sky. They have a coherent etiology, and the public debates in both the Quebec and Ottawa assemblies touched on all the normal causes for crisis elaborated by Aristotle in Book v of *The Politics.*[17] The main argument of the NDP was that the FLQ developed as a result of economic exploitation. 'The base of the FLQ lies in the disadvantaged and unfortunate people in the province of Quebec,' Douglas said.[18] The Conservatives took the line that, whatever the cause, it had not surfaced during the night of 16 October, and consequently must have been the results of a long-standing and evidently wrong policy.[19] In Quebec, the weakness of Bourassa as a leader and of the Liberals as representatives of Quebec aspirations was attacked.[20]

In Ontario, we witnessed the curious spectacle of John Robarts declaring 'total war.'

Even if Robarts' foolishness appears less than serious, the grim undertone must be acknowledged. Whatever the mixture of vanity, arrogance, imagination, stupidity, and good will in the soul of a politician, one should not be astonished to see him panic when he experiences support for him and his government draining away; hence Trudeau's outburst against Lewis. At the same time, however, his recognition of reality could not become explicit because it would entail the public acknowledgment of confusion and uncertainty. A compromise between fantasy and frankness was struck with the notion of a 'type of erosion of the public will' that, Turner said, was 'more disturbing' than the kidnappings, bombings, thefts of dynamite, and murder.[21] The formula was repeated early in November when the Public Order Act was debated. At one point Lewis asked for clarification of what was meant by 'erosion of will.'[22] No answer is recorded in *Hansard*. In the National Assembly, Bourassa decoded the Ottawa cypher: there were, he said, 'many days of discussions between Mr. Demers [the government negotiator] and Mr. Lemieux [the FLQ negotiator]. This was painful for the State and, I believe, for every Quebecker to see, on television, the State ridiculed by Mr. Lemieux. Numerous times each day he humiliated the State of Quebec. We accepted it, we tolerated it because we wished to save the life of Pierre Laporte.'[23] If we ignore the more outrageous embellishments of the 'erosion of public will' such as Trudeau's view of a 'provisional government,'[24] his fear of another Kent State, where civilians would be shot by military and police officials, and his obsession with a 'parallel power,' we are left with a symbol strong enough to raise fears and imprecise enough to prevent any reference to empirical events whereby the grounds for fear could be ascertained.

A commonsense observation would be that the clever politicians were being Machiavellian; they saw their support slipping away and manipulated the public into accepting the terms of debate – *either* for the FLQ and 'anarchy' *or* for the government and order. There may have been some cunning involved, but reading over the debates in the two houses and, if memory serves, listening to news broadcasts – on 16 October the 7:00 AM news on CBC began 'You have no rights' – the overwhelming atmosphere was one of nervous posturing. The lying of politicians and journalists was not Machiavellian. Machiavelli was not a PR man. He counseled lying only when the object was deception, and deception assumes that the deceiver can distinguish between truth and its opposite; it is by no means clear that the government possessed such insight.

Indeed, there is a good deal of evidence to suggest just the opposite. Precisely because the content of the term is so scanty,[25] 'public will' can be

declared anything, and those who declare it to be whatever it is have nothing
beyond their own opinions by which to judge. They know it, and this knowledge is unsettling. It would not be too misleading to interpret Trudeau's
'Operations Centre' and Bourassa's plaints of *lèse-majesté* as evidence of concern for a political image rather than with the relatively straightforward
demands of the FLQ. Perhaps it was the influence of public relations and a
concern with 'images' of 'public will' that made it so easy for men such as
Bourassa, Trudeau, and Turner to slide from the 'manipulation' of the electorate through slogans to the 'manipulation' of the electorate, or at least part
of it, through the army. An additional argument that supports the notion that
images rather than facts governed the response to the crisis is found in the
occult logic of the 'scenario' adduced at various times to justify the government's deeds. The first thing to note is that the word itself has been borrowed
from the theatre, a fine complement to a concern with images. And, as with
an image, scenarios are invulnerable to factual repudiation; the playwright can
always add another act. Evidence that the government was obsessed with a
scenario of increasing 'escalation' can be found in Turner's justification of the
War Measures act and the Public Order act, in Trudeau's national television
address, and in his inappropriate Kerensky analogy; it dominated the statements of Bourassa as well.[26] The point is that if we are to call the federalists
'Machiavellian' it is only in most vulgar sense; Machiavelli's teaching was more
graceful, more interesting, and above all more realistic.

Simply in terms of technique, government spokesmen employed arguments from definition (as in the very terms of the enabling proclamation),
from analogy, and from cause-and-effect. There was a single major flaw in all
such arguments, however, that the appropriateness of the definition, analogy,
and causal relationship was dependent upon external evidence and so was
open to independent judgment. The arguments of the opposition in Ottawa
and Quebec by and large were articulated in terms of a different reading of
events, demands for more coherent justification, and so on. The opposition,
in other words, exclusively employed what Aristotle called enthymeme. To
the extent that the government replied in the same mode, that is, to the
extent that it entered *debate,* the opposition was clearly superior. In addition,
the government relied upon the argument from authority or testimony, as the
examples of scenario and escalation show. There were also explicit statements
that perhaps the 'whole story'[27] never could be told and, curiously, statements that 'everybody' already knew the story anyhow and that the 'value
judgment' of the government was on the record, to be defended, presumably,
at the next election.[28] A final curiosity that deserves attention is that while
authoritative scenarios of escalation were given currency cabinet officials
were also denying the possibility that the FLQ were serious in their demands

for negotiations.[29] At no time was it clear that negotiation was rejected because it was hoped that the FLQ would free their victims (which would give the lie to the 'ruthless escalation of terror' image) or because the victims were already written off as dead.[30] The premise that the hostages were dead men from the time of their abduction is nothing if not consistent with the image of the FLQ that the government sought to 'sell.' Finally, the concern with images, scenarios, and the deadly, abstract logic that integrates them may sustain the often criticized inflexibility of the government.[31] If you 'know' the scenario already, if you are concerned with the condition of your image, what place is left for such traditional political virtues as flexibility or prudence?

The argument from authority is not necessarily a base argument: 'The sound maxim is that an argument based on authority is as good as the authority.'[32] A rationally discriminating attitude towards what is authoritative may support not simply order but good order. Now, the claim to authority that is not based upon rational discrimination but upon formal or legal office is, obviously, less able reasonably to demand our obedience. When the argument from authority is justified by appeal to feelings and imaginations, to excessive imagery and immoderate emotion, there is nothing legitimate about it; sensationalism in political debate is simply the obverse of silence. Both degrade the user and his audience and run the tremendous risk of arousing the enthusiasms of brutality and thoughtless solidarity. The government used such methods of rhetoric during the Quebec crisis; what we still must understand, unless we attribute this cheapness to the smallmindedness of the men involved,[33] is why such methods are employed and why, in some sense, they may be appropriate. One explanation is, of course, that the only way to fight terrorism is with the army and special police powers; but then we must also understand the significance of terrorism.

Much of our confusion in such matters stems from the specifically modern way we understand political affairs. But the modern understanding cannot appear as modern unless it is seen from another perspective. Classical political science provides not only a non-modern view of politics but, we shall argue, a more intelligible one. What we propose to consider are a number of distinctions to be made when talking of the relationship between politics and violence, and the modification of political self-understanding wrought by the introduction of non-political symbolisms. Within the text of official argument, the response to the FLQ violence, no less than the opening move on Redpath Crescent, was founded upon distinctly non-political premises. We conclude by suggesting a few insights to be gained from the Quebec crisis and from violence as an assertion of individuality in a situation where, increasingly, individual self-articulation is seen as destructive either of other people or of an organization that fails to recognize individuality.

According to the Greeks, or more exactly to Aristotle, the capacity that men have for political activity was to be understood not only as different from the activity of the 'natural association' whose locus is the home and the family but, in a fundamental way, as opposed to it. The doorway of a citizen's home was literally the threshold between private and public; moreover, the activities of the household had to have been taken care of before the citizen could emerge into the street. When something has to be done it is a necessity, so it is no surprise to learn that the household was concerned with biological life and the continuous processes needed to sustain it. On the other hand, there was nothing necessary about the activity that went on in public. Liberation from the bonds of economy meant a choice of ways of life. Two of these ways of life, Aristotle, in common with most Greeks, thought worthy, and two he thought perverse. The first two included the life of leisure devoted to thought and contemplation and the life of political action; the second, perverse ways of life, included the chrematistic or acquisitive life and the life of a voluptuary.[34] Certain activities which we would naturally consider to be 'ways of life' are not so considered by Aristotle. Manual labour was a 'household' activity often performed by slaves; merchants, and 'metics,' foreigners who had to pay a special tax (*metoikion*) to live within the polis and so could understandably be excluded from citizenship, Aristotle also would exclude artists who were certainly much more respectable than the rabble of hucksters in the marketplace, and even the poor. They were excluded since Aristotle thought them incapable of achieving the 'excellence of the citizen' because they lacked leisure. There was no reason to give unleisured men citizenship. The rather tortuously achieved point of all this is that politics and, *a fortiori,* dialectic, was conceived as the activity of man 'in-between' the level of mere biological life and the divine.[35] That is why Aristotle calls politics *to eu zēn,* 'good life' and not simply *to zēn,* 'biological life.' What was 'good' about politics, Aristotle argued, was that it permitted the actualization of the specific generic differences between men and beasts, a capacity for speech and for action, *and* it permitted the appearance of the individual self as a distinctive person, recognized as such by others who were his equals. On the other hand, since slaves were men, and as it sometimes happened that those who 'naturally' were fit for political life were born slaves, slavery could rest on mere legal convention and bodily force (*nomon kai biastheisi*), and not upon common interest. Such a situation Aristotle thought disadvantageous for both master and slave.[36] Apart from relations with other poleis and apart from the bastard form of government, tyranny, 'force' was an interhuman category only in the context of an unjust master-slave relationship.

It is a long way indeed from Aristotle's view of the relationship between politics and 'force' to that of Max Weber: politics is 'the relation of men dominating men, a relation supported by means of legitimate, (that is, considered to be legitimate) violence.'[37]

We may begin to see what has changed in the way men understand their living together by an exploration of the kinds of activity that Aristotle saw as being appropriate for violence and then raising the question as to whether in contemporary reality these same kinds of activity are termed 'political.'

We noted earlier that Aristotle was of the opinion that not all slavery rested upon 'force' but that under some conditions it was in the interest of both master and slave to uphold their mutual relationship. Whether enforced or not, however, the slave was an 'instrument' and, moreover, a necessary one at least until such time as a shuttle should weave of itself, and a plectrum should play its own harp.[38] But even if there were technological changes such as Aristotle never dreamed, the slave would still be 'functionally' required, for the slave, unlike the shuttle is more than an instrument of production (*poiesis*); he is also an instrument of action (*praxis*). And since 'life is action and not production' the slave is a servant of the sphere of action.[39] But what happens if we consider life to be production and not action? That is, what kind of an answer may we expect to the question, what does life produce? The answer of course is 'nothing.' Indeed the question is absurd since mere life is presupposed in order that there be production, so we must ask a different question, but one that appears to hide the original absurdity.

The key term is production. What is produced is a 'thing' or, more specifically, an object to be used. The intellectual trick is to conceive of life as a use-object, and the way to do it is to advance the opinion that man has the ability to adjudge the meaning of everything in terms of its utility. Plato saw the problem created by such an opinion, namely the dissolution of all criteria of rational judgment;[40] but the problem is surely with us as well, under the heading of 'values.' Now values are not 'natural.' In one way or another they are the result of an exchange between men – whether an exchange of opinions or of goods is, for the moment, irrelevant. But whereas use-objects can be denoted with certainty and precision the 'value' of a use-object cannot, since use is variable. The utter futility of the search for an 'absolute value' has not inhibited men from looking; of interest in the present context is the observation that what is gained by the belief that one has attained an absolute value or standard is the certainty and precision that otherwise would accrue only to the activity of producing use-objects.[41] Another aspect of this nonsensical perspective is that one is ever aware that the absolute value involved is, in principle, 'human' rather than either natural or divine. When men

who conceive that they know, or have, or are the absolute value also believe
that other men must be made to conform to it, the intrinsic relationship
between violence and production becomes apparent. In the production of
use-objects violence must be done to nature; one kills the tree to build the
chair. Likewise in connection with human affairs, one 'moulds' the 'human
material' so as to create the desired 'object.' In so far as the instrumentality
of production is concerned, the distinction between 'making' good citizens
through propaganda and 'making' good citizens through terror vanishes. More
generally, instrumentality presupposes acceptance of the notion that life is
production and politics is resolved into the question: 'what kind of politics
do you wish to make?'

A second area, distinct from production and focally related to interhuman
affairs that was considered as a field of violence was what we might call
international relations. Thucydides' account of dialogue between the
Athenians and the Melians is a particularly dramatic exposition. 'You know,
as well as we do,' the Athenians said, 'that in human discussion justice enters
only where the pressure of necessity is equal [as it was within but not without
the polis]. For the rest, the strong exact what they can and the weak grant
what they must.' Trying to justify the promise that the Athenians would
slaughter the men and enslave the women and children if the Melians did not
submit, the Athenians continued: 'Of the gods we believe, and of men we
know, that by a necessity of nature they rule wherever they can. We neither
made this law nor were the first to act on it; we found it to exist before us
and shall leave it to exist forever after us; we only make use of it, knowing
that you and everybody else, if you were as strong as we are, would act as we
do.'[42] The Athenians were not wrong in their estimation and when their own
city was taken after Aegospotami it was only the restraint of Sparta that
saved Athens from 'such treatment as they had visited upon the Melians.'[43]

A final area where violence was to be expected is under tyranny. The
characteristics of the tyrant are as well known as the reasons for getting rid of
them. Tyranny is preserved by the tyrant isolating himself from his subjects,
literally by domesticating them and ruling as the father rules the household.
Force, in the form of a bodyguard, secret spies, and so on, is employed to
prevent the tyrant's subjects from either coming together or, if assembled,
from voicing their opinion on public matters.

It has already been noted that violent actions may easily be predicated
upon attitudes of instrumental rationality. When instrumentalism is linked
with the class of problems dealt with by Aristotle in Book v of *The Politics,* a
rather heady mixture is concocted. It is not so much a matter of justice and
equality any more as it is of correct plans correctly executed. The common-
sensical qualification that 'good' plans must be implemented by 'consent'

rather than by violence leads to a kind of Kantian paradox about means and ends, for if the plan is 'good' then one is obliged to implement it by *all* means available. In political philosophy the most outstanding example of the characteristically modern view of human affairs is Hobbes, whose Commonwealth is an artifice constructed by the new science initiated, he said, with the publication in 1642 of *De Cive*.[44] To the extent we are all Hobbesians, we will be plagued by the problem of the 'value' of our political works. Hobbes' answer, which effectively undercut the problem rather than answered it and which remains the principle answer of modern man, was to declare, in a backwards sort of way, that life was the highest 'value.'[45]

We have already seen that life must be presupposed for 'values' to exist and that the indulgence that allows us to use the term 'value' with respect to human affairs results in the understanding of politics in terms of bartering the results of fabrication; of equal importance is the way the absurd consequences have been ignored. To use a term of some local currency, government is conceived not as the actualization of 'life' but as the guardian of 'possessive individualism.' So conceived, the purpose of politics is exhausted in 'the protection of ... property and ... the maintenance of an orderly relation of exchange.'[46] The contemporary Western variant, which we might call 'possessive corporatism' and the contemporary eastern variant which has been called 'possessive collectivism'[47] are alike in so far as they seek nothing beyond liberation from necessity, conceived as the domination of nature. Moreover, they are alike in so far as they conceive of any obstacles that appear in the course of a futile and frenetic activity as the result not of the burden of biological necessity but as the result of a deliberate violation by other man, a conscious 'political' act. Marx was, without doubt, the most equivocal of thinkers who blended the threshold between public and private. As Arendt observed, he transformed more than anyone the point of political change: 'the role of revolution was no longer to liberate men from the oppression of their fellow men, let alone to found freedom, but to liberate the life process of society from the fetters of scarcity so that it could swell into a stream of abundance, Not freedom but abundance became now the aim of revolution.'[48] Lack of abundance was, in consequence, the result of unnecessary violence and paradoxically, violence, now conceived as necessary, would be required to establish abundance.[49] Considered in Aristotelean terms (see note 39) the modern view of revolution, whether violent or not, seeks the public respectability of man's 'slavish' character. If 'slaves' are properly *servants* of the sphere of action and not themselves actors, to the extent that we all are tied to the realm of production and consumption we exhibit our own 'slavishness.' Thus, while 'slaves' are in some sense necessary for the appearance of the political man (*polites*) or the 'real' man (*aner*), it is by no means true that the existence of 'slaves' is sufficient. Quite the opposite is true, as the evidence of our own society shows. Indeed, it is one of Marx's more intelligible insights to point out how both bourgeois and capitalist could become 'slaves' to capital.[50]

Two points need to be made. First, if it can be accepted that we live in a regime of 'possessive corporatism,' however it may violate Aristotelian notions of politics, it is by no means clear that on its own admittedly base, or vulgar, or perverse terms such a regime is anything but a great success. The point may need stressing since it is often neglected: for a good number of North Americans, most of whom are here because they or their ancestors sought relief from European misery, the dream of the poor, endless abundance, has been proximately achieved. Moreover, and this is the second point, an important, and perhaps the decisive factor in the creation of a society of abundance has been the large-scale organization of productive life governed by the formal norms of bureaucratic efficiency. Such norms are patterned after the experience of making plans, setting down rules, and executing the plans according to the rules. Thus, we may expect from the perfect bureaucrat as much sympathy for those to whom he applied the plans, according to rule, as we would expect from a carpenter for the tree he violates in building a table. There is, in addition, an informal norm of bureaucratic organization that, while militating against efficiency, actually enhances the tendency to violation and violence. Recently it has been pointed out with characteristic wit by men such as Galbraith and Townsend that the primary real goal of bureaucracy is self-preservation and the foremost way of assuring preservation is through growth. Now growth and productivity, which are daily chanted by political and economic bureaucrats as the 'goal' of society, are easily comprehended by way of familiar biological metaphors. This is hardly surprising since the cycle of production and consumption is what sustains life and all of us know that we grow up. But taken as a general metaphor of human affairs it may be dangerous for two distinct but related reasons: first, while violence is inevitably part of the struggle for life in the animal kingdom, to infer that violence is necessarily a prerequisite to the survival of man carries with it the temptation to conclude that men are simply 'rational animals' whose 'reason' simply makes them more clever, and thus more dangerous, but no less beastly. A second reason why this is a bad metaphor is, as has often been observed, that nature is profligate. A similar profligacy in human affairs is a sanction for large-scale murder sanctified by some imaginary law of nature which has jurisdiction over men as well as beasts. Finally, we may note that bureaucracy is a kind of slavery without a master, or, as Arendt said, a tyranny without a tyrant.[51] When we all must follow bureaucratic rules, the banality of life, in the precise etymological sense, is unreleived with the hope of rebellion or tyrannicide, and violence becomes little more than a paroxysm.

The structure of modern society, with its class and ethnic antagonisms, no less than the principles which inform its organization, such as production, administration, and growth, certainly serve as predispositions to violence. There is, in addition, a somewhat exogenous factor which may be identified, perhaps inadequately, as the lust for apocalypse. The experiential core of this passion is rather different from the desire to master the earth by remaking it or the dream of endless consumption and painless, joyful, creative, production. The origin of apocalyptic expectations lies in Old Testament prophetism and the Book of Daniel. The circumstances surrounding the origin of these documents is of political as well as theological interest. We will take but a single example to illustrate the curious state of the psyche involved. In 734 BC the Kingdom of Israel was at war with Syria and the city of Jerusalem was in considerable danger. The king, inspecting the city water supply in anticipation of the seige, was approached by Isaiah who told him he had nothing to worry about because 'The Lord Yaweh says this: / It shall not come true; it shall not be' (Is. 7:7). And, furthermore, if the king failed to trust in Yaweh and his prophet, he would be defeated: 'If you do not stand by me, / you will not stand at all' (Is. 7:9). Thirty years later, this time in a war against the Assyrians, he gave equally odd military advice, advising the king not to bother sending for Egyptian reinforcements because 'The Egyptian is a man, not a god, / his horses are flesh, not spirit; / Yaweh will stretch out his hand / to make the protector stumble; / the protected will fall / and all will perish together' (Is. 31:3)[52] Isaiah's point is not that trust in Yaweh would make the Israelites fight better, but that it would be a substitute for fighting at all. The guarantee, as it were, is found in the prophet's opinion that he has intimate knowledge of the divine plan, and its pragmatic impact is the result of the prophets ability to compel Yaweh to transform empirical reality and assure a military victory in the absence of soldiers. The magical component in all this is obvious, and it is still focal in the modern secular variation. The only important difference is that whereas Isaiah performed his magic on the basis of his 'knowledge' of God's plan, modern apocalyptics do the trick on the basis of their 'knowledge' of 'history' or 'nature' or some other world-immanent factor. The encyclopaedists found the agents in the French *haute bourgeoisie* of the eighteenth century; Schiller picked the liberal, middle-class civil servants for the job; Marx called up the proletariat. This last representative of human fulfilment made some kind of empirical sense until the beginning of this century when the empirical existence of complex social stratification proved Marx's prognostications to be in error. The result was a new carrier of apocalyptic hope, the 'third world.' But the third world cannot fix things either and now we find an emphasis on a magic that has a minimal empirical content.[53] All of the secular apocalypses whose bewildering succession during this century may make the most prosaic historian rather dizzy have emphasized violence as a crucial component of their grimoire.

The summary conclusion to be drawn from this brief analysis is that the modern view considers politics to be a factional struggle for domination of other factions through the instruments of violence. The rewards for victory are a larger share of material abundance, and the means to assure it is to integrate the whole society into a single cooperative unit. This is called 'progress.' Sometimes 'progress' is sought through magic. With respect to the Quebec crisis, the rhetorical incantations of the government and their brutal deeds did nothing so much as match the apocalyptic lusts of the FLQ.[54] But if we consider what violence can ever achieve in politics, namely short-term goals, the FLQ activities must be judged a qualified success: they did not secure the release of the prisoners or the satisfaction of their economic demands, but, as Trudeau feared, they did gain publicity, particularly through the publication of the manifesto.

As a purely practical matter, the danger to us all lies not with the despair of the FLQ but with the confident acolytes of 'progress' who do their best to transform a struggling political regime into the progressive paradise of reliable administration. It may be true that violence is the only way to interrupt the administrative process once the whole social family has been organized,[44] and it may be true that the only way to be rid of apocalyptic fanatics is through violence, but we, in Canada, are not yet the victims of total organization, and our politicians are not yet totally enslaved to their dreams. There are, moreover, reasons why hope for change may not entirely be vain. Local organizations are the most obvious empirical examples. It is certainly true that the success of such organizations is what prompts the wrath of municipal politicians, such as Drapeau, but it is also true that the action taken in local groups is the only genuine politics. The fact that the concern of most such organizations is simply economic should not obscure the recognition that what they do constitutes the substance of social change. The only alternative would be to constitute themselves into a faction and reinforce the social order they wish changed.

There is also a theoretical reason to anticipate more reasonableness in public affairs: men can imagine reality to be anything they wish, but their imaginative projection still occurs within reality. Thus we can *speak* of social 'progress,' an end to suffering and the like, but in the end we change our mood from joy at the imaginary promises we hold out to ourselves to despair because we know they can never be fulfilled. Sooner or later we give up the quest for final solutions and return to common sense. Consciousness of the magic component in the rhetoric of contemporary politics, which I have tried to suggest in the essay, may constitute a modest contribution to the restoration of rationality in public affairs; whether it helps diminish the proclivity of moderns to use violence is not for political science to say, but for men to do.

NOTES

* I should like to thank Ken McRoberts, Melvyn Hill, and Howard Adelman for their comments on an earlier version of this paper.
1 According to Aristotle: 'A dialectical problem is a subject of inquiry that contributes either to choice or avoidance, or to truth and knowledge, and that either by itself, or as a help to the solution of some other such problem. Moreover, it must be something about which people either hold no opinion at all, or the many hold an opinion contrary to the philosophers, or the philosophers to the many, or each among themselves.' *Topics,* 1046 1ff.
2 *Language is Sermonic* (Baton Rouge 1970), 205
3 The principle is established at *Republic,* 368c-d and applied to Athens at *Republic,* 492b.
4 The elaboration comprises nearly all of Book IV of the *Republic.*
5 *Rhetoric,* 1354a13ff
6 *Rhetoric,* 1355a6ff
7 Richard M. Weaver, *The Ethics of Rhetoric* (Chicago 1953), 56
8 Vallières' statement concerning the 'lessons of October' entitled *L 'Urgence de choisir* has not, at the time of writing, appeared. Chapter 2 only has appeared in the form of a two-part article in *Le Devoir* 13 and 14 December 1971; an English version has appeared in the *Canadian Forum* (Jan-Feb 1972). Vallières' statement is ambiguous because, while he speaks of his earlier naiveté, the main reason why he abandons violence is that under the circumstances as they presently exist it doesn't work. One implication may be that under different circumstances violence might work. But see also his statements in *Point de Mire* 3 (Mars 1972), 8-12, concerning his reasons why he took a job with the federal government. I owe this reference to André Blais.
9 The notion of human self-creation, *prima facie* so laughable, is a symbolism derived from certain specific religious experiences which became secularized by German idealism and Marx. For details, see E. Benz, 'Die Mystik in der Philosophie des deutschen Idealismus,' *Euphorion,* 46 (1952), 280-300; H.U. von Balthazar, *Prometheus* (Heidelburg 1947), 139ff, 265ff; N. Lobkowicz, *Theory and Practice* (Notre Dame 1967), 159-81.
10 See 'Le PQ ne peut promouvoir les intérêts des travailleurs,' *Le Devoir,* 5 Jan 1972; 'Le parti des masses sortira de leurs lutte,' *Le Devoir,* 6 Jan 1972. I owe this reference to Ken McRoberts.
11 Because we must rely on public documents, the analysis is confined to the federal and Quebec politicians; the Montreal municipal government is, by and large, outside our focus.
12 Canada, Parliament, House of Commons, *Debates* 3rd Session, 28th Parliament, 255, 261, 275, 283; Québec, Assemblée nationale, *Journal des débats,* 1st Session, 29th Legislature, 1621-2
13 *Debates,* 223-4
14 Ibid., 210, 214
15 Ibid., 250-1
16 Ibid., 200. Compare the comments of Stanley Knowles, 330, and T.C. Douglas, 892. The identification of the FLQ as the 'military arm' of the PQ was quite common in the Quebec National Assembly. See the remarks of Robert Bourassa, *Journal des debats,* 1539-40, Gabriel Loubier (Union Nationale), 1554-5, and Guy Fortier (Liberal), 1621.

The Créditistes, true to form, saw the FLQ linked back to *Cité Libre* (Yvon Brocher), 1625. See also the complaints of the Péquiste deputy Charles Tremblay, 1690-2.

17 Very simply, Aristotle's argument turns upon the question of equality and justice: when equals are treated as unequals they consider it unjust, as do unequals when treated as equals. Out of a sense of injustice they begin to form seditious factions.

18 *Debates*, 200; see also Lewis, *Debates*, 218-20

19 Stanfield, *Debates*, 195-6; Diefenbaker, *Debates*, 203ff

20 Laurin, *Journal des débats*, 1528-31

21 *Debates*, 212

22 *Debates*, 879 (Turner); 926-7 (Lewis)

23 *Journal des débats*, 1533

24 In the National Assembly, Bertrand explained to Bourassa that 'provisional government' could mean either the replacement of the existing government 'by a *coup de théâtre* or *coup de grace*,' or it could mean the reinforcement of an obviously fragile existing government. Phillipe Demers, also of the Union Nationale, suggested that what might be implied was a 'union' government. Bourassa clearly preferred the first, most alarming construction, *Journal des débats*, 1498. Denis Smith gives a plausible and thoroughly constitutional argument of what a 'provisional government,' under the circumstances, probably would have meant. See his *Bleeding Hearts ... Bleeding Country: Canada and the Quebec Crisis* (Edmonton 1971), 82-99

25 Smith, *Bleeding Hearts*, is the most shrewd analysis, in either French or English, that I have read.

26 For Turner's remarks, see *Debates*, 210-11; 879-80. The relevant parts of Trudeau's address are in Smith, *Bleeding Hearts*, 53ff. The Kerensky statement is in *Debates*, 511. Bourassa's scenario and the Péquiste criticism is in *Journal des débats*, 1479, 1527, 1534.

27 *Debates*, 212, 215 (Turner); Crétien quoted in *Debates*, 685

28 *Debates*, 510-11, 547 (Trudeau)

29 Sharp, 2nd Session, 28th Parliament, *Debates*, 8836; Turner, 3rd Session, 210; *Journal des débats*, 1529

30 Trudeau's argument that the 'government had no responsible choice' but to invoke the War Measures Act was based in part upon the 'expiration of the time offered for the release of the hostages,' *Debates*, 194.

31 *Debates*, 219 (Lewis), 319 (Nowlan); *Journal des débats*, 1524 (Laurin), 1572 (Lessard).

32 Weaver, *Language is Sermonic*, 216

33 And even if the despotic tendencies of the powerful are emphasized, we still must account for their public respectability.

34 The data for this summary can be found in *Politics*, 1252a1 ff; *Nicomachean Ethics*, 1095bff; *Eudemean Ethics*, 1215a20ff. I might add in passing that 'to be leisured' was understood as an activity: *skolēn agein*. Hence, for example, Aristotle's curious way of justifying contemplation as containing to a greater degree all the supremacy of 'political life' over the *erga anangkaia* in *Nicomachean Ethics*, 1177a18-b26.

35 Aristotle, *Politics*, 1253a 3-4. Plato, *Republic*, 478e; *Timaeus*, 49e-50e, 90a-d; *Symposium*, 202e. A recent elaboration of the Platonic 'in-between' (*metaxy*) is E. Voegelin, *Anamnesis* (Munich 1966), 266ff, 304ff.

36 *Politics*, 1255-b4-15; *Nicomachean Ethics*, 1161b5ff

37 'Politics as a Vocation,' in *From Max Weber*, ed. and trans. C.W. Mills and H.H. Gerth (New York 1946), 78

38 *Politics*, 1253b 36-1254a1

39 *Politics*, 1254a7ff. For the Greeks, this was more than 'functionally' true; most slaves were servants who sustained the life of the household rather than a labouring class for the whole society. See H. Arendt, *The Human Condition* (Chicago 1958), 119.

40 *Theaetetus*, 152aff. The same problem has been treated recently by Stanley Rosen, *Nihilism: A Philosophic Essay* (New Haven 1969).

41 Consider Aristotle, *Nichomachean Ethics*, 1142a7ff.

42 Thycydides, *Pelopnnesian War,* V, 89, 105
43 Xenophon, *Hellenica,* II, ii, 3
44 Hobbes, *English Works,* ed. Molesworth, I ix
45 Hobbes put the question the other way around: the greatest evil was violent death. It took little imagination or insight to vulgarize Hobbes' own vulgarization of the aristocratic virtue of honour: the greatest good, soon enough, was understood as the comforts of abundance, the depraved life of Aristotle's 'apolaustic' man.
46 C.B. MacPherson, *The Political Theory of Possessive Individualism* (Oxford 1961), 3
47 The term is Howard Adelman's.
48 *On Revolution* (New York 1963), 58
49 Hence Marx's aphorim, 'violence is the midwife of every old society pregnant with a new one.' *Capital* (Modern Library ed.), 824. Incidentally if Marx were serious, violence is the 'midwife' of historical change itself, which is acceptable enough if one were also to allow the opinion, inherited from Hobbes, that history (or perhaps 'pre-history') can come to a stop.
50 See Marx, *Early Writings,* Trans. and ed. T. Bottomore (New York 1963), 29, 85, 115, 179, 191, 193-4: consider also A. Kojève, *Introduction à la lecture de Hegel,* 2nd ed. (Paris 1947), 189ff.
51 *On Violence* (New York 1970), 81
52 The translation is from *The Jerusalem Bible.* A more extensive analysis of the political problems involved is in E. Voegelin, *Order and History* vol. I, *Israel and Revelation* (Baton Rouge 1956), 447-58.
53 Roger Garaudy recently spoke of a revolution in 'knowledge' for example; Reich writes of a new 'consciousness.' Perhaps the Surrealists are only being frank with their conscious embrace of alchemy.
54 Daniel Latouche has documented the identical vocabulary employed by contemporary federal anti-separatists and traditional *Canadien* messianists. 'Anti-séparatisme et messianisme au Québec,' *Canadian Journal of Political Science,* III (1970), 569ff
55 Arendt, *On Violence,* 79ff

Melvyn A. Hill

Political judgment and
the viability of institutions

The state ... is stable only when public and private ends are identical. It has
often been said that the end of the state is the happiness of the citizens. That
is perfectly true. If all is not well with them, if their subjective aims are not
satisfied, if they do not find that the state as such is the means of their satisfaction, then the footing of the state itself is insecure.

HEGEL

In thinking about social change one is in effect considering the possibilities for change in the way of life of a society, with the clearly implied premise that the change we are concerned with will lead to a better life in society. I would call social change in this sense reform, which is to be distinguished from revolutionary change where one considers not merely a better way of life but also a new beginning for society. Between the phenomenon of social change and that of revolution we encounter emancipation, which implies a radical change in society achieved not necessarily by revolution, a new beginning, but by a degree of change over time that leaps from an accumulation of change to an entirely new way of life. There are thus three categories of change that I would distinguish: reform, emancipation, and revolution. The question is, how can we judge which is at hand.

I think it is wise to begin by clarifying two of the major elements of concern in the ongoing process of any society. Both of these have been reiterated in one way or another by the major Western theorists of society and politics. On one hand there is the concern for what is called the viability of the state, for the endurance of the institutions of society, to provide for continuity in the way of life, and in particular for the transmission of the culture from one generation to the next, so that the old may decline in the knowledge that their work will be taken up by the young and the world maintained as they have built it, while the young may mature in the knowledge that they will come into possession of the means to maintain and live in the world, and also, it is hoped, to act within it out of their own initiative. The viability of the state and the institutions of society not only offers security to old and young alike that the world will be handed on and that it will not be allowed to disappear back into nature, but it also provides an essential security against the possibility of hostilities breaking out among citizens of the same state. The viability of the state is in this respect as much a guarantee against civil war as it may prove to be against foreign invasion.

The second major concern that I should like to emphasize is the problem of the relation of the individual to the order of politics and society in the contemporary western state. Here there are two sets of interests that have to be reconciled. Firstly, how does one reconcile the private interest of the individual with the common or public interest of the state? How does one achieve a rational ordering of the institutions of society out of the conflicting private interests of the many individuals who make up a society?[1] Secondly, and here we encounter the obverse of the same problem, how does one reconcile the authority of the state and its institutions with the rights of individuals in the state? For while private interests may clash and so prevent the possibility of establishing a common interest, the public interest of the state expressed in the intentions of its legislation and its executive authorities may conflict not with individual interests but with individual rights, which is to say the rights agreed upon as the common patrimony of every citizen regardless of their private interests. Briefly, I would describe the first aspect of the problem, the reconciliation of individual interests with the public interest when it appears on the political stage, as the problem of power, whereby the state requires the support of its citizens to be able to carry out its business at all; and I would describe the second aspect of the problem, the reconciliation of the authority of the state with the rights of individuals, as the problem of administration, whereby the state requires authority over its citizens in order to put its legislation into practice.

The two aspects of the problem of the relation of the individual to the state, namely, power and administration, cannot be understood simply as two sides of the same coin, for they do not support each other. On the contrary, without power there can be no authority, while on the other hand, administration can extend itself so far that it eliminates the possibility of power arising at all. From these extreme possibilities it is clear that the relation between power and administration is by no means complementary. I would call it dialectical. There is an ongoing tension in any society between the interests of individual citizens and the public good represented (to the degree it is) by their institutions, and between the authority of the administrators of a society and the rights of the citizens. If the rights of the citizens are eliminated, so are the wellsprings of power. On the other hand, if the clash of interests among citizens precludes the establishment of a public domain, then power itself also disappears. For men to create power they need to act, to come together, and they have to be free to be able to come together. For institutions to be effective they require authority, but for their authority to survive it has to be maintained by the support of the citizens.

The viability of a democratic or bourgeois state stands or falls on the interplay between individuals and institutions within it. It was Burke who argued that a political order incapable of change could not survive. Conversely, the survival of a society does not only depend on the transmission of the way of life across the generations by virtue of the authority vested in its institutions. It depends also on the readiness of the executive authorities to be mindful of the ongoing tensions between institutions and members of society and to develop policies responsive to these pressures. Except for totalitarian regimes and tyrannies, one could argue that the viability of a social and political order derives from the means it develops to cope with the interplay between individuals and institutions. Totalitarian regimes and tyrannies survive to the extent that they can control or eliminate not only individual rights but also the initiative of individuals in their own interests. For it is the conjunction of interests and rights that leads to the generation of power.

In this connection an interesting lesson in the judgment of social change can be drawn from the contradictory interpretation of the French Revolution offered by Burke and de Tocqueville. Burke objected to the Revolution because it gave occasion for the free expression of violent and conflicting passions that it is otherwise the task of the traditions of a society to channel within its institutions by inculcating a gradual affection for familiar practices, just as affections are channelled within a family. The weight of Burke's criticism does not stem from his objection to violence as such, but rather from his argument that it might have been avoided, and yet the goal of freedom achieved, had the French seen fit to restore the tradition of liberty embodied in the Estates General. Burke's critique of the French boils down to the capitulation of the Estates General. De Tocqueville, on the other hand, points out that Burke did not realize that the Estates General, which had not met for over a century, no longer represented a viable tradition among the French, who had in the meanwhile forgotten what the exercise of freedom and power meant. It was precisely because of their lack of the experience of political action within institutions that constitute a realm of freedom that Frenchmen could not appreciate the demands and the limits of freedom and power when, for a brief while, they revived the public realm. Consequently, according to de Tocqueville, they gave up their freedom for the sake of the effectiveness of a centralized administration. He goes on to point out that an administration not responsible to the power of free men inevitably becomes tyrannical. Thus he argues that by sacrificing power for the sake of authority the French established a new despotism that put out the brief flame of freedom in their great Revolution.

While the French Revolution is certainly marked by an increasing recourse to the authority of the Committees in order to execute the will of the Assembly, and then gradually simply to get decisions made, this shift from the free exercise of power to the free exercise of authority was *not* the result of a lack of political experience. Perhaps the lack of experience in government may have made the shift easier to accomplish because few if any realized where it would lead. But the major cause of the shift lies, of course, in the pressures from the counter-revolution and the invasion, which were not political, but military. And surely not even Burke, let alone de Tocqueville, would argue that an assembly can direct a civil and a foreign war. Similarly, in the contemporary US, the shift from the power of Congress to the authority of the White House has taken place in the context of sustained military campaigns. While critical attention was directed at the 'military-industrial complex,' a succession of presidents shifted the weight of government from the legislature to the executive. De Tocqueville's error, interestingly enough, is to ignore the profound effect that war has on government. It leads to the increase of authority at the price of power. A return to peace also requires the redress of that balance, if freedom, action, and power are to be restored to the citizens.

Even more to the point for our discussion of the problem of viability in relation to the interplay of individuals and institutions, is de Tocqueville's observation that it was not the failure to reform the institutions of France in the light of its old tradition of freedom that led to the 'failure' of the Revolution, as Burke had maintained; but, on the contrary, he argues that it is precisely because any reform at all was attempted that the fundamental injustices and malpractices of the old regime entered public discussion and became the focus of attention, thereby making them all the more intolerable. Thus the grievances of the citizens became the theme of the day and their conviction that they were each victimized under the old regime was now legitimized by the public recognition of injustice. It is this recognition and consequently reinforcement of the sense of grievance that de Tocqueville singles out as the efficient cause of the arrival and the course of the revolution. Indeed he goes so far as to call the revolution inevitable, a term we would usually trace to Marx in this connection.

The debate, so to speak, between Burke and de Tocqueville, about the origin and course of the French Revolution serves to define the difference between social reform, or even emancipation (which Burke clearly had in mind in his sympathy for the French) and revolution. It is when the attempt at social reform leads inevitably to the overthrow of a regime that we encounter revolution. This concept of inevitability which we find in de Tocqueville has to be clearly distinguished from the concept of inevitability that we find in Marx. De Tocqueville's concept of inevitability derives, as I have attempted to show, from the point at which political institutions can no longer accommodate the pressures for change within a society that, at the same time, they can no longer control or eliminate. Paradoxically, he and Burke agree on this point, if we recall once more Burke's notion that a political order that cannot accommodate change cannot survive. Whereas Burke, being an Englishman, did not realize that this point of inevitability had been reached in France, de Tocqueville, writing with the benefit of hindsight, concluded that it had. Marx, on the other hand, posited the inevitability of the proletarian revolution within the context not of a theory of institutions but of a theory of history. For Marx had placed the rise and fall of institutions within a theoretical framework that accounted for conflict and revolution in a society by referring it back to the underlying contradictions between the means of production and the relations of production that accounted for the transformations of society and politics throughout history. Consequently Marx, for example, viewed the French Revolution as the

breaking out of the bourgeoisie, who now owned the new means of production, from the old relations of productions that remained virtually unchanged
since feudal society. Similarly he foresaw the proletarian revolution as inevitable once the contradiction inherent in the private ownership of social
means of production became evident to the proletarians. For Marx the inevitability of revolution derived from the contradictions within any society
between the means of production and the relations of production as he
conceived them. The ideologies of the various social and political institutions
served merely to disguise the underlying economic interest of the ruling class,
which defined and received the surplus from production. Whereas for de
Tocqueville it is the coincidence of freedom with the initiative that derives
from private interest that leads to action, and in certain cases, revolutionary
action, for Marx it is largely a matter of becoming conscious of the precise
nature of exploitation that will inevitably lead the proletariat to revolt. Marx
judged the possibility of revolution primarily from the perspective of the
exploited who had no rights. De Tocqueville, who was conscious of the
injustices of the old regime, combined this awareness with an analysis of the
role of power and authority in the viability of institutions, in his interpretation. In de Tocqueville's judgment, in a world without inequality there would
be little cause for a revolution, while in a world with inequality revolution is
inevitable only when the political institutions can no longer deal with pressures for change. While Marx based his judgment of the inevitability of revolution in bourgeois society on the likelihood of pressures for change arising
among the proletariat, de Tocqueville would suggest that we add to that
a judgment based upon the theory of institutional viability.

In the judgment of the revolutionary potential in a political situation de
Tocqueville's analysis can certainly offer a more comprehensive and possibly
a more reliable paradigm to guide us. For what one can say is that even the
so-called Communist revolutions have occurred in countries and at times that
one would hardly have judged likely in the light of the degree of contradiction between the means and relations of production in those societies at those
times. Given that this contradiction can be found in every society, including
the European communist countries today, it is not at all clear from the
criterion of the class struggle when it will reach revolutionary proportions. I
offer this sceptical view of the sufficiency for political judgment of Marx's
concept of inevitability as an indicator of revolution, only too conscious of
the fact that my criticism does not touch upon the ground of the concept
in the Hegelian notion of dialectic. I am concerned here with the value
of both de Tocqueville and Marx for political judgment, and not with
tracing the development of their thought, or, for that matter, its systematic coherence.

I shall now expand my remarks on de Tocqueville's analysis of the viability of a state. In his *Democracy in America,* de Tocqueville treats the question of the viability of institutions in considerable detail. *Prima facie* there were two characteristics of the American Union that struck him as having a major bearing on the problem of viability: the first supporting the possibility of endurance and the second placing it in jeopardy. The relatively equal distribution of wealth among white Americans distinguished the social condition of the country from anything de Tocqueville had seen in Europe. Basically he remarked upon the relative lack of a clearly articulated class structure, which followed from the general prosperity, if not wealth, in the country, and from the consequent mobility between the classes he observed. This de Tocqueville believed augured well for the viability of the Union. On the other hand, the size of the country and the unavoidable differences in regional interests within its enormous territory suggested that the Union might one day be faced with a divisive and irresoluble conflict. In this his judgment was, of course, borne out, and not too long after. But the problem of the size of the Union raised a further and perhaps even more decisive question concerning its viability. This had to do with maintaining the authority of institutions over a population so widespread, and at the same time of maintaining the freedom and the power of the people in determining the course of their own affairs. While de Tocqueville admired the love of freedom that he encountered among Americans, and which he observed in their readiness to accept public office and political responsibility, he also remarked the informality of bureaucratic procedures and the irregularities of practice in their administration. Although he was pleased to note the absence of the typical arrogance of European officials and the coincident mistrust and contempt in which they are held by the people – the Americans were on friendly terms with their officials – de Tocqueville wondered whether in fact the government, and in particular the federal government, had sufficient authority to exercise its responsibilities in relation to foreign powers, whether in war or peace. Here he cites, for example, the inability of the federal government to put its orders for conscription into effect in certain states during the War of 1812.

De Tocqueville admired the American federal constitution because in its recognition of the rights of the states and of individual citizens it ensured the decentralization of institutions and the realm of freedom necessary if the people were to engage fully in their own public affairs. It was because of the generous measures taken to ensure the participation of citizens, and the checks and balances of power within the constitution, that de Tocqueville believed that there was little or no suspicion of authority in the country. As one reads the first volume of *Democracy in America* it becomes clear that de Tocqueville is offering a description of a social and political order among

white Americans where political alienation is hardly to be found. He detects
nowhere in America the idea that individual citizens have interests that contradict the structure of power or the authority of their institutions. And it is
precisely because of the high degree and general practice of participation in
those institutions that the Americans experience freedom. This freedom
among white Americans, along with the absence of a clearly articulated class
structure among them, was a primary indication in favour of the viability of
the state. What de Tocqueville described amounts to the free play between
individuals and institutions in a society, with the virtual coincidence of
authority with power and the virtual absence of conflict between private
interests and the public good.

In this connection de Tocqueville singles out the phenomenon of voluntary associations which he found so widespread in America. He admired the
way Americans did not wait for their authorities to recognize and act upon
problems or interests that arose among themselves. On the contrary, if they
discovered a common interest they would meet and a group would organize
itself and take action to further their interest, whether directly, should this be
within their competence, or through lobbying and persuading others, should
they require the support of legislators and other citizens. In this readiness to
accept responsibility de Tocqueville found the basis for the love of freedom
among Americans. They were a people who had gone as far as possible to
eliminate the ancient distinction between the rulers and the ruled, by participating themselves in their own government, and by themselves taking
responsibility for determining their common interest and acting upon it
wherever possible.

The prevalence of voluntary associations among Americans provided de
Tocqueville with a clear indication of the absence of political alienation
among the people. As I have suggested, he saw in their voluntary associations
the determination of a people to accept the responsibility for their own
destiny and thereby to insist upon their dignity as free citizens. I believe there
is a further point that emerges from the phenomenon of voluntary associations that has a direct bearing upon the problem of viability. This has to do
with the reconciliation of private interests with the public good. For the
voluntary associations mediate between the established institutions of society
and the particular interests of men as they arise outside of the chambers of
public institutions. They serve to reinforce the belief that private interests can
indeed be brought to bear upon public policies, and even coincide with them.
The citizen is saved from the prospect of the alienation of his interests in
society since he is assured that his interests contribute to, influence, and
inform the public interest. It is as if the voluntary associations serve to

eliminate the apparent distinctions between private interests and the public interest that is a fundamental source of division in society and a fundamental aspect of the problem of viability.

In order to clarify still further the importance of the voluntary association in de Tocqueville's analysis of American democracy, let me briefly compare the way it works there with Rousseau's analysis of the determination of the general will in the *Social Contract*. Rousseau also confronted the relation between private interest and the public good as a central problem in the establishment and viability of a democracy. But he was interested more in the menace of corruption in a society where private interests enjoy greater sway than does the public good than he was in the problem of power and administrative efficiency which occupies the foreground in de Tocqueville's analysis. According to Rousseau, the general will, or the public good, can only be judged by the citizens when they consciously alienate private interests from their minds and then proceed to deliberate on the public good. Only then are they free to determine the general will, as opposed to the conflicting multiplicity of particular wills otherwise prevalent. Rousseau, in other words, posits a conscious step of alienating oneself from one's private interests as essential to the operation of a viable democracy. Only through this step of self-alienation can the citizens hope to arrive at a viable basis for agreement among themselves on which to build the authority of government.

If we contrast Rousseau's concept of alienation with the stress on the importance of voluntary associations in de Tocqueville, the following point emerges: the voluntary association is a unique means of securing the viability of a democracy without demanding the alienation of private interests in politics but, on the contrary, by channelling them into the mainstream of political life. In de Tocqueville's analysis, democracy thrives on the conflicting multiplicity of private interests once they are given free play through voluntary associations. Consequently the necessity for alienating private interests posited by Rousseau is not merely obviated but turned around, whereby it becomes necessary to provide free scope for the organization of private interests and their articulation through action. In American democracy de Tocqueville found no conflict between particular wills and the general will, and still less the need for the alienation of particular wills in order to arrive at the general will. The general will is simply established by the free play of conflicting particular wills acted upon through the voluntary associations that can then register rival pressures among legislators, officials, and citizens, with the understanding that decisions arrived at through the political process in this way are binding as long as they remain on the books. The fact that decisions in a democracy are never final, but are changeable, guarantees

flexibility at the level of legislation and administration, which ensures that
the activities of voluntary associations are always informed with the hope of
effecting change.

It is this combination of the freedom to act upon private interests through
the voluntary associations and the prospect of effecting change guaranteed by
the flexibility of the laws and administrative practices established in a democracy that accounts for the integration of private interest and public good, the
reconciliation of power with authority in de Tocqueville's analysis. The price
paid for this method of integration was the amateurish nature of administration that de Tocqueville observed in America. For the administration was
confronted on one hand with the changeability of the laws and on the other
with the constant need to ensure that its measures enjoyed the support of the
citizens. By contrast, where the administration ignores the interests of
citizens and acts upon authority, unless the citizens have consciously adopted
Rousseau's step of the self-alienation of private interests, government builds
on the distinction between the rulers and the ruled, with the result that the
rulers alienate the ruled from the political institutions.

Rousseau and de Tocqueville provide us, therefore, with two conflicting
models by which to judge the viability of a state. In Rousseau's case, the state
would be viable if the citizens in exercising their political judgment make sure
to step outside of their particular interests in order to see the public interest.
Then the general will would be constituted by the agreement of the citizens
as to what would be best for all. De Tocqueville, however, saw in America a
society where it is precisely by organizing into voluntary associations which
exert pressure on the legislatures to further their private interests that citizens
are integrated into the life of the state. How are we to understand these two
contradictory positions?

Surely one has to say that de Tocqueville's model of the coincidence of
power and authority through the role of voluntary associations was drawn
from a society in which (among white Americans) he observed a relative
degree of social equality. Consequently one might say that the lack of marked
or rigid class distinctions made it possible for private interests to gain free
play in the political realm without leading to the breakdown of authority.
When the issue of slavery emerged, however, civil war followed. From our
point of view, de Tocqueville's model of voluntary associations confers
viability in the context of a soceity where relative equality prevails. Where it
does not, the free play of power among citizens would either prove ineffective, or lead to considerable disruption of society and the political order. This
leads us to Rousseau's model, which was drawn up in the light of his experience of France before the Revolution, a society marked not only by clear
class distinctions, but also by corruption on a grand scale accompanied by

and made possible by the virtual absence of political freedom. Rousseau's concept of the alienation of private interest in order to determine the general will would not only preclude class domination in the exercise of authority but in particular it would eliminate corruption, the use of authority to secure private ends.

Whereas de Tocqueville's model of voluntary associations would indicate the viability of the state where equality prevails, Rousseau's model of the alienation of private interests in determining the general will would appear to indicate viability when social inequality prevails but corruption does not. Rousseau's model remains an ideal, especially for bourgeois democracies. But what are we to make of the veritable renaissance of voluntary associations that we have witnessed in Canada and in other Western democracies over the past few years? Is this an indication that power and authority are on good terms, that our institutions are open to social change, and that the citizens accept responsibility for and take initiative in the determination of their way of life? Is liberal democracy indeed viable because of the generous interplay of its citizens with its institutions?

Certainly de Tocqueville's model of voluntary associations does not obtain among us, for the simple reason that we live in a society with a clearly articulated class structure, still largely determined by the criteria that Marx pointed out long ago. The major change has come in the development of the service sector of the economy, and, associated with it, the expansion of government services and offices. Consequently we have a large middle class who do not own the means of production, but hold down jobs in offices or perform specialized services. And the leadership of the new voluntary associations appears to be coming largely from this middle class. Quite often the leadership of a voluntary association becomes the extension of somebody's professional work, or job, or becomes a middle-class job in itself. And while a fair number of these associations are concerned, in Canada, with the 'under-privileged' or 'minority groups,' a large number of the most successful voluntary associations serve middle-class interest groups: ratepayers associations, tenants associations, anti-American and nationalist associations, professionals organizing into 'trade-unions,' and associations concerned with the problem of pollution and 'the quality of life in our cities.' Certainly the extent of these voluntary associations shows that citizens are sufficiently hopeful for change to come together and create the power to act, and that they look forward to the success of their efforts within the institutions of society. One measure of this success, at the municipal level, has been the election of the 'reform' city council in Toronto on the crest of efforts by voluntary associations to change the policies of the city government. How are we to understand the role of voluntary associations in a society that does not meet de

Tocqueville's condition of equality? How are we to judge the significance of these voluntary associations for social change?

In de Tocqueville's analysis the voluntary associations served to integrate private interest with the public good. For our purposes this has the following implication: that the action of voluntary associations is always to further particular interests within a social system, and through the processes pre-scribed by its institutions. In brief, it means that their action does not have radical implications for a society, but can be accommodated, by and large, through the re-allocation of resources on a marginal scale, and through the revision of certain policies and designs that affect the quality of everyday life, whether aesthetically, or in terms of security, and so on. The consciousness of society implied in the efforts of voluntary associations does not indicate a radical awareness of the underlying structures of society, nor, for that matter, a concern to transform them. Thus, for instance, the election of the reform slate to the Toronto City Council indicates that their supporters want them to use the appropriate channels for change within the institutions to effect certain adjustments in the policies of the city administration. Although they may find themselves in open conflict with councillors who represent the interests of, let us say, the realtors, their platform does not include, for example, a fundamental revolt against the economic basis of the real estate business in the city. It does not go to the heart of the structure of the economy of the city and the relation of this economic structure to the political institutions in the city. The voluntary associations and their representatives and lobbyists work well within the predefined institutions of liberal democracy, they attempt to revive the potential for participation implied in these institutions and thereby to establish a base of political power that will enable them to bargain more effectively for marginal changes in the conduct of affairs. It is from these quarters that I believe we may expect the more significant social reforms to come, and at the same time I believe that they will not be changes of a revolutionary order. The question that remains in my own mind is whether they will be changes whose cumu-lative effect may indeed prove emancipatory for society as a whole.

My first point, then, is that the political effect of our voluntary associa-tions is essentially conservative. By working through the legitimate channels for change within the institutions of society they give them new life. And despite the fact that the old guard, who then lose control of these institu-tions, may call the newcomers 'radicals' or 'revolutionaries,' they are re-formers whose work will preserve the institutions and traditions that they will change from within. Secondly, however, they will bring about change. Since the reformers come largely from the new middle class of professionals and jobholders, their leverage in society is not property but simply the fact of their coming together and so creating a new source of power. This suggests both the dynamic source and the structural limit set on these organizations. Where they come into direct conflict with those who direct capital expansion their power is bound to reach its limit, unless they gain access to the direction of capital. The voluntary associations may well serve to integrate the new middle class into the institutions on the basis of their participation. They are unlikely, however, to lead to radical change. I think they can best be judged in the light of the old debate about trade unions.

In assessing the potential of voluntary associations for emancipatory change, we are confronted once more with the phenomenon of trade unionism, which has now been adopted as a method of action on a far wider scale. And although voluntary associations preceded the organizations of trade unions historically, I think we can safely treat the problem of judging the effects of voluntary associations on society within the context of that problem as it arose in the case of trade unions. In other words, the gist of the debate that we need to revive before being able to judge the implications of the present form of voluntary associations is precisely the debate over trade unionism in Marxist circles in the past.

The crux of the argument was that the trade unions pursued the private interests of the workers without organizing for a revolutionary change in the social structure that alone would guarantee the transformation of the fate of the workers in society. In other words, they settled for the betterment of the condition of the workers, instead of attempting to revolutionize society so that there would no longer be a proletariat as it is found under capitalism. The attack on trade unionism from the left has traditionally been a result of its failure to realize that the true interest of the proletariat is revolutionary, and not the mere palliatives or marginal re-allocations that can be achieved by exerting pressure within the system. The left argued that trade unionism is based upon an inadequate consciousness of the historical structure of society, that it proceeded upon the assumptions about reality contained in the ideology of the capitalist system instead of penetrating to the historical contradictions in capitalism and the revolutionary role the proletariat might play in transcending them.

The trade unionists and the revolutionaries confront us with two contrasting conceptions of political action. The Marxist revolutionaries argue that political action has to be based upon a historical understanding of the inevitable direction of the class conflict, and not upon the appearance of possibilities for change within the present order of society and politics. The trade unionists, on the other hand, believe that by exerting sufficient pressure for change within the institutions of society they may in effect achieve emancipatory change, that is a change so radical in its cumulative effect that it amounts to a transformation of the way of life within the framework of the ongoing institutions. Here the belief is simply that the present order of institutions can survive since they can indeed accommodate the full degree of change necessary to establish justice and equality.

The issue boiled down to the question of whether the private interests of the workers are such that they cannot be realized within the present structures, that is to say, whether the class structure in society embodies contradictions so radical in nature that equality and justice can only be achieved by overthrowing the institutions of society in order to be able to reach the structural inequities. Here we can refer once more to the first of de Tocqueville's *prima facie* observations about America, that it was a society based upon relative equality. Consequently, private interests would not represent a revolutionary danger once they entered the political realm. In the left critique of the trade union mentality, the argument ran that trade unionists repressed the revolutionary extent of the workers interests in order to persuade the bourgeoisie that they could be trusted within established institutions, there to effect gradual change. In other words, in a situation of radical injustice the trade unions were considered inadequate organizations of even private interest, since in those situations private interests are revolutionary in import.

In applying this debate to voluntary associations there are two arguments to be made. Firstly, one might argue that these associations do not realize the radical implications, or simply the roots, of the problems they are organizing to resolve. They show their inadequate understanding by their belief that they can effect the necessary change within the institutions. Or, secondly, one might argue that the problems that the voluntary associations have recognized, and the interests they champion, are not in fact of radical significance for society. In my view both arguments hold true for various associations. For instance, one could probably make Toronto a pleasant city to live in, at least for the middle class, by enforcing the laws already on the books, and spending the taxpayers' money intelligently. But the problem of pollution inevitably leads to a confrontation with those who manage the capital of our society. Or, again, while it may be a small step in the direction of common sense to press for and organize the recycling of newspapers in the city, it hardly approaches the root of our abuse of nature. By and large I would argue that the rise of voluntary associations will enable the new middle class, who, unlike the rich, cannot buy their way out of the discomforts and inequities of our society, to modify them sufficiently in order to feel more at home.

On the other hand, the slim chances for revolution can be judged from the fact that democratic participation seldom leads to the articulation of revolutionary consciousness. People are far more inclined to demand immediate interests than to take a historical perspective on the present situation which has given rise to their grievance. In order to become revolutionary in consciousness and action a degree of the alienation of one's own interest has always been required, usually in the form of sacrificing one's life to the cause of the revolution. Such has been the informing principle of the lives of our great revolutionaries. But can this be expected from the people? And since patently it cannot, how does one get the people to transcend their private interest and become aware of the historical role they are called on to play? How does one get the people to engage in Rousseau's alienation of the particular will in order to realize, if not the general will, certainly the consciousness of the need for revolution? As we all know this debate was never concluded with a unanimous vote. Lenin organized his revolutionary vanguard while Rosa Luxemburg went along with a democratic, revolt of the proletariat. In both cases the attempt to bring revolutionary consciousness to bear upon the political realm, either through the vanguard or through popular uprising, resulted in the defeat of the revolutionary cause, in Russia through a totalitarian regime founded upon Bolshevik authority, and in Germany through the failure of the Spartacus rising.

This brief survey of the situation of the left, as it developed in relation to the debate over the trade union mentality and the possibilities for a proletarian revolution, serves as a reminder, on the one hand, of the limitations of the trade unions in effecting change, and on the other, of the unresolved dilemma of the revolutionary left in their attempt to effect a structural revolution based upon historical consciousness, with the support of the people. In both cases, albeit from different perspectives, the crucial problem is one of engaging the private interest of the people in the possibility for change, without being limited in the strategies for action by their perception of their own immediate interest.

After all, to put it at its simplest, political action is not the domain of social and political theorists, who are supposed to be capable of bearing the larger picture in mind, even in addressing themselves to immediate problems; nor is it the exclusive domain of revolutionaries, ready to sacrifice their private interests and even their lives for the sake of an historical transformation, a new beginning, of society. And furthermore, if the theorists and the revolutionaries do indeed manage to dominate the political realm and determine its course, there is little cause for optimism on the basis of our experiences in the modern age. The noblest social and political ideals pursued without regard to the free interplay of power and authority can lead to the most frightful and frightening social and political orders.

I have attempted to show that the revival of voluntary associations in Canada, and in the liberal democracies in general, indicates the overcoming of political apathy among the middle class in particular, and consequently that we may expect that this system of society and government will remain viable by making marginal changes. That these will amount to an emancipation from the present way of life seems unlikely. On the other hand, I have attempted to show that theoretically grounded movements for revolution have yet to resolve the dilemma of reconciling participation with the authorities of revolutionary consciousness, which lies behind the tragic fate of most modern revolutions.

NOTE

1   The attempt to wrestle with the problem of relating private interests to the public good is modern. It presupposes the distinction between civil society and the state that we find clarified in Hegel. It was previously implied in Rousseau's distinction between the private interests and the general will. Both theorists looked towards a political order where the public good would be judged by citizens who deliberately suspended, or controlled, their private interests in order to be able to judge from the point of view of the public good. It was Marx, of course, who indicated the futility of this hope. He simply showed that the distinction between civil society and the state grows out of the progressive alienation of men in bourgeois society and indicates the contradiction between the state as the agent of the private owners of the means of production and the fact that the means of production are social. The state, in other words, is an extension of the private realm of the capitalists from which the interests of everybody else are excluded. The state and civil society are at odds because the state is public only in name, but not in character. From this one could conclude that the distinction between the state and civil society is made precisely when the public realm has been taken over by certain private interests and has therefore, to all intents, disappeared! For an indication of this argument see *The German Ideology* (London, 1965), 265 sqq.

William Leiss

The false imperatives of technology

I

Criticism of society because of its failure to realize possibilities for improving the conditions of human existence is as old as social theory itself and is a pervasive feature of contemporary society. Almost everyone, regardless of political persuasion, now believes that the state as the instrument of 'society' must encourage the maximal exploitation of the available productive resources and must assume responsibility for an increasing number of problems (urban environment, pollution, transportation, and so forth).

The analysis of the general phenomenon of technological change is being approached more and more from this point of view. The dramatic rate of technological innovation and application, and the social changes associated with it, seems to require a greater degree of public control; in the words of one recent author, 'the political imperatives of technological change call for institutional innovation in the direction of mechanisms responsive to the enlarged scope of public decision-making in our society.'[1] In the United States, government-sponsored studies have been undertaken in order to discover the length of time that elapses between the completion of basic scientific research in an area, the perfection of the technological innovation (the 'product idea') based on that research, and the marketing of a new device.[2] The US government currently spends more on 'research and development' (most of it in the form of a subsidy to private industry) than do all private firms combined.[3]

This situation is now the usual context within which one of the more pervasive issues of the present – the evaluation of the social consequences of technological progress – is considered. An intense interest in this subject, manifest in academic treatises (the fruits of vast research programs exclusively devoted to it), official governmental reports, and journalistic forays of varying competence, reflects the converging concerns of abstract social analysis and concrete public policy. The specific historical situation of this recent literature is of some relevance. The subject became prominent as a specialized area of investigation after the horrors of the Second World War, when the massive destructive capabilities of modern industrial technology were amply demonstrated. A symposium sponsored by UNESCO represented one of the first systematic treatments of this topic and illustrated many of the approaches which were later pursued in more detail.[4]

One can safely assume that the question of the social consequences of technological progress will be extensively examined in the coming years. Yet a glance at the present state of the subject will reveal, in addition to some valuable insights, an unnecessary amount of conceptual confusion and dubious prognosis. The following pages have been devoted to some critical comments on recent literature in this field, with the intention of clarifying the issues that might shape future investigations.

This critique deals with the basic theoretical context of the problem and with several subsidiary matters. As far as the first is concerned, I shall try to show that the confusions prevalent in the recent literature arise from a failure to treat the particular question (namely, the social consequences of technological progress) within its real historical context (the attempt to shape *social behaviour* according to rational standards and freely chosen goals). Secondly, the subsidiary topics taken up below will include, among others: (1) the kinds of abstractions used in the predominant theories, especially the concepts of 'man' and 'society'; (2) the cause-and-effect explanations employed in the theories; and (3) the familiar question of the 'neutrality' of technology.

II

Almost every aspect of technology is being investigated at present.[5] In addition to the regular outlets for the reporting of this research, specialized projects devoted exclusively to this subject area have been initiated. Since 1960, for example, a learned journal (*Technology and Culture*) has been established and major projects on technology and society (Harvard University) and on technology and values (University of Pittsburgh) have been undertaken. The particular problem with which the present essay is concerned has received much attention under the heading of 'technology and social change.' Many contributions to this literature, however, encompass a relatively narrow domain, concentrating on immediate social problems or on the short-range effects of certain technological innovations; others are superficial surveys or restatements of familiar knowledge. Although there are individual points of value in all of them, for the most part they do not offer an adequate basis for rigorous theoretical analysis.[6]

A few authors have cast the problem in wider terms and have seriously attempted to evaluate the general relation between technology and society. Those who have done so, and whose writings will be examined in the following pages, are R.J. Forbes, Emmanuel G. Mesthene, John Kenneth Galbraith, and Jacques Ellul.[7] The inclusion of Ellul in this list might occasion some surprise, since he has been stereotyped as the extreme example of the 'pessimistic' analysis of technology; I will try to show, however, that the basic conceptual approach of the more 'optimistic' thinkers is practically identical with Ellul's. Since we will be concerned here with certain broad issues, the divergences among the members of this group on particular points will not always be noted.

What is the hallmark of their body of thought? Its basic conception is indicated in a set of familiar phrases: technological order, technical civilization, technological society, technological man, and so on, even to the 'technetronic society.'[8] The major implication of this terminology is that modern technology itself brings into being a form of society qualitatively different from all previous types; that is to say, this technology has a peculiar dynamic which necessitates far-ranging adjustments in social and individual behaviour. Almost all of these writers refer to the 'imperatives' of technology.[9] To a greater or lesser degree they suggest that we are experiencing a radical discontinuity in human history, a sharp break with the past and the preparation of a far different future.

Their language is often dramatic. Forbes writes: 'Technology can no longer be viewed as only one of many threads that form the texture of our civilization; with a rush, in less than half a century, it has become the prime source of material change and so *determines* the pattern of the total social fabric.'[10] For Ellul, too, the technological order (representing the integration of specialized techniques from all aspects of social behaviour) comes to assert a determining influence over the separate features of society, imposing a uniform mode of organization on the whole.[11] The evaluation of this development in positive or negative terms is, according to Ellul, less important than the appreciation of it as a form of social organization which is different from everything in the past. Mesthene's attitude is rather more joyous, but the basic point is similar: 'Technology, in short, has come of age, not merely as a technical capability, but as a social phenomenon. We have the power to create new possibilities, and the will to do so. By creating new possibilities, we give ourselves more choices. With more choices, we have more opportunities. With more opportunities, we can have more freedom, and with more freedom we can be more human. That, I think, is what is new about our age. We are recognizing that our technical prowess literally bursts with the promise of new freedom, enhanced human dignity, and unfettered aspiration.'[12]

The first step to be taken in evaluating this hypothesis is to inquire what is meant by the term 'technology.' The authors are straightforward in their definitions. Mesthene regards it as 'the organization of knowledge for the achievement of practical purposes.' Galbraith concurs: 'technology means the systematic application of scientific or other organized knowledge to practical tasks.' Forbes notes the definition offered by *Webster's Third New International Dictionary* ('the science of the application of knowledge to practical purposes'), which is almost the same as those given by Mesthene and Galbraith, and then formulates his own: 'technology, then, is the product of interaction between man and environment, based on the wide range of real or imagined needs and desires which guided man in his conquest of Nature.'

Ellul distinguishes technique and technology, chiefly because the latter term misleads us into thinking that the technical phenomenon is only an aspect of society, whereas in reality (for Ellul) it pervades the whole. He finds Harold Lasswell's definition of technique – 'the ensemble of practices by which one uses available resources in order to achieve certain valued ends' – the most acceptable.[13]

Quite obviously, these definitions are rather broad and loose; one can trap myriad types of evidence in such liberally constructed conceptual nets. Some time ago Stéphane Bernard, in a careful theoretical treatise on the topic under discussion in this paper, warned against this tendency and argued that unless some reasonable delimitation were imposed on the concept of technology one could not even attempt to analyse the problem of the social consequences of technological progress. He distinguished a loose and a restricted sense of the term and suggested that the restricted sense be employed in the treatment of the above-mentioned problem.[14] Judging from the evidence of recent literature, his advice has gone unheeded. But the conceptual latitude takes its revenge in the theories we are discussing, for the ecumenical definition of technology serves chiefly to magnify their inadequacies and contradictions.

The fundamental liability is their tendency to obscure the workings of the social process within which technology functions – not directly, to be sure, but by virtue of their selective emphasis and their methodology. If technology is the organization of knowledge for practical purposes, what we need to know is *who* organizes it and how it is organized. Or, if we look at Forbes' definition, we must ask, *who* guided the conquest of nature and for what purposes? Lasswell's conception, accepted by Ellul, prompts us to inquire, *what* ends and how are they selected? An immediate rejoinder might be to argue that such problems are outside the realm of technology itself and thus that these matters must be formally distinguished from one another. But such a rejoinder would be inappropriate because it would contradict one of the primary assertions of these very theories – namely, that modern technology is a broad social phenomenon, that it pertains to the 'total social fabric,' that it imposes itself on the totality of society's institutional arrangements.

If modern technology must be viewed as a general social phenomenon, rather than merely as the technical capability of society (that is, the material instruments of production), then the genesis of this pervasive factor must be explained, not taken for granted. To put the question bluntly: whence come these 'imperatives' of technology? Ellul treats the question most extensively, relating it to a 'change in attitude on the part of the whole civilization.' After asserting that the 'ultimate reason' for this dramatic change 'escapes us,' he lists five factors whose convergence resulted in the appearance of the novel technological order.[15] All of these factors in turn require explanation, especially the one which Ellul calls the most decisive ('the plasticity of the social milieu'), and although he recognizes this requirement and briefly attempts to satisfy it this remains one of the weakest features of his book. The technological order, 'autonomous' and 'self-augmenting,' shrouds its own dynamic and tends to restore an aura of mystery to the workings of society.

For Galbraith the imperatives of technology are related to the structure of the 'industrial system.' This, in turn, possesses a highly deterministic character: 'it is part of the vanity of modern man that he can decide the character of his economic system. His area of decision is, in fact, exceedingly small. He could, conceivably, decide whether or not he wishes to have a high level of industrialization. Thereafter the imperatives of organization, technology and planning operate similarly ... on all societies. Given the decision to have modern industry, much of what happens is inevitable and the same.'[16] Something inherent in the 'nature' of modern industry sets the limits of human options once it is adopted. The underlying reasons for this situation (for example, the possibility that it reflects the impact of an authoritarian societal structure on the productive organization of the industrial system) are not explored, and the failure to investigate them results in a reified conception of society's productive process.

The framework of Mesthene's analysis differs in emphasis, but not in substance, from that of Ellul and Galbraith. His method is to trace the impact of technology *on* the various facets of societal existence, as is clearly shown in the subheadings of one of his essays: 'How technological change impinges on society,' 'how society reacts to technological change,' 'technology's challenge to values,' and so forth.[17] The nature of his approach is indicated in his attempt to explain the process of technological change. He writes, 'I do not depreciate the interaction between technology and society ... Nevertheless, once a new technology is created, it is the impetus for the social and institutional changes that follow it.' Of course we need to know what is responsible for the creation of a new technology. Mesthene tells us that 'the initiative for development of technology in any given instance lies with people, acting individually or as a group, deliberately or in response to such pressures as wars or revolutions.'[18] This can hardly be accounted an *explanation* in any sense, however. The entire analysis is designed to trace the immense impact of modern technology on social behaviour. We are told, in a passage quoted earlier, that 'our technical prowess literally bursts with the promise of new freedom, enhanced human dignity, and unfettered aspiration'; and we are asked to believe that a great flowering of individuality is to be expected.[19] All of this is to be attributed to the actions of 'people.' Once more, the analysis of this supposedly vital force dissolves into commonplaces and circular propositions.

Of course Mesthene would readily agree – and so would everyone else – that technology and society 'mutually interact.'[20] But what must be delineated precisely is the structure and process of this interaction. Mesthene notes: 'With few exceptions, technologies in our society are developed and applied as a result of individual decision ... In deciding whether to develop a new technology, the individual decision maker calculates the benefit that he can expect to derive from the new development and compares it with what it is likely to cost him. If the expected benefit to himself is greater than the cost he will have to pay, he goes ahead.'[21] In plainer and briefer English, *profit* is the dynamic element in technological development and application; and of course, in contemporary society the 'individual' calculus referred to in this passage is primarily that of the large corporations. Yet if technological change is itself rooted in profit, how is it possible to attempt to trace the social consequences of technological change without relating it to its socio-economic 'ground'? How can one even separate the two at all, and arbitrarily concentrate the analysis of social change (as Mesthene does) on the alleged impact of technology?[22] To be faithful to the viewpoint expressed in the quoted passage above, Mesthene would have to analyse the particular effects of the dynamic interaction of technological advance and profitability (including the *distortions* imposed on the process of innovation) in its widest dimensions.

Forbes devotes comparatively little space to this problem. As we have seen, he understands technology as the product of the interaction between man and the environment based upon the collection of 'real and imagined desires.' But unless we understand the process by which these desires are expressed and socially legitimated, we will not comprehend in turn the genesis of our technology. Forbes remarks that relative differences in technological development across cultures may be related to the 'consensus as to the demands and aspirations of the society' in each case and that the modern Western technology 'was created primarily by response to the challenges of the environment in Western Europe from the 12th century on, and in North America, beginning three centuries later.'[23] Yet the existence of such a consensus in society, past or present, is doubtful, and in any case the basis for the assertion of demands and aspirations itself requires investigation; moreover, the two explanations (consensus and environment) are to a great degree mutually contradictory.

The manifest weaknesses of these theories might lead one to dismiss them out of hand were it not for the intrinsic importance of the subject matter and for the fact that these theories are representative of widely shared attitudes. Modern technology *is* indeed a general social phenomenon, and no competent social theory can afford to misinterpret its function in the totality of the societal process. The essential error in these theories is to isolate one aspect of this totality (technology) and then to relate it back to the totality in a mechanical fashion; accordingly, the cause-and-effect network is resolved upon analysis into a set of circular propositions. The result is that a 'technological veil'[24] is cast over the social process which obscures both the general dynamic of advanced societies and the specific role of technology in that dynamic. A discussion of a few selected points in the literature under review may serve to illustrate the functioning of this technological veil.

III

Among the most popular theses of this literature are two interconnected propositions: (1) the chief social function of technology is to create new possibilities for human activity; and (2) in terms of its social effects technology is 'neutral,' the fruits of technological progress may be used 'for good or evil,' depending upon the ends in the service of which they are employed. The first proposition has been championed most consistently by Mesthene. He writes, for example, 'the first-order effect of technology is thus to multiply and diversify material possibilities and thereby offer new and altered opportunities to man.' And in another place he links the two propositions: 'technology ... creates new possibilities for human choice and action, but leaves their disposition uncertain. What its effects will be and what ends it will serve are not inherent in the technology, but depend on what man will do with technology.'[25] Forbes concurs: 'the technologist can only argue in defense of his art that his creative act produces an end that is neither good nor bad. Technological problems, like those of science, recognize only a correct or an incorrect solution; the value judgments of "good" or "bad" come only when the solution is applied to the affairs of men.' Likewise, Ellul says: 'but a principal characteristic of technique ... is its refusal to tolerate moral judgments. It is absolutely independent of them and eliminates them from its domain.'[26]

These quotations illustrate the two interconnected propositions mentioned above, which can now be analysed in turn. In the first place, these conceptions, if compared with the citations given earlier in this paper, illustrate a basic contradiction in the theory, a contradiction between the idea of technology itself and the actual social process of technological development. As shown earlier, technology is defined in these theories as the 'organization of knowledge for practical purposes.' Technology is thus one of the great manifestations of human *activity* in the world. But in the description of the process of technological development, the predominant impression is one of human *passivity:* technology 'offers' possibilities to men. Reviewing Forbes' book, one of Mesthene's research associates remarks, 'man's rationality and his ability to develop ever more potent and sophisticated technologies which will *bring* mankind new and greater opportunities for choice and decision making are not questioned either.'[27] The bold formulation of another writer makes explicit this outlook: 'But, as we are learning, technological innovation belongs to us less than we belong to it. It has demands and effects of its own on the nature and structure of corporations, industries, government-industry relations and the values and norms that make up our idea of ourselves and of progress.'[28]

Through a curious process of inversion, the means (technological innovations) come to govern the ends (values and norms). Human beings become the 'objects,' rather than the 'subjects,' of their own activity. It is not that individuals are experiencing an essentially novel phase of social development, for most have passed through the historical record as the objects of forces which they neither comprehended nor controlled; the paradox is that this persistent condition should be *revalued* and now be regarded as bursting with 'the promise of new freedom.' The element of passivity in these conceptions of technological development is the unintended admission of the truth that most individuals remain the objects of their practice, that is, that their productive activity results in new circumstances to which perforce they must adapt themselves. This passivity is clearly expressed in the notion that individuals must 'learn how to take full advantage of the humane potentialities of technological progress,'[29] a formula which implies an adaptive mode of behaviour and which confuses means and ends.

It would seem that the suppressed social dimension of the problem, the concrete social context of technological development which these theories stubbornly ignore, forces itself into the analysis at this point. According to these theories, individuals experience technological progress as the discovery of new possibilities 'offered' or 'brought' to them; but *how* these possibilities reach them presumably remains a mystery. In other words, the theories fail to show how technology, conceived as organized human activity for practical purposes, results in the *specific* allocation of the world's material resources and the *specific* possibilities now being planned for the immediate future — possibilities which are *presently existing* features of the advanced societies. Despite the fact that much is made of the alleged difference between an 'optimistic' or a 'pessimistic' viewpoint by these theorists, the deeper affinity among them reveals itself here.[30] Ellul has merely given an extreme formulation of their basic analysis, in which the growing technological apparatus appears to set out the options and limitations of choice in a more or less autonomous fashion.[31]

The peculiar association of activity and passivity in this account of technology is a consequence of the abstract way in which 'possibilities' are conceived. Taken by itself, the idea that the principal outcome of technological progress is the creation of 'new possibilities' is at worst tautologous, and at best uninformative. In order to arrive at a proper assessment of the matter, we would need to know not only which possibilities had been created, but also which had been simultaneously denied or distorted. (The family farm as a socio-economic unit and a sense of craftsmanship in labour are examples of the latter.) The point is not to attempt to 'balance' the loss against the gain, for there is simply no adequate measure which would permit this.[32] Of the greatest importance, however, is the character of the process by which new possibilities are opened and older ones closed: is it a response to human needs that have been articulated in a relatively non-manipulative and non-authoritarian framework, or rather just the opposite? And if the latter is the case, what effects have the *distortions* of human needs on the course of technological progress itself?

With reference to these kinds of problems, it is clear that the proposition concerning the 'neutrality' of technology merely begs the question. The depiction of a set of possibilities opened up by certain innovations is indeed a currently fashionable pastime for the futurologists – although, it must be said, the suggested vistas are often rather trite. Far more difficult, but ultimately also more insightful, is the attempt to delineate the forces that determine which specific innovations are encouraged and perfected and which are delayed or suppressed. This 'background' context of technological development is not at all a neutral sphere, but on the contrary is an arena of often violently conflicting social interests, both national and international in scope.[33] And since every step in technological advance occurs within a specific background context, it is the nature of the *whole* context (including the technological innovation as one of its components) that must be evaluated as a stage in the evolution of specific human societies.

Moreover, the notion of the neutrality of technology introduces a formal contradiction into these theories, for technology cannot simultaneously be neutral on the one hand, and on the other exhibit 'imperatives' and entail positive 'consequences.' If it is really and completely neutral – if it involves 'only possibility' (as Mesthene puts it) – no positive results *at all* can be attributed to it. Whatever imperatives in present-day society are discovered by the theorist and whatever consequences seem to be associated with the existing level of technological accomplishment must be traced to non-technological social forces. According to the proponents of the neutrality thesis, it must be remembered, no determinate ends (either good or bad) can be associated with technology itself. Thus, strictly speaking, no consequences at all (and likewise no imperatives) flow from technology; and the possibilities which are allegedly 'opened' by it are in reality determined by the nature of the social order as a whole.

Let us take an example. Edward Shils advances the proposition that 'individuality has been greatly fostered by the development of a science-based technology.'[34] By individuality Shils means a greater range of choices in consumption, occupation, residence, and so on; and he finds evidence of an enlarged political role for the individual in the increasing attention paid to public opinion polls by political leaders. But to this list of circumstances could not one say, plus ça change, plus c'est la même chose? What does all of this have to do with individuality? None of the factors cited by Shils would be inconsistent with the thesis that the individual remains subjected to a productive system over which he has no control, no matter how large the range of his 'choices' within the system.[35] The problem is that Shils is using the concept of individuality uncritically, and it is instructive to compare his treatment with that of John Stuart Mill in *On Liberty*. Mill's searching discussion shows convincingly, in my view, that the level of technological achievement is by no means a decisive feature of individuality. Thus Shils can only link the two by introducing a highly questionable notion of individuality; in the light of a more sophisticated notion, very little of any import seems to follow from the present level of technology itself.[36]

Mesthene's theory tries to rescue itself from this dilemma concerning the consequences of technological progress with the concept of 'negative externalities.'[37] He explains the existence of the 'negative effects of technology' (pollution, ecological damage, threats to individual privacy, and so forth) by the fact that no social agency is responsible for dealing with such problems. Since we are concerned here only with the basic conceptions of the theory and not with political considerations, it will suffice simply to note that this theory again becomes contradictory at this point. If technology 'spells only possibility,' it is incorrect to link any of these problems with the study of technology, for they must be (according to the theory) formally extrinsic to it. Technology cannot have any negative effects for the same reasons that it cannot have any positive consequences. If Mesthene were to be consistent within his own theory, he would have to regard the benefits of technological progress – for example, the factors which promote individuality – as 'positive externalities.'

Moreover, as McDermott has pointed out, the concept of 'negative externalities' is highly arbitrary and subjective. *For whom* are these negative effects 'external,' and for whom have the negative effects of advanced technologies constituted the primary (and even exclusive) experience of them? The South Vietnamese peasant has never known the beneficial application of herbicides, but on the contrary has suffered their utilization as an instrument of destruction. What is a negative externality for the advanced societies (for example, the deleterious effects of widespread application of DDT) is not at all an externality for Vietnamese society. These theories can continue to regard such matters as incidental only at the risk of excluding much of the prevailing reality from their purview.

An analysis of the theories under discussion here uncovers the curious fact that none of the theoretical pegs upon which the elaboration of their arguments depend – the idea that technology exhibits certain imperatives, the autonomy of modern technology, the notion that technology only involves possibilities, and the neutrality of technology – ever receives the consideration of a well-argued demonstration. This deficiency arises, I believe, because the framework of their analysis is far too narrowly conceived. A much fuller theoretical model is required, one which relates concretely the human struggle with nature (in which technology appears as the set of instruments devised for the mastery of the natural environment) with the intense social struggles.[38] This latter aspect of the over-all problem is almost wholly absent from the theories analysed here; a look at this deficiency and its consequences will complete this critical review.

IV

One of the hallmarks of theories about technology and society is their concern with the possibilities awaiting 'man.' In technical terms, man is the 'subject' of the process described by the theories, the agent and presumably the beneficiary of the growing technological apparatus. In a passage cited above Mesthene remarks that technology's effects 'depend on what man will do with technology'; and Forbes writes, for example, 'man is not only free to choose his technology; he can also control the rate at which it absorbs previously human functions.'[39] These are typical examples of what is for them a routine mode of expression. And yet one is compelled to object that the putative subject does not yet exist. The appearance of a universal 'man' in history, the fulfilment of the ancient idea of 'humanity,' is still awaited. One cannot explain the significance of technological progress in terms of a non-existent subject; rather, the actual, concrete subjects of the process – particular groups of individuals engaged in the bitter struggle with nature and with each other – must be the basis upon which the role of technology is assessed.

Indeed this point seems too obvious to require mention. Yet the fact remains that it is not recognized in these theories and that instead they employ an abstract concept which helps to distort the account of technology and its social consequences. It ought to be equally obvious that the 'freedom of choice' that individuals supposedly possess vis-à-vis their technologies is similarly unreal. The tempo of technological change (a worldwide process) is part of an essentially anarchic situation. 'Society,' too, becomes a grand abstraction in these theories, assuming the guise of a theatre for mutual effort; of course this image eliminates the fact of persistent and intense conflict. Everything seems so simple, for example, when Forbes notes that technological thinking pertains to 'operations to effect certain changes in the environment which society in effect has commissioned the technologist to perform.'[40] The phrase 'in effect' introduces an equivocation that enables the theory to avoid any consideration of the *actual conditions* under which decisions affecting the nature of technological advances are made. To ignore those conditions, however, is to misrepresent the character of the whole process, of which technology is an integral but subordinate component.

The basic issue under discussion is epitomized in the problem of the relation between the rationality of the part (technology) and the rationality of the whole.[41] The growth of technology, especially in the past few centuries, is a phenomenon of transparent rationality; in other words, the continued successes in the application of exact knowledge to 'practical' problems and the dramatic vistas thereby unfolded (both in the alleviation of labour and in the satisfaction of wants) are conclusive demonstrations of the human ability to provide an adequate material basis for the traditional utopian visions. But the rationality possessed by technology as an independent factor cannot be 'transferred' intact, as it were, to the general social context in which it develops. The rationality or irrationality of the whole is the outcome of the intersection of many contributory factors, and it is the ongoing (unstable) resolution of these multiple forces which in turn largely determines the role which each of them plays in the totality. Thus in order to examine any particular aspect of this dynamic – for example, the social consequences of technological progress – the primary focus of the analysis ought to be directed at the relation between the partial aspect and the whole.

The enormous difficulties involved in assessing the 'rationality of the whole' should not be underestimated, of course. Such difficulties are responsible for the fact that for most of human history the social order has appeared as the product of mysterious, uncomprehended forces and its workings traced to the activities of the gods or Nature. The contributions of philosophy and social theory, which sought to delineate the conditions under which society might be radically reorganized according to the dictates of human rationality (for example, Plato's *Republic*), remained immeasurably distant from the actual historical situation. It was Hegel who first claimed to be able to demonstrate in systematic fashion a connection between the development of rationality and the chaotic, brutal, mass struggles of human history. Hegel characterized this in the famous notion of the 'cunning of reason,' by which he tried to explain the fact that the actions of individuals and groups often transcend the immediate interests which motivate them and thus prepare the way for the emergence of different social conditions.

Marx adopted this idea and attempted to explore it more fully, especially with reference to modern society. His remark that 'men make their own history,' but not under freely chosen circumstances, is a restatement of Hegel's conception.[42] For Marx the period of human development when the great majority of individuals are at the mercy of forces (natural and social) which they neither understand nor control should be labeled the 'prehistory' of mankind; the true 'history' of mankind will be inaugurated when the conditions of existence are confronted by the associated individuals within a framework of rationality and freedom. But it is the structure of events in the 'prehistoric' phase which governs progress towards the 'historical' phase, and this means that the forging of those instruments and institutions which are to provide the basis for the enjoyment of freedom takes place within the context of pervasive unfreedom and irrationality.

Technology, in the broadest sense of this term, is one of those instruments. The developing characteristics of the industrial revolution, which demonstrated the immense productive powers of sustained technological innovation and increasingly skilled labour, was primarily responsible for the widening expectation that a form of society qualitatively different from those of the past could be brought into being. Like many of their contemporaries, Marx and the other nineteenth-century socialist thinkers were profoundly influenced by the actual course of the industrial revolution during this period. However, unlike some of their contemporaries (such as the Saint-Simonians) and unlike most writers on technology in our time, Marx and a few other thinkers of the nineteenth century (Charles Fourier, for example) never attempted to treat technological-industrial progress as an independent or semi-independent factor that could be analysed apart from the entire ensemble of social relations.

The theories under discussion here mark a retreat in the realm of social theory by attempting to isolate the rationality of technology from the rationality of the whole. The task of contemporary theory is not to search for new opportunities or possibilities 'brought' by technology, but rather to inquire whether our most urgent needs can be realized within the structure of existing institutions. In other words, modern technology does not really challenge us most 'by guiding us in the reformulation of our ends to fit our new means and opportunities.'[43] Rather, it demands that we alter the way in which our ends are formulated and reformulated, that we radically improve the social decision-making process which governs the character of technological progress. This is most certainly not a matter of 'arresting technological development,' at least not as George Kateb has described it.[44] It concerns the formation of a social order that would liberate technology from its far too competent service in the cause of human conflict.

NOTES

1 E.G. Mesthene, 'Comment,' Symposium on the Role of Technology in Society, *Technology and Culture,* X (1969), 536
2 Illinois Institute of Technology Research Institute, 'Technology in Retrospect and Critical Events in Science,' I (Washington, DC, 1968)
3 'Research Spending Heading for a Record,' *New York Times,* 18 May 1970, 47-8
4 *International Social Science Bulletin,* IV (1952), 243-399. Of special interest are the articles by Georges Friedmann, 'The Social Consequences of Technical Progress' (243-60), and S. Herbert Frankel, 'Some Conceptual Aspects of Technical Change' (263-9).
5 One could go further and remark that the situation is almost out of hand. So many aspects of social development are being causally related to technology that one wonders whether Martin Nicolaus exaggerates at all when he writes: 'For nearly a decade, the entire official spectrum of analysts, critics and columnists has been pointing to "technology" and "inflation" as the root causes of one or another troublesome phenomenon. These are the "ether" and "phlogiston" of contemporary socio-economic criticism, the residual, fictional categories into whose murky depths escape all those who fear the sunlight of critical, radical thought ... The problem with "technology" and "inflation" is that as explanations they include *too much;* they can be used to explain everything, and therefore end up explaining nothing.' *Leviathan,* I, no. 5 (September, 1969), 16
6 In this category I would include: *The Technological Order,* ed. Carl F. Stover (Detroit, 1963); Donald Schon, *Technology and Change* (New York, 1967); *Technological Innovation and Society,* ed. D. Morse and A.W. Warner (New York, 1966); *Technology and Social Change,* ed. Eli Ginsberg (New York, 1964). For an exhaustive but unselective bibliography see Victor Ferkiss, *Technological Man* (New York, 1969), 295-327. In my view almost all of the recent contributions to 'futurology' fall into this category; the extent of this literature is indicated in the bibliography in *Values and the Future,* ed. K. Baier and N. Rescher (New York, 1969). See R.A. Nisbet's incisive comments on futurology in 'The Year 2000 and All That,' *Commentary,* XLV, no. 6 (June, 1968), 60-6.
7 Forbes, *The Conquest of Nature: Technology and its Consequences* (New York, 1968). Mesthene, 'How Technology Will Shape the Future,' *Science,* CLXI (12 July 1968), 135-43; 'Technology and Wisdom,' *Technology and Social Change,* ed. Mesthene (Indianapolis, 1967), 57-62; 'The Role of Technology in Society,' *Fourth Annual Report 1967-1968,* Harvard University Program on Technology and Society, 41-74 [reprinted in *Technology and Culture,* X (1969), 489-513]; *Technological Change: Its Impact on Man and Society* (New York, 1970). Galbraith, *The New Industrial State* (Boston, 1967). Ellul, *The Technological Society,* trans. John Wilkinson (New York, 1967). Ellul's book was first published in French in 1954 (*La Technique,* Paris), but it attracted wide attention only in the 1960s. For summations of the problem much different from the one given here see F.R. Allen, 'Technology and Social Change,' *Technology and Culture,* I (1960), 48-59; and Irene Taviss, 'The Technological Society: Some Challenges for Social Science,' *Social Research,* XXXV (1968), 521-39.
8 The neologism is a product of 'technology' and 'electronics': Zbigniew Brzezinski, 'America in the Technetronic Age,' *Encounter,* XXX, no. 1 (January, 1968), 16-26.
9 Galbraith, chap. 2; Mesthene, passage cited in note 1 above; Ellul, 210 and elsewhere. Forbes (x, 75) speaks of an 'environmental imperative' to which human technology responds.
10 vii (my italics). Forbes takes great pains to distinguish his views from those of Ellul (72-6), but this passage is perfectly in accord with Ellul's thesis!
11 See especially 78-147 of *The Technological Society.*
12 'Technology and Wisdom,' 59
13 Mesthene, *Technological Change,* 25; Galbraith, 24; Forbes, x; Ellul, xxv-xxvi, 13-18
14 *Les conséquences sociales du progrès technique: methodologie* (Brussells, 1956), esp. 124ff

15 44-60
16 403
17 'The Role of Technology in Society,' passim. The recent book, *Values and the Future* (above, note 6), is subtitled, *The Impact of Technological Change on American Values.*
18 This and the preceding quotation are from 'How Technology Will Shape the Future,' 136.
19 On the last point see 'The Role of Technology in Society,' 23-4, 62-3.
20 He writes, 'It is important to recall that technology is not independent of the society in which it develops and flourishes,' (*Technological Change,* 20). On this point cf. George H. Daniels, 'Reply,' in Symposium on the Historiography of American Technology, *Technology and Culture,* XI (1970), 33.
21 *Technological Change,* 38, 39
22 Recently George H. Daniels has suggested reversing the prevailing emphasis, arguing that 'the direction in which society is going determines the nature of its technological innovations.' He adds further: 'If the pattern of invention thus depends in large measure upon socio-economic change, we see once more why it is futile to attempt to trace social changes to technological inventions.' 'The Big Questions in the History of American Technology,' *Technology and Culture,* XI (1970), 3, 8. This is not an ideal solution, since Daniels' hypothesis is also one-sided and mechanical, but it is a valuable antidote to the conventional wisdom.
23 x, 54
24 Herbert Marcuse, *An Essay on Liberation* (Boston, 1969), 11-12
25 'How Technology Will Shape the Future,' 136; *Technological Change,* 60. Cf. 'Technology and Wisdom,' 59: 'Technology spells only possibility, and is in that respect neutral.' Since Marcuse is classified by Mesthene and others as one of the 'pessimistic' antagonists of technology, it might be instructive to compare a recent statement by Marcuse with others just quoted: 'is it still necessary to state that not technology, not technique, not the machine are the engines of repression, but the presence, in them, of the masters who determine their number, their life span, their power, their place in life, and the need for them? Is it still necessary to repeat that science and technology are the great vehicles of liberation, and that it is *only* their use and restriction in the repressive society which makes them into vehicles of domination?' (*An Essay on Liberation,* 12; my italics). Compare this passage with a similar one written by Marcuse nearly thirty years earlier in his essay 'Some Social Implications of Modern Technology,' *Studies in Philosophy and Social Science,* IX (1941), 436-7.
26 Forbes, 67; Ellul, 97. Cf. Ellul, 'The Technological Order,' in *The Technological Order,* 33: '*Our* thesis is that technical progress contains simultaneously the good *and* the bad' (author's italics). And Mesthene (*Technological Change,* 26): 'New technology creates new opportunities for men and societies, and it also generates new problems for them. It has both positive and negative effects, and it usually has the two *at the same time and in virtue of each other*' (author's italics)
27 Irene Taviss, review of Forbes, *The Conquest of Nature,* in *Technology and Culture,* X (1969), 306-7; my italics
28 Donald Schon, *Technology and Change,* xiii
29 W.E. Howland, in the symposium 'Technology for Man,' *Technology and Culture,* X (1969), 6; cf. the critical comments by James C. Wallace, *ibid.,* 17-19, which are especially relevant to the problem of passivity
30 For Mesthene, Forbes, and others Ellul is the prime representative of the 'pessimistic' outlook, even though Ellul (xxxvi) explicitly rejects such considerations. It seems to me that the dichotomy of optimism or pessimism depends upon highly subjective and superficial criteria. For example, Taviss (see note 27) finds even so genial an observer as Forbes too gloomy.
31 Of course the others would reject this association of their views with Ellul's. But I do not think that they may justly do so without incorporating in their theories some conception

of how the process of technological development — considered as a global phenomenon — might come under the control of rational human activity.

32 A discussion of the inherent limitations in the influence of technological progress on human activity would take us too far from our subject. For an excellent brief introduction to this question see René Dubos, 'Adaptation to the Environment and Man's Future,' *The Control of Environment,* ed. John Roslansky (Amsterdam, 1967).

33 See Richard Hinners, 'Vietnam: Technology v. Morality,' *Continuum,* IV (1967), 221-34. Hinners writes (231-2): 'For any technology the primary questions should be not, what is it and what can it do, but rather, whose technology is it and what are their purposes and interests in it? Technology is always the production by men for or against other men; it is never humanly or morally indifferent, however much we may wrongly persist in believing in its neutrality.'

34 Harvard University Program on Technology and Society, *Fourth Annual Report 1967-1968,* 23-4. It should be noted that this publication presents only an outline of Shils' thesis.

35 'With technical progress as its instrument, unfreedom — in the sense of man's subjection to his productive apparatus — is perpetuated and intensified in the form of many liberties and comforts.' Herbert Marcuse, *One-Dimensional Man* (Boston, 1964), 32. In an earlier essay Marcuse commented specifically on the relation between modern technology and individuality: 'Some Social Implications of Modern Technology,' 414-39 passim.

36 In his paraphrase of Shils' argument, Mesthene (the author of the *Report* cited above, note 34) says that modern technology *'presents* the individual with a more complex society that *offers* him a wider range of experience ...' (24, my italics). It should be clear by now how deeply rooted is the element of passivity in these theories.

37 *Technological Change,* 38ff. See the critique of the concept in John McDermott, 'Technology: The Opiate of the Intellectuals,' *The New York Review of Books,* XIII, no. 2 (31 July 1969), 25-35.

38 See my book, *The Domination of Nature* (New York, 1972), especially chapter seven.

39 Mesthene, *Technological Change,* 60; Forbes, 61. Ellul would seem to dissociate himself from this practice (390): 'The technicians' myth is simply *Man* — not you or I, but an abstract entity.' But his entire study uses the concept 'man' precisely in this abstract manner.

40 Forbes, 88

41 See Jürgen Habermas, *Toward a Rational Society,* tr. J. Shapiro (Boston, 1970), 81-122, esp. 94ff.

42 'Men make their own history, but they do not make it just as they please; they do not make it under circumstances chosen by themselves, but under circumstances immediately present, given, and transmitted to them.' *The Eighteenth Brumaire of Louis Bonaparte* (New York, N.D.), 13, translation changed

43 Mesthene, 'How Technology Will Shape the Future,' 141

44 *Utopia and its Enemies* (New York, 1963), 79-82

Howard Adelman

Wrong turn: youth and social change

In the autumn of 1971 the Committee of Youth report commissioned by the government of Canada was published under the title *It's Your Turn.* As an analysis of youth, the report is a miasma of illogic. Young people are celebrated for the serious intellectual challenge that they provide to conventional institutions to enable those institutions to undertake basic reforms; the institutions must reform if the young are to accept social roles. On the same page, young people are celebrated as instigators of a very different type of change; as adumbrators of new *attitudes* (rather than advocates of new reforms), opting out of institutions altogether in order to obtain novel perceptions denied by the very nature of institutions. A reader faces an immediate dilemma. Do the institutions reform themselves in response to criticism or do they dissolve in order to provide the freedom and flexibility of the new sensibility cult?

In both versions, the young are considered superior in either critical comprehension or sensibility to the rest of society; both views depict young people as visionaries. But the report also considers them the most victimized part of the working class suffering from a disproportionately high unemployment rate (primarily among those without the benefit of senior secondary or postsecondary education); it considers them a special part of an economic class victimized by particular political policies affecting the government of the economy – in spite of its stated claim on the first page that it rejects considering youth in terms of class analysis. To add to the confusion, the young are considered in terms of cultural as well as economic victimization. 'Youth question traditional family patterns while experimenting with other communal relationships,' but society provides no support for these experiments which challenge its most sacred institution, the family. According to the report, the young should be treated as children and supported in their experiments to revolutionize the whole foundation of society and overthrow its paternalism.

Are young people the *economic* victims of the overt anti-inflationary policies of a capitalist society? Or are they the *cultural* victims of a paternalistic society which refuses to support their anti-paternalistic experiments? Are they economic or cultural victims at all, or are they visionaries, as the report also states – the latest emanations of either economic or cultural emancipation?[1] However illogical the report is in its internal contradictions, it does seem to bring together (without, of course, being conscious of it) four variations on the theme of youth as the vanguard of social change.

The Committee of Youth report is only one example of the way in which these various perspectives on youth and social change have been brought together. A similar function is performed in the United States by a book published in the Markham Series on process and change in American society entitled *Youth and Social Change* by Richard Flacks (1971). Like the Youth Report in Canada, Flacks sees technology as the basic impetus behind the changing role of youth in society. The contradictions between technology and the social and cultural systems thrust the young into the vanguard of social change. 'The basic theoretical perspective taken here is that the revolt of youth is a *symptom* of a fundamental socio-cultural crisis. In general terms, the crisis involves a substantial conflict between the emergent technological potentialities of a society and the established social order and cultural system' (p. 6).

There are four distinct ways in which youth is thrust up into this vanguard, though Flacks does not recognize these as distinct perspectives. First, 'youth' is a sociological expression of a new stage in maturation provided by the affluence of a technological society. 'The society created a new social type, called youth, and then provided very few ways for these people to live in terms of the aspirations and feelings they developed. Youth has hope to the extent that it can believe that the future is open – open for social change, and open for personal opportunity' (p. 136). Young people possess a superior critical understanding which society heretofore lacked.

Secondly, 'youth' is an anthropological expression. 'Youth' is not so much a new stage in the maturation of the individual; it is a new stage in the evolution of society as a whole. Following Margaret Mead, Flacks argues that, 'youth constitutes the most viable model of cultural adaptation. In such a "prefigurative culture," young people are the guides of their elders rather than the reverse' (p. 72). The superiority, in Mead's analysis, however, does not arise from a superior intellectual comprehension of the current state of society, but from a new sensibility that heretofore did not exist in man's social evolution. It is not that the young are most ready to change, but that the new technology has already changed young people to create a new breed.

Young people are depicted as victims as well as visionaries. In one definition, the young are members of a new class. 'Technological changes have created new social roles – new classes – whose occupants experience discontent with old ways and established cultures' (p. 6). In another version, the young are cultural victims as they adopt unisexual modes of cultural expression. 'As boys adopted the long hair, necklaces, headbands, and bright colours that were traditionally feminine, girls bought their clothing in the men's departments and abandoned their makeup ... The new youth fashions ... quickly became labeled as a direct challenge to deeply held cultural values with respect to the sex role, work, sensuality and efficient use of time and money ... Thus, the fully dressed "hippie" youth became a target of verbal insult, physical abuse and discrimination in many communities. Also, he was likely to experience forms of harrassment from law enforcement agencies' (p. 67).

Thus, Flack's book is the academic equivalent in the United States to the Canadian government commission report on youth. Both the Canadian report and the American book are united by a common presumption that young people are the vanguard of social change. Both documents attribute this development to technology. Both documents fail to distinguish, and indeed confuse, four different ideological variations on the theme.

This article is intended to clarify a profound misunderstanding of the nature of the relation of the young to social change. This misunderstanding will be revealed through an analysis of four variations on the basic theme. The study points out the common premises of these variations, as well as the dynamic of the contradictions which prevail between them.

YOUTH AS THE VANGUARD OF SOCIAL CHANGE

The general argument can be stated very simply. The agency of social change is technology; the agent of social change is youth.

The basic condition which creates the necessity for change is change itself as embodied in technology. Change is not based on a desire to reach the 'new Jerusalem' and, thereby, utopia; nor is it a result of either constitutional change or material change, primarily. What stimulates the need for change is technology – the embodiment of change itself.

Youth is the principal agent of change. Change is not to be left either in God's hands or in any accepted human authority. Nor could it even be vested in men in general through invisible laws – either natural laws which created a balance of individual wills for the good of the masses or historical laws which gave priority to certain individual wills, also for the sake of the masses. The young, those most in the process of change and most susceptible to external changes, are vested with the responsibility for change.

The thesis can be examined by a detailed analysis of its four variations. The four variations can be grouped into two sets. In the *reformist* ideologies, technology has resulted in a qualitatively new historical phase with a unique form of youth emancipation. In the *radical* ideologies, technology is continuous with the past except that the newest victims are the young. The believers in the emancipation and in the victimization of youth can each be divided into two subsets depending on whether social change is considered to be primarily political or primarily cultural. The four ideological visions of youth can be designated as follows:

Reformist ideologies: youth as visionaries
1 / politically emancipated youth
2 / culturally emancipated youth
Radical ideologies: youth as victims
3 / politically victimized youth
4 / culturally victimized youth

POLITICALLY EMANCIPATED YOUTH

The analysis of the basic theme begins with the theory which vests its faith on a politically emancipated youth hailed as the vehicle of social change to drive society into an even better future. The driver of the vehicle was the New Left of the early and mid-1960s which operated on C. Wright Mills' principles articulated most succinctly in his 'Letter to the New Left,' originally published in the *New Left Review* in 1961 (no. 5). It involved a moral and non-party political stance in which the mind, independent of the political and power processes, served as a critical intelligence to ensure that political leadership was both responsive and responsible in the conduct of human affairs. Knowledge had a clarifying and corrective function, and youth, unencumbered by the power process, could use knowledge to be the conscience of society.[2]

But the clearest articulation and apology for the conscience role of youth emerged in Ken Keniston's study of the Vietnam Summer of 1967 at the climax of New Left activism before it took a more radical turn. In his study, *Young Radicals,* subtitled *Notes on Committed Youth,* published in 1968, Keniston hailed the New Left youth as *the* means to transport us into the future, declaring 'that post-modern societies especially need these men and women ... as the essential basis for social change.'[3] The reason young people are available to do this job is because of technology. Technology produces affluence to free an elite group of privileged youth to act as social critics; technology also poses the omnipresent threat of destruction in general and of the destruction of individuality in particular. Technology provides both the opportunity and the threat which necessitates that the opportunity be taken up.

The ideology of youth as a political vanguard of reform is based on a more general theory of social change which is rooted in a theory of individual development or maturation.[4] Social maturation is dependent on individual maturation, but new possibilities of individual maturation are created as society develops. With affluence, adolescence – the *psychological* stage of maturation when a child outgrows his ties to his parents – has been made possible. More recently, affluence has introduced another stage of individual maturation, *social* maturation. The individual not only outgrows his ties to his parents but he takes on individual independence and social responsibility in his own right. Previously, because they had to work, men adopted social roles without time to reflect critically on those roles. The stage of social maturation has now become a distinct (though only emergent) phase with the development of real affluence, at least for the children of the affluent who dominated the New Left of the early and mid 1960s. 'The stage of youth ... as a separate phase of life is only now becoming visible ... and is available only to a small though growing minority of post-adolescents.'[5]

Thus, the responsibility for social change is associated with individual maturation and the development of a youth stage in that process, which, in turn, is due to previous technological developments which emancipated an elite group of youth from the labour market. That elite can be concerned with the gap between the principles and practices of the society in order to bring the practices of society into line with its principles. 'Those who enter a stage of youth are clearly an elite – psychologically, socially, and economically privileged, and often possessed of unusual talent and vitality.'[6] They are not only an elite but the *least* alienated section of youth, sharing the credal values of their parents yet going beyond their parents as a conscience to point out the differences between creed and practice. 'Affluence is producing more and more families who bring up their children to be idealistic, responsible, and serious about the credal values of our society – children who are therefore dismayed and outraged when they discover the societal lapses between principle and practice.'[7]

In Canada, the New Left conscience began as a critique of Canada's posture as an international peace mediator while the government was obtaining nuclear warheads from the United States. After American Bomarcs were introduced into Canada, the Student Union for Peace Action (SUPA) in replacing the Combined Universities Campaign for Nuclear Disarmament (CUCND) followed the American lead to haunt the Canadian domestic dream of an affluent society with the exposure of the plight of the natives and the poor.

As the third phase of the development of the New Left in Canada, the conscience issues and tactics of American life – race and community organizing – were Canadianized. The government nationalized the ideology true to its heritage as the representative of the benevolent state. The Company of Young Canadians (CYC) was established in 1966. The 'Short, Unhappy Life of the C.Y.C.' was recorded by Marg Daly in *The Revolution Game* (New Press, 1971).

Daly traces the New Left transformation of the CYC from the government's conception of a safe 'bandaid' operation into a crown corporation dominated by the New Left ideology, for the New Left won the battles for both the key executive posts and the appropriate formal legislation. In the process, however, the bureaucratic battles, the battles over the administrative and regional structures, were neglected, and sympathetic governmental officials were alienated. These administrative losses were complemented by a straw foundation resulting from a haphazard selection of projects and volunteers.[8]

The root of the problem was an overinsistence on change versus continuity. The resurgence of old-fashioned individualism gave the New Left the flexibility to defeat the executive legislative ploys of a conformist bureaucracy; it also prevented the reformers from accepting administrative coherence. Since bureaucracy was seen as destructive and ultimately authoritarian, the details of continuous management were neglected, initial bureaucratic allies were alienated, and administrative issues became a form of destructive conflict. The overdevelopment of the superstructure occurred at the expense of the substructure – the personnel and the programs of the organization.

The New Left's stance was non-party and non-political. Yet in its desire to remain unencumbered by the corrupting effect of power and to retain a pure conscience, it was tied to an individualistic bourgeois ideology – as a conscience of the corporate conformity of technological society; this was in spite of the fact that it was the wealth of that technological society which gave youth the opportunity to perform as a superego to bourgeois liberalism. Youth matured to outgrow parental power but failed to outgrow parental ideology. Thus, where mastery was relevant in the legislative and executive arenas of combat, the young emerged victorious; where service was the key, in bureaucratic management and sustenance of a grassroots organization, they failed. The worship of novelty and innovation was directly correlated with the neglect of tradition and continuity.

The root of this problem can be seen in the theory. Keniston not only espouses a doctrine of youth as a prime vehicle of social change rooted in a particular view of technology, but also provides a theoretical underpinning. Social history is both rooted in and determines the possibility of individual maturation, so that only in contemporary history has the progress of technology made possible an elite group of individuals who can serve as a conscience for the destructiveness of that technology as judged by the creed of individualism which underpins that society. And the behaviour of the young radical is perfectly consistent with that liberal creed. For the prime tenet of the bourgeois creed is the necessity to master nature, to master time and space and create a world made by him to satisfy his own individual needs. 'For the young radical, mastery consists of an effort to give direction to social change, creating a meaningful future more in accord with his own basic principles and needs.'[9] The direction and criteria of change are rooted in individualism and the goal of that change is mastery by the individual. A paradox underlies the desire to restore individualism as a conscience of both technology and the growth of corporate conformity. For bourgeois individualism is the beginning of the quest for technological mastery.

Keniston does not examine this problem. Nor does he examine the paradox of viewing youth both as outgrowing his parents to achieve a new stage of maturation and as failing to outgrow the ideologies, or the paradox of viewing youth as learning what is most valuable from his parents but, at the same time, learning most by identification with his peers in opposition to previous generations. The problem of reconciling collective mastery through technology and individual freedom, the problem of defining maturity as outgrowing the past while defining maturity and the means to achieve it by the criteria of the past becomes most difficult when Keniston declares that what is most important is style, change for change's sake, and ideology of '*new* forms of adulthood,' 'a *new* orientation to the future,' '*new* pathways of personal development,' '*new* values for lives,' '*new* styles of human interaction,' '*new* ways of knowing,' '*new* kinds of learning,' '*new* concepts of man and society,' '*new* formulations of the world,' '*new* types of social organization,' '*new* tactics of political action,'[10] – an ideology of newness which is one of the essential tenets of traditional bourgeois ideology.

CULTURALLY EMANCIPATED YOUTH

The advocates of a *culturally* emancipated youth differ from the advocates of a *politically* emancipated youth. The former declare that the new youth has outgrown the bourgeois ideology of maturation through peer-group identification, has outgrown the ideology of stuffing new content in old forms since the very forms of change have altered. Both the relation between generations and the very forms of technology (and not merely its results) have been radically transformed. For Margaret Mead, youthful sensibility rather than the New Left provides transportation into the future, an electronic rather than a mechanical means of historical development.

Margaret Mead describes three different perspectives on the relation of youth to social change. In McLuhan's analysis, these three stages are clearly related to three stages of development of the different forms of expression of technology. The source of change is not in the results of technology, as the advocates of a politically emancipated youth claim – affluence or a propensity to conformity – but the very character of the technology itself. The basis of social change is not individual maturation (à la Keniston) but the maturation of technology itself and the social organization which reflects that maturation.

In pre-print cultures (pre-bourgeois or agricultural society), we have a postfigurative system of dealing with youth and social change. The young man or young woman emerges into adulthood by emulating both the sexual behaviour and the social role of the parent of the same sex. A boy does what his father did; a girl does what her mother did. Essentially, it is a passive and incorporative approach to social change. A person grows into adulthood by receiving, accepting what is received, and when he is mature contributing in some small way to the organic development of the social whole. The main character of such a system is the dependency of youth on age; the dominant institution to reinforce the dependency is religion.

By contrast, 'A cofigurative culture is one in which the prevailing model for members of the society is the behaviour of contemporaries ... in which ... old and young alike would assume that it was "natural" for the behaviour of each new generation to differ from that of the proceeding generation ... In all cofigurative cultures the elders are still dominant in the sense that they set the style and the limits within which configuration is expressed in the behaviour of the young.'[11] Cofigurative cultures are peer group cultures in which old forms acquire new content epitomized by pioneering situations which are regularized 'so that age grading, youth rebellion, intergeneraion conflict, and the expectation that children will regularly depart from the parental model are built into the culture.'[12] The archetypal cofigurative (and bourgeois) culture is Jewish culture based on 'change within changelessness.'

Postmodern culture for Mead is neither postfigurative or cofigurative but prefigurative. It is characterized by a world community (McLuhan's new tribalism) initiated in this century by the scientific revolution or, more specifically, the electronic revolution in the creation of radio and television as means of communication. As a result of the radical nature of the change we all become immigrants in time just as the members of cofigurative cultures were immigrants in space. But 'our thinking still binds us to the past – to the world as it existed in our childhood and youth. Born and bred before the electronic revolution, most of us do not realize what it means.'[13] Young people 'live in a world in which events are presented to them in all their complex immediacy; they are no longer bound by the simplified linear sequences dictated by the parental world.'[14] If postfigurative youth owes allegiance to the past and cofigurative youth owes allegiance to the future, for prefigurative youth the future exists in the immediate present. Prefigurative youth embodies the future in the present as a new culture, as a new sensibility symbolized by an unborn child in the womb whose sex, appearance, and capabilities are unknown. In the prefigurative culture, 'the young, free to act on their own initiative, can lead their elders in the direction of the un-known.'[15] What we are presented with is an intellectual rationale for the 'blind leading the blind.'

Erikson and Mead are apologists for theories of historical progress in which the young, because of their emancipation, are the vanguard of that progress. For Erikson this is attributed to technology, which produces both affluence as a condition of freedom and a propensity to conformity as a condition threatening to engulf the individual; for Mead, it is not the results of tech-nology but its essential character as electronic which is responsible for the change, for electronic technology is worldwide and immediate, creating a new sensibility and a new tribalism. In the doctrine of emancipated *political* youth, youth plays the role of a social conscience to point out discrepancies between the past fundamental virtues of the liberal ideology and its present practice. In the doctrine of emancipated *cultural* youth, ignorance becomes a virtue and the elders who are entrusted with the past are advised to follow the young, who are emancipated from the past. In the political doctrine, the young lead man to an increased mastery of space and time which will somehow be more individualistic. In the cultural doctrine, openness to the future rather than control of it becomes the aspiration.

Nor is the role of leader restricted to an elite peer group of the New Left. All young people will be more sensible and sensitive than their forebears; it is not one's peers but the group that is even younger than oneself who will be the source of new insight. But whether the young are seen as masters of their fate or governed by it, whether as a peer group or as individuals obsessed with those younger than themselves, whether espousing a new individualism or a new tribalism as a form of social change, whether serving a role of conscience or a role of the blind leading the blind, there is a belief in history as progress, technology as the instrument of emancipation, and style as opposed to ideology as the essential means of change which youth are to employ. Youth is hailed as the vehicle of social change to drive society into a better future; alternatively, youthful sensibilities and attitudes are lauded as forecasts of the new future. Whether as buses or barometers, a complete stratum of society is acclaimed as a modern Moses. If the young don't lead us to the promised land, they at least anticipate its character.

POLITICALLY VICTIMIZED YOUTH

There is a *radical* vision as well as a reform one. In this variation of the theme, youth is the vanguard of social change, not because the young are more emancipated, but because they are more victimized. In the political version, youth is the new class. Technological progress again is seen as the responsible source, but not because of its results (affluence and a propensity to conformity) or its electronic form, but because of its superstructure or institutional encrustation. Technology is controlled by the capitalists.

Michael Miles[16] in *The Radical Probe* focuses on a basic change in the infrastructure of capitalism in shifting its resource allocations more and more towards the service industries and the knowledge industry in particular, the sector responsible for the production and distribution of knowledge and information which in its broadest sense now absorbs 30 per cent of the gross national product in the USA. Student rebellion is rooted in the industrialization under capitalist forms of education, knowledge, and culture so that the institutions of learning become more and more to be operated on industrial models with its weighing of inputs and outputs, its economic measures of productivity, and its impersonalism; the postmodern world offers us a super-industrial society in which even schooling and intellectual life are completely organized in a capitalist institutional mould. The means of social change is a rebellion by an alliance of the new and old working classes, the students and the blue-collar workers. Like the industrialization of the physical labour, the industrialization of intellectual labour results in regimentation and exploitation both within the system and in the unemployment resulting from it.

The route to social change is the path of conflict and revolution rather than reform. The young are not masters of their destiny but inevitable victims of the destiny of capitalism. Rather than the alliance of peer groups, or of elders and the new sensitive youth, intellectual labour, particularly the exploited youth section, must ally itself with the physical labouring classes in a new revolutionary class consciousness and a neo-Marxist revolutionary ideology in order to become masters of the work place, in order to develop a truly classless society where everyone is a peer, in order to free the individual from the coercive forces of capitalism, and in order that youth might put substance in place of style as part of the Radical Left.

CULTURALLY VICTIMIZED YOUTH

However, there is also a radical cultural ideology in contrast to the political ideology which sees youth as the latest and greatest crop of historical victims. The ideology is radical because it is revolutionary, demanding a total transformation of society, but in an Aristotelian rather than a Marxist sense, a sense in which revolution is not an historical development in the modern tradition but a circular motion, like the hands of a clock, returning to the place of origin. The cultural revolutionaries call for society to return to the truth of its youth as opposed to its present stage of technological senility where the blind lead the blind. Technology has not emancipated man through its affluence or brought man a new sensibility because of its new character. Technology has victimized man. And this is not simply a result of a capitalist superstructure and super-industrialization but because of the very essence of technology itself, whatever form it takes. The capitalist structure is merely the dominant North American embodiment and the electric medium its most recent historical form.

The mastery of space and time Keniston calls for, the new sensibility of the McLuhan-Mead worshippers, and the new slave consciousness of Miles which insists on a revolution in order to become masters as well, are all equally apologists for the technological religion for 'they all effectively subscribe to society's faith in mastery.'[17] The goal of the world-wide religion of technology which is advanced though state or corporate capitalism is to create a universal and homogeneous state with its resultant homogenization and dehumanization of man as he pursues power over others rather than control over himself.

Technology by its very nature is the source of the problem. The worship of technology is linked to the worship of mastery – the mastery of nature and of other human beings. The technological religion and love of mastery is directly related to the power of the state, whether that state is called capitalist or communist. And the central function of the state is, ultimately, to foster the values of consumerism, even if the state is neo-colonial. 'Current nationalism is merely the affirmation of the right of colonial elites to repeat history and follow the road travelled by the rich toward the universal consumption of internationally marketed packages, a road which can ultimately lead only to universal pollution and universal frustration.'[18] And the focus of the cultural revolution is schooling, the system whereby the young are brainwashed into consumer values, where the high cost of schooling itself turns education into a scarce resource in order to rationalize a hierarchy of superiority and inferiority. The primary instrument of the state to foster values of mastery and the technological religion is schooling.

What is the alternative to the worship of technology, of mastery, of the tyranny of the state, and of compulsory schooling? As a counter-weight we require the wisdom and faith of the historical youth of Western civilization to save the youth of today from the monstrosity of technology, consumerism, and power. 'The Greeks were suspicious of technical activity because it represented an aspect of brute force and implied a want of moderation. Man, however humble his technical equipment, has from the very beginning played the role of sorcerer's apprentice in relation to the machine. This feeling on the part of the Greeks was not a reflection of a primitive man's fear in the face of something he does not understand (the explanation given today when certain persons take fright at our techniques). Rather, it was the result, perfectly mastered and perfectly measured, of a certain conception of life. It represented an apex of civilization and intelligence.

'Here we find the supreme Greek view (self-control). The rejection of technique was a deliberate, positive activity involving self-mastery, recognition of destiny, and the application of a given conception of life. Only the most modest techniques were permitted – those which would respond directly to material needs in such a way that these needs did not get the upper hand.'[19]

Technology must serve wisdom; the brain must not be made a slave to technology. If a revolution is to be really fundamental it must focus on overthrowing the technological religion which is fostered by statism and, according to Ivan Illich, the state's primary instrument, compulsory schooling. The response of youth to this distrust of technology itself is to attempt to preserve what is natural by a flight into 'spiritual' living, a flight into quasi-religious institutions as refuges or new monasteries to preserve and rebuild a humane society independent of the state. Organized on the rule of the virtuous rather than the rule of the many as a basis for seeking out the *natural* boundaries within which and from which creative expression arises, these new communities pursue their personal and historical youth in order to oppose the natural to the artificial.

Dennis Lee's article, 'Getting to Rochdale'[20] provides a theoretical backdrop for analysis of a preeminent example of the role of youth in social change. Lee begins his article with an account of his gut disaffection from a university which no longer promised a challenge to 'the texture and the reaches of our mind and imagination and spirit' and debased itself by discouraging such attempts through the very temper and method of the university. What Lee envisioned in Rochdale was a centre of liberal education which had been predominant at the end of the nineteenth century but had been submerged with the emergence of the multiversity.[21] 'By "liberal education" I meant any study which liberated a person from unreflecting reliance on the assumptions, structures, models, categories that he had soaked up from his family, school, church and society. It encouraged him to steep himself as deeply in a discipline ... that his mind and imagination came to recapitulate the structures and categories and models that entered in that discipline ... and it brought him through the educational processes – I saw them in terms of an idealized Oxbridge education.'[22]

The escape from inherited models, structures, and assumptions was really the return to the models, structures, and assumptions of the university when it stopped being a propaganda agency for the mediaeval church and became a centre of a (bourgeois) nationalist high culture. For Lee, the existing multiversity was technological, 'encouraging the transfer of discrete units of information and theory, rather than liberal.'[23] The goal was liberation, not mastery. But it was a liberation from contemporary society and the dominance of technique over essences. Schooling had to be free, not compulsory. 'Members can give or take lectures, seminars, tutorials, make films, agitate on the streets, start construction firms or publishing houses, vegetate; no staff, though anyone can teach; no exams, though anyone can be examined if he can find an examiner; no entrance criteria and no criteria for learning.'[24]

What was the result? 'The frustrations of the physical and adminsitrative environment and the people attracted by the experimental education programme could not mesh to resolve problems. Instead, paranoia began to stalk the halls of Rochdale in spite of the friendliness of the people in the building. Rochdale with its initial disorganization and the character of the publicity it received became a crash pad for dope users, teenage social drop-outs, bikers, and crashers.'[25]

Rochdale reputedly became the centre of drug distribution in Toronto. The administration was replaced numerous times. The ground level of the building was covered with a hodgepodge of posters and the rugs with a hodgepodge of cigarette burns. By 1970, Central Mortgage and Housing Corporation, the first mortgager, initiated proceedings to take over Rochdale.

Though Rochdale was blessed with articulate poetic visionaries and though the founders of Rochdale managed both to obtain the initial requisite amendments of the National Housing Act to make them eligible for a loan and to obtain the loan itself, they failed to establish either a base for administrative continuity or even the means to keep the physical facilities clean and in good repair. On the issue of ends and the formal means of obtaining the ends – success. On the issue of means, both basic and bureaucratic – failure.

THE FOUR VARIATIONS COMPARED

A summary and comparison of the views of those who believe that youth is primarily the vanguard of political or cultural emancipation or the victim of the present political or cultural structures can now be made. The one element all four perspectives stress is the primacy of the role of technology. However, they all focus on different aspects of technology – either its results, its characteristic forms of expression, its means of control, or its essential nature.

The political emancipators stress the results of technology. Technology has provided the affluence to permit a large group of young people to criticize the society in which they live, spurred on in that criticism by the dire threat technological development seems to hold over their lives. These two conflicting results of technology, affluence and fear of annihilation, become the basis for the belief that youth can be the leader in a new political emancipation.

The cultural emancipators stress the form in which technology is expressed rather than its results. Modern electronic technology is instantaneous and world-wide; print culture is linear and mechanical. As a result, the young are more in tune with what is really happening than their elders and must lead their elders into the new world of electronic awareness.

The belief that youth have become the new class of economic victims is linked with the industrialization of the school system. Neither the results of technology nor its expression constitute the basis for the creation of youth as leaders of social change. Instead, the superstructure used to control technology, in particular the capitalist appropriation of the school system, put the young in the role of victim rather than visionary and, as such, make them the newest class of the exploited upon whom the revolution could be built. The school is a system to convert raw physical labour into a refined machine tool, the skilled labour necessary to the capitalist production system. Not only is the function of the school analogous to that of the factory as a production enterprise, but human beings are revealed more starkly than ever as the raw material to serve that function. Thus, the young, as the key raw material of modern technological capitalism and not only as the physically exploited labour to process the raw material, constitute the new class of exploited upon whom the revolution was to be built.

Finally, the believers in youth as cultural victim stress that the very essence of technology – not simply its results, form of expression, or methods of control – is the root of the problem. The young are victims not because a particular capitalistic system controls the school system, but because the school system is inherently technological. Schools teach passive obedience to authority, the values of manipulation divorced from the realities of a natural life, but most of all, the values of consumerism. Students are socialized into accepting a technologically artificial world; in schools, students are conditioned to be the consumers of its products.

In all four interpretations of the role of youth in social change, the progress and development of technology perceived from different aspects (results, form of expression, control mechanisms, or essential nature) has determined that role. It is as if the concept 'technology' has become for our contemporary North American thinkers what the concept 'nature' was for seventeenth century Europeans. Technology has become divine; technology has become the key to the root of all good and all evil.

If technology is the root of the tree, the fruit is change, and the different qualities of that fruit can now be more precisely examined. The basis for change in both *political* theories, whether reformist or revolutionary, is the *individual intellect*. In the reform view, the young have the time to develop a heightened critical awareness; in the revolutionary view, the critical consciousness has been dulled by the routine processing of the brains of youth in the university sausage factories. The basis for change for the *cultural* theorists is a new *collective sensibility* rather than the traditional individual intellect, but the new sensibility of the cultural reformers is an immediate and exhilarating electronic contact with the rest of the young who are tuned in, whereas the cultural revolutionaries view the new collective sensibility as the worship of insensitivity and the training of youth to adapt to the cold impersonal world. They celebrate the restoration of the interpersonal and intrapersonal sensitivity that is quickly being lost. In all four variations, the basis of change is in perception – in the mind or in the senses.

If the bases of change are various forms of perception, the mechanisms of change rest either in social institutions or in individuals. And it is interesting that the political theories which stress *individual* intellectual consciousness focus on *collective* forms of social action to instigate change, whether they be non-violent reformist actions or violent strategies to achieve revolution. By contrast, the cultural theorists, which stress *collective* sensibility, focus on *individuals* as the mechanisms of social change, whether those individuals instigate change by sending out and receiving electronic messages in a new version of the oral tradition, or by laying on of hands, by personal tactile communication in order to foster the 'sympathetic understanding of the heart.' As Illich states, 'An objective study of the ways in which meanings are transmitted has shown that much more is relayed from one man to another through and in silence than in words.'[26]

In a consideration of the basis and mechanism of change, the cultural views, while differing, are more comparable and contrast with the political views. The comparison of attitudes to change becomes more complex when one considers the form in which change is to be made and the end it is to achieve. In these respects the reform political position is comparable to the revolutionary cultural position, while the reform cultural position is comparable to the revolutionary political position.

In comparing the theoreticians who greet youth as a conscience of society to permit its reform and those who see youth as the victim of a compulsory school system, one finds that both groups see change proceeding through legal mechanisms; but, for the political reformers, improvements to the law are necessary, whereas, for the cultural revolutionaries, the existing universal compulsory laws must be dismantled. The procedures for social change for the cultural reformers and political revolutionaries focus on extra-legal violent behaviour. The cultural reformers violate our sensibilities and intelligence. The political revolutionaries are extremists in that they perform violence on our political representatives.

A similar comparison can be made about the end of change. The political reformers and cultural revolutionaries (like liberals and conservatives) both stress the individual as the end of change. For the political reformers, reform is directed to equalizing the opportunities for acquisitiveness or consumption for all, whereas the cultural revolutionaries aim to enable each man to become humble enough to receive from another and gracious enough to give of himself to another, stressing, thereby, the spiritual rather than material quality of the individual. The cultural reformers, on the other hand, see as the end a new tribalism comparable to the new collectivism envisioned by the political revolutionaries; but in the tribe, man will be linked by quasi-mystical bonds of unity, whereas the equality in the ownership and use of material goods will be the sign of the new collectivity of the political revolutionaries.

In sum, for the political reformers, society is rooted in the individual, and the development of individual critique serves society in order that individualism may be maintained. The beginning and end of social action is the individual, and society is only a mediating organism. For the cultural reformers, the beginning of new forms of social behaviour resides in a collective sensibility, and the ultimate goal of that change is to create a new form of tribal culture in a mystical sense in which all men are linked as beads on a magical electronic thread. The political reform position begins and ends with the individual, a transaction mediated by social action on state law and institutions. The cultural reform position begins with a new collective awareness and ends with the collective organization of society into a new tribal culture.

The political radicals base the forces of change in the individual's consciousness of the victimization; however, the development of the consciousness is not intended to maintain an individualistic philosophy but to create a new collectivity. The transaction is from the individual through the mediation of collective but anti-state action to the creation of a new collectivity. The cultural radicals base the forces of change in the nature of institutions (schools, the state). Since those forces are corrupting, those institutions must be destroyed. The method of destruction is a prophetic voice and a personal touch. The end of the destruction is the restoration of education, the interpersonal exchange and transaction which is corrupted by collective systematization.

In both the reform and the radical *political* positions the method of instigating change is rooted in collective action even though the object of the reform position is increased individualism and the object of the radical position is a new collectivity. In both the reform and the radical cultural positions the method of instigating change is rooted in individual sensibility, even though the object of the reform position is a new tribalism and the object of the radical position is a restored personalism.

Thus, the four variations on the theory of youth as the vanguard of social change can be contrasted in their perspectives on technology and their different stresses on the individual and the social organism as a whole in discerning the beginning, method, forms, and ends of social change. Not one of these variations satisfactorily attempts to examine technology in all its aspects. None attempts to seriously wrestle with the epistemological questions at the root of change, the relation between individualism and collectivism and the problems in the philosophy of law in the methodology and goal of change. The variations, however, do reveal their own inadequacies when a comparative analysis is undertaken.

YOUTH AND SOCIAL CHANGE

If the root of the tree of the knowledge of good and evil is technology and the fruit of the tree is social change, much of contemporary ideology and practice envisions youth as the trunk of the tree. On the shoulders of the young and not on the wisdom, detachment, skill, or suffering of their elders rests the resolution of the problems of North American culture. It is as if the older generation is busy rationalizing its abrogation of responsibility for the contemporary dilemmas of North American culture.

The belief that youth is a politically emancipated group which, because of affluence, can act as an independent voice of criticism of contemporary society is an ironic but revealing contrast with previous bourgeois history. In the nineteenth century the conscience of English-speaking societies was not the young. In England itself the conscience of that society (though, by no means, the source of fundamental criticism) was the prerogative of a redundant aristocratic class. Men such as Lord Shaftesbury in England led the struggle to ameliorate the hardships of the process of industrialization in Great Britain.[27] What had been the function of a redundant aristocratic class in the nineteenth century has now devolved upon bourgeois youth in the twentieth century when industrialization is in its maturity. The difference between the roles, however, is that bourgeois youth functions as a *haunting* conscience to point out discrepancies between the promises and the performance of the bourgeois system, whereas the aristocrats were a *critical* conscience (though not a critical force) pointing out the difference between humane values and bourgeois practices. Thus, the young, who were to be the ends justifying all that bourgeois sacrifice, become prematurely aged and invested with the role of detached observers and commentators. One way to castrate the creative energies of the young is to give them roles as an impotent conscience.

In the political emancipator's view, the creative energies which were to flow towards youth are drained away by giving youth an impotent function. In the cultural emancipation thesis the critical skills, which are a precondition of making use of those creative energies, are discouraged as historical ignorance is acclaimed as the end of history. Instead of the wisdom of ages, age is associated with ignorance and ignorance with insensitivity to the new electronic medium of communication. In this way the responsibility for wise and crical guidance is devolved on the young with no expectation that they can be wise or critical.

Further, in the shift of the frontier thesis of American civilization from geographical to historical pioneering, one suspects a rationalization of the shift from an emphasis on imperialism in geographical terms to an emphasis on imperialism in time. For the nation which controls technology and, thereby, the direction of change, controls the surrounding nations. Technological imperialism or neo-colonialism is more subtle but no less destructive than its earlier equivalents.

The politically emancipated view of youth says that young people have real power, but envisions the exercise of that power in the role of an impotent haunting conscience, a role reserved a century earlier for the remnants of a redundant aristocratic class. The culturally emancipated view of youth acclaims the young as prematurely wise and condemns them to perpetuating ignorance. Thus, in attesting to the visionary qualities of youth the political and cultural reform theorists endorse either castrating the young or poking their eyes out.

The view of youth as victim rather than as visionary entails an inverse paradox. For the visionary theorists greet the young as heroes but intend them as victims; the victim theorists pity the suffering young, but then give the suffering of youth a superior role relative to the suffering of the rest of the population; in one way or another the suffering is deified.

The 'youth as a class' theorists say that the schools are being turned into factories for the production of skilled workers for the capitalist system. The cultural revolutionaries view compulsory schooling itself as inherently evil in training the young as consumers rather than producers, in giving them artificial values rather than real skills. In either case schooling is a process of victimizing youth. In the political view, the young are victimized by teaching them technical skills to be used in a capitalist system; the cultural view asserts that 'the contrary is probable: schools select those already inclined toward such technical knowhow,'[28] thereby perpetuating and reinforcing class divisions and rationalizing different levels of consumption.

It would appear that the political view of youth as victim says that youth is the new working class and the school is the method of making youth conscious of its class status, but this *means* that the division between youth in the schools and workers in the factories is made even greater. For instead of giving those in the youthful intelligentsia the role of serving the workers, it raises their status as revolutionaries. They themselves are an exploited class; further, they suffer from a newer and more intense form of exploitation. Thus, the slogan of allying the intelligentsia and the workers takes on a new meaning, for in the new form of alliance the driving force of the revolution shifts from the workers to youth and workers become the rear guard in the battle. In declaiming the victimization of the young and their need for a renewed alliance with the working class, these theoriests greet the young as the heroic martyrs of revolution, but doom them to a fruitless martyrdom since placing the young on a pedestal in this way increases their alienation from the working classes as the traditional force of modern revolutionary change.

The cultural view of youth as victim says that the young are being systematically trained as consumers. Substitutes, such as the restoration of apprentice training or of the value of personal tutoring, are also examples of earlier forms of education. The intent of this radical revisionism is to force man to face reality instead of concentrating on transforming reality into an artificial realm and then educating the young at great cost to adapt to that fantasy. It is a call to personal witness rather than collective engineering where 'The expanding dignity of each man and each human relationship must necessarily challenge existing systems. It is a call to the service of faith rather than the mastery of reason, the restoration of the primacy of spirit rather than the primacy of the material realm. The paradoxical view of youth becomes clear when the claim that youth is the greatest victim of technology in its imprisonment in schools is revealed as a claim that youth is the most expensive and materially indulged group in the society. The young are victims because they are indulged idols of a corrupt religious practice. Characterizing them as indulged idols reinforces society's withdrawal of some of its gifts to turn the social forces against youth as a creative force of change; it divides the conservatism of the elders from the creativity of youth as surely as the political view of youth as a class of heroic martyrs divides youth from the working class as a revolutionary force. The reformers say the young are visionaries but would castrate and blind them; the revolutionaries say the young are victims but would separate them from the rest of society as heroic martyrs or indulged idols.

Thus, the roots of technology lead to institutional branches in which the fruit of the tree appears to be four varieties of change. But the trunk holding up those branches and supporting the heavy responsibility for the fruit of change is youth. And youth, whether as visionary or victim, while hailed for its strength, is really having its weakness reinforced. This is the real sign of a hollow and rotten trunk incapable of sustaining the forces of change swirling around it while repeating in different ways themes of our inherited culture.

The result is that the application of the theories to practice yields the appearance of change – executive and legislative change – without any roots or the conditions for bureaucratic continuity. Youth, in the name of social change, is performing the role of a conservative conscience – either a liberal or romantic conscience or a communist or classical conscience. Youth is not the instrument of social change, but the instrument to act out the various antipathies to the rapid changes in contemporary society.

CONCLUSION

I have attempted to clarify and expose the difficulties of adopting the position that youth is the vanguard of social change – whether youth is seen as emancipated or as victimized. These difficulties were shown to arise on two levels: the normative and the empirical. As well, the four variations of the thesis, when juxtaposed to one another, were discovered to be contradictory, ironic, paradoxical, and mistaken. What has not been provided in this context is an alternative explanation of the nature of social change. Nevertheless, the essentially 'negative' character of the criticism in this study does not preclude the possibility of creativity.

To set the driving force of social change in technology is to root change in change. Nature has been distinguished from artifact. Nature is identified with the given and unchanging. Technology is identified with the dynamic and changing side of life. Technology is the mastery of change over *stasis*. A theory of social change cannot be rooted in choosing change over rest but in choosing both change and rest, creativity and preservation. The choice is not one of either/or but of both/and. The dilemma of man as an historical being is the question, how do I preserve what is most human in my past? The choice is not change versus preservation, or change over rest, for such a choice is simply to act out a state of restlessness and rootlessness. The choice is really what is worth preserving and what needs transformation in order to allow what is preserved to grow.

In this view, change does not depend primarily on perception either in alterations in our individual intellects or in our collective sensibilities. Action must precede thought. Consciousness does not direct action but rather checks it. We must use our *collective* wisdom and intelligence and our *individual* sensibilities to constantly monitor our actions. But they will not be able to direct those actions.

Thus change cannot be rooted in the technological realm of artifact nor based on mental perception. Change must be rooted in the dialectic of history and be based on concrete actions. The question of whether such change will necessarily be legal (either reformist and revisionist) or extra-legal (radical or conservative) is to misconstrue the problem. For true change is only derivatively a legal matter; it is much more a problem of judgment rather than law.

Finally, acting out is not a sign of change but a symptom of a need for very basic change. To put such a responsibility on one group of adults, and the most youthful and inexperienced, is merely the admission that adults in general are unwilling to take genuine responsibility for the changes that are really needed, changes which require individuals involved in and committed to action in order to preserve man as an historical being, a being with both a past and a future.

NOTES

1 The conception of the young as either victims or visionaries in contemporary social theory has been pointed to frequently but without further analysis into its subcategories or the conceptual basis for the different views. For example, Joseph Adelson notes 'the two dominant imaginings of the young – as victims and as visionaries' [*Commentary*, 51, no. 5 (May 1971), 43], but only uses this to castigate the violence of youth and demonstrate his own intellectual impotence by confessing that the analysis of young radicals 'may well be a task beyond us.'

2 See C. Wright Mills, *The Sociological Imagination* (Oxford, 1959), for a full articulation of this perspective. I.L. Horowitz characterizes Mills' views as the *classical* liberal critique of contemporary corporate liberalism. *The New Sociology: Studies in Honor of C. Wright Mills* (New York, 1965)

3 (New York), 272

4 The general theory is developed by Erik Erikson in his volume *Childhood and Society* (New York, 1964) and is applied explicitly to social issues in a series of essays published as *Identity: Youth and Crisis* (New York, 1968).

5 Keniston, *Young Radicals*, 266

6 Ibid., 273

7 Ibid., 265

8 For a more detailed analysis see my article, 'Politics of the Counterculture,' *Canadian Forum* (March 1971).

9 Keniston, *Young Radicals*, 266

10 Ibid., 287-9

11 Margaret Mead, *Culture and Commitment* (New York, 1970), 32

12 Ibid., 59

13 Ibid., 74

14 Ibid., 75

15 Ibid., 94

16 For an earlier less-developed version of this thesis by two Americans who were expatriates in Canada at that time, see 'Youth as a Class' by John and Margaret Rowntree, *Our Generation*, Vol. 6., nos. 1-2 (1968). This thesis is not to be confused with Marcuse's vision, later retracted, of youth as a catalyst of revolutions.

17 George Grant, *Technology and Empire* (Toronto, 1969), 113
18 Ivan D. Illich, 'A Constitution for Cultural Revolution,' 171, in *Celebration of Awareness* (New York, 1970)
19 Jacques Ellul, *The Technological Society* (New York, 1964), 29. Cf., also *The Political Illusion* (New York, 1967)
20 Cf. *The University Game*, ed. H. Adelman and D. Lee (Toronto, 1968), 69-94. Rochdale College was both a residence and a very controversial 'student'-run college in the spirit of the 'free university' current in the sixties. An eighteen-storey structure built in the northern perimeter of the University of Toronto on fashionable Bloor Street, Rochdale was a physical mix of commercial, educational, and residential facilities. The college was initiated by the Campus Co-operative Residence, a student-owned and operated residence which had by then a 30-year history at the University of Toronto of providing cheap accommodation in a convivial atmosphere for approximately 100 career-oriented students. But Rochdale College broke away from its roots. The author of this article was involved in the leadership of the co-op and was a founding member of Rochdale.
21 For a detailed account of this history, see my book, *The Holiversity* (Toronto, 1973).
22 *The University Game*, 84
23 Ibid., 74
24 Ibid., 81
25 H. Adelman, *The Beds of Academe* (Toronto, 1970), 191
26 'The Eloquence of Silence,' 31, *Celebration of Awareness*
27 See K. Polanyi, *The Great Transformation* (Boston, 1957).
28 Illich, 'Sexual Power and Political Potency,' 139 *Celebration of Awareness*

Donald E. Willmott

Voluntary associations: the view from radical humanism

We need a revolution! After more than a century of 'economic development' we still have poverty and mindless consumerism. After more than a century of 'democracy' we have a growing concentration of power. After more than a century of 'nationhood' we still feel colonized. And the international system of which we are a part appears to have neither the wisdom nor the capacity to avert war, ecological disaster, or the coming onslaught of the have-not nations against the haves.

These obvious problems require radical solutions. But what of the less visible state of the human spirit? The humanist sees a need for transformation there too. 'Possessive individualism' must be replaced by a more collective ethic in the public sphere, and commercialized conformity must give way to creative individuality in the private. In short, both institutions and values must be transformed. The system of corporate capitalism must be replaced by an egalitarian, libertarian society – by a kind of socialism appropriate to Canada. We need a revolution.

Such is the mood of the radical humanist today. But he needs more than mood. He needs knowledge and theory, lest he be led into futile activity or defeatist inactivity. He must confront the reality of the society around him with an understanding which suggests a plan of action.

REVOLUTIONARY POTENTIAL

When I say 'revolution,' I mean a transformation in the basic institutions and values of society. History identifies revolutions by the overthrow of regimes and the consequent changes of institutions. But, as Mao Tse-tung warned and the Chinese are now demonstrating, mobilization for revolutionary change in values must start well before such historic events and must continue long after. The development of revolutionary consciousness, of popular commitment to both institutional and value transformation, is generally a slow process, though it accelerates in times of institutional breakdown or change. In my view, the significant element in this consciousness is not violent hostility, or even militancy, but a strong desire to change institutions and values at their roots.

I ask the reader to keep in mind that by 'revolution' I mean only radical transformation. The change may be fast or slow, with or without violence; but these important questions are beyond the scope of the present paper.

With these definitions in mind, it can be said that Canada has several small revolutionary groups and a wider pool of people with growing revolutionary consciousness. The significant fact, however, is not the number of such organizations and persons, which is still relatively small, but their immense diversity and disparity.

The Canadian Party of Labour, the League for Socialist Action, and even the Women's Liberation movement are typical of groups that provide a fairly comprehensive revolutionary ideology. Other groups, such as the Vietnam Mobilization Committee or New Feminists, have revolutionary programs limited to specific areas. These various groups usually have at least some of the following characteristics: small membership, relatively short lifespan, severely limiting rhetoric and vocabulary, isolation from their potential constituency, inability to cooperate with other radical groups and even hostility towards them, and inadequate understanding of the political process and potentialities in Canada. For these reasons, and for others to be mentioned below, it is clear that none of these organizations will be leading a mass revolutionary movement in the near future.

Revolutionary consciousness is, however, by no means confined to these organized groups. Alienation and dissatisfaction have reached the point of desire for fundamental change among many members of disadvantaged groups in Canadian society: the poor, women, French Canadians, Indians, intellectuals, farmers, and workers in some industries. In the middle class, a 'counterculture' of anti-establishment values and life styles is steadily growing, especially among youth. Again, however, the disparity of ideologies, interests, values, and strategies is so great that one cannot imagine a powerful, unified movement emerging from this scattered revolutionary consciousness.

Some have theorized that while labour has become generally committed to seeking a greater share in the status quo, youth has emerged as a new class and has inherited from labour the historic mission of spearheading revolutionary change. Trends a few years ago made this theory seem plausible and attractive. But it has become clear that because of their organizational weakness, their susceptibility to ever-changing fads of orientation, their conflicting ideologies, and the continuous turnover of both leadership and membership (due either to growing older or to being 'co-opted' into the status quo) the young cannot become the primary vehicle of revolution in the foreseeable future.

Revolutionary change in Canadian society in the next five or ten years is rendered unlikely by a number of other factors which seem to persist. The goals of the middle class and of that part of the working class which identifies with it are being met sufficiently well to assure a large measure of complacency. Public opinion polls, surveys, and other observable indicators show that the majority of Canadians, in spite of various particular dissatisfactions, believe that their social and political system is a good one, in general, or is well on its way to becoming so. Among those disadvantaged groups which do not share this positive view, fatalistic apathy is widespread.

If unemployment, us domination, or economic hardship were to reach proportions sufficient to seriously discomfort a majority of the population, and if the government appeared to be doing nothing about these problems, one might anticipate a full-blown revolutionary movement. But our liberal establishment is not entirely intransigent. It effects continuous modifications in the system in order to maintain itself. And it generally has the support of the instruments of public opinion, the mass media.

Considering, then, the weak, scattered, and disunited nature of revolutionary consciousness and the seeming viability of liberal capitalism in Canada today, it is conceivable to me that the transformation of society that I should like to see may take as many years in developing itself to completion as did the institutional and value changes of the 'industrial revolution.' Such a revolution is not without conflict and clashes, but one system is replaced by another in stages, without being overthrown by sudden overwhelming power. There are, however, two other possibilities.

One is that external or international events could alter the situation inside Canada in such a way as to bring about a strong convergence of revolutionary potential here. For example, it now seems possible that the 'third world' will turn increasingly to communist solutions, inspired by China, and that this and internal problems will bring into being an even more reactionary, imperialistic, and perhaps even totalitarian regime in the United States. The sociologist Philip Slater has suggested that the black movement and the rapidly spreading challenge of the 'counterculture' may in themselves instigate a reactionary counter-revolution there.[1]

In addition, international war is an ever-present possibility, with unpredictable effects in Canada. Eventual ecological disasters, economic crisis, urban chaos, or separatist movements, if met with incompetence or intransigence on the part of government, could also result in revolutionary situations.

A second kind of revolutionary possibility (again, suggested by Slater) is the piecemeal but rapid transformation of institutions and values, one by one. For example, under various pressures – and here students might well be the 'spearhead' – universities as we know them may well be replaced by alternative forms of 'higher' education. A pattern of dissatisfaction, mobilization, confrontation, and finally transformation might occur in one after another of such institutions as local governments, newspapers, broadcasting stations, professional organizations, or productive enterprises. This might or might not lead to counter-revolution, and thus eventually to general revolution again.

These various nebulous and uncertain possibilities of future rapid change do not offer solid ground for the active engagement of the radical humanist, especially when he considers that not all revolutions have beneficial outcomes. So let us examine the alternatives.

VOLUNTARY ASSOCIATIONS AS
VEHICLES OF DEMOCRATIC CHANGE

Few social scientists consider that democratic elections assure responsive government. But there has been a widespread conviction, going back at least to de Tocqueville, that voluntary associations provide continuous links between the citizen and his government which safeguard his interests and guarantee his freedom. For example, the American sociologist Arnold Rose maintains that voluntary associations 'distribute power over social life among a very large proportion of the citizenry' and provide a 'powerful mechanism for continually instituting social changes.' He goes on to say: 'through the voluntary association the ordinary citizen can acquire as much power in the community or the nation as his free time, ability, and inclinations permit him to ...'[2]

Are voluntary associations, then, the means by which radical humanists can hope to transform society? An answer to this question requires a thorough assessment of the functions of associations in society today and of their potentiality as vehicles of social change.

There is a countless number of voluntary groups in Canada. In a prairie town of about 1000 population a survey turned up 59 clubs and societies. In a railway town of 2600 people 144 organizations were found. The white and yellow pages of the Toronto telephone directories list at least 1500 associations, and this does not include the plethora of smaller organizations which abound in churches, universities, schools, community centres, service agencies, and people's homes.[3]

We must note, however, that only a small fraction of these associations are designed mainly to take political action; that is, to influence government or to change public opinion. A telephone survey of the listed organizations in Toronto, for example, showed that only about 6 per cent were political action groups – for example, the Yonge-Bloor-Bay Association, the Socialist Labor party, and the Stop Spadina and Save Our City Co-ordinating Committee. In the prairie towns mentioned above there were no political action groups, except the party organizations which surfaced at election time. In nearby rural communities there was an occasional branch of the Saskatchewan Farmers Union.

Aside from political action groups, many voluntary associations organized for other purposes sometimes do take political action or involve themselves in public affairs in some way. In prairie surveys, about 15 per cent of town and country organizations reported having taken at least one stand on public issues in recent years. Just over 60 per cent of the Toronto associations surveyed had taken public stands or attempted to influence government. But if groups without telephones could have been included in the Toronto sample, the percentage probably would not have differed significantly from the smaller towns. Only about half of the actions reported were described by organization officers as 'major' attempts to influence public affairs.

As for the effectiveness of the political action taken by voluntary associations, I have concluded from interviews with politicians, civil servants, and political scientists that most of it achieves no direct results. The usual 'action' consists merely of sending resolutions to appropriate authorities. Briefs and delegations are reported to be somewhat more effective, but even these are often ignored. The Transportation Committee of the Metropolitan Toronto Council sat through 222 briefs on the Spadina expressway issue, and then voted against the position taken by 210 of them. Harold Kaplan has made a study of how 55 municipal issues were resolved in Toronto. He found that 'in almost 90 per cent of the issues considered ... the outcome would have been the same if no groups had intervened.' The neighbourhood associations, he said, had a 'consistent record of failure.'[4] I conclude that in most political decisions, the politicians' personal views, presumed obligations, and electoral interests prevail over organizational pressures.

On the other hand, group action does sometimes significantly affect the political process. The Spadina expressway was stopped. A reluctant cabinet was pushed into appointing a royal commission on the status of women. The 1971 tax legislation was described as virtual capitulation to the hundreds of business and professional associations which sent briefs, delegations, and lobbyists to the government after the report of the Carter Commission and again after Mr Benson's White Paper.

Laura Sabia and her Committee. A brief to the Carter Commission on Taxation presented by the Grand Orange Lodge. What was the Committee on the Equality of Women without Ms Sabia? How many Orangemen participated in preparing 'their' brief on taxation, or even knew about it? We must remind ourselves that when an organization takes action, this usually stems from an internal core elite and therefore reflects primarily its own views and interests. In voluntary associations, as in business and government institutions, we often find elitism, vested interests, and bureaucracy.

Surveys have consistently shown that the leaders of voluntary associations are disproportionately drawn from business and professional circles, and that membership too is concentrated in upper socio-economic levels of the population – with the exception of labour unions and fraternal societies.

Looking at the over-all picture, then, we can conclude that only a very small proportion of all voluntary associations is organized for political action; a small but significant minority of the remainder makes frequent or major attempts to affect the political process; a larger number engages in minor political activity from time to time, and probably the majority never takes action on public issues. When organizations do take action, it is usually ineffective. Even when an association exercises successful influence, the policies advocated generally represent primarily the ideas or the interests of the officers or 'inner circle.' Manual labourers and their families, and especially those with very low incomes, are disproportionately absent from organizational activity and almost never assume leadership positions. Hence, to the extent that voluntary associations participate in the political process, the interaction may be seen as a small voluntary elite talking to a small political elite, both of which represent primarily well-to-do groups and the status quo.

Even when we add to this scenerio the 'revival' of voluntary associations of which Professor Hill[5] speaks — that is, the increasing activity of new groups of ratepayers, tenants, welfare poor, women, and so on — it does not add up to the picture of widespread participatory democracy implied by Arnold Rose. It is, I believe, too soon to assess the ultimate effectiveness of the new groups. Their record so far has shown only a few scattered and perhaps temporary victories against the bureaucracies and vested interest groups which usually ignore them. The 1972 elections in Toronto and other municipalities reflect a dramatic strengthening of citizen participation, but whether this can last, and whether it represents more than a liberal middle-class movement, remains to be seen.

In my opinion, if liberal democracy is proving viable and political alienation is decreasing, as Professor Hill suggests, it is not because the majority of ordinary Canadian citizens has gained a new sense of efficacy through voluntary associations, but because generally favourable economic conditions and a generally tranquilizing mass media have created widespread complacency. In short, Tocquevillian optimism about Canadian society today seems misplaced, or at best, premature.

VOLUNTARY ASSOCIATIONS FOR AND AGAINST CHANGE

In the previous section, I have argued that voluntary associations, in so far as they engage in the political process effectively, are primarily instruments of conservative elites. I feel I must add a few more measures of seemingly pessimistic realism before trying to single out the social change leverage points which offer some hope to the radical humanist. In this section, then, I shall try to show that voluntary associations have inherent characteristics which make them more effective vehicles for defending than for changing the status quo.

The defining characteristic of voluntary associations is their voluntary nature. Although the term 'voluntary' poses certain psychological and philosophical difficulties, these need not concern us here. If we define voluntary associations as those non-governmental organizations through which members pursue common interests in part-time, unpaid activities, it should be evident that they are voluntary in at least one of several ways: entry to membership is a matter of individual choice; members may resign or simply drop out whenever they wish; the voluntary organization does not provide renumeration which is essential to the livelihood of members, and therefore participation is not made mandatory; or, the activities of the group are engaged in during the 'free time' of members. This means that voluntary associations have the special problem of motivating people to join and to contribute their time and resources.

The requisite motivation for voluntary activity may derive either from direct private interests or from some commitment to the public interest. Of these two, given the individualistic orientations of Canadians today, only the former can sustain the membership or participation of relatively large numbers of people. Thus the generally conservative occupational groups, such as trade associations, professional societies, and labour unions, are bound to be stronger and more long-lasting than idealistic groups working for public causes such as peace or pollution control.

For property-owners, businessmen, and professionals there is more at stake in governmental decisions than for others; the day-to-day decisions of legislatures and government departments affect more of them more frequently than is the case with other large groups. For this reason, and because of their social-class origins and the selective process for entering such occupations, these individuals tend to have a much more activist orientation to life and politics than most people.

On the other hand, people in routine occupations who are accustomed to playing subordinate roles – and this applies to young people and many women, as well as to certain ethnic groups and the working class generally – tend to develop a more fatalistic or apathetic orientation towards society. The motivation for political action among these groups is dampened by their life experiences. Social psychological studies of social and occupational groups show up significant differences with regard to 'achievement motivation' and 'alienation.' Hence any attempt to increase the participation of presently disadvantaged groups will have to include changes in aspects of the social and institutional environment which affect motivation.

Other characteristics of voluntary associations give automatic advantages to the conservative, upper socio-economic groups in Canada. For political efficacy, an association needs organizational skills, political know-how, and influential personal contacts. Because these advantages are concentrated among businessmen and professionals, their organizations are assured of greater effectiveness.

The advantages of wealth are as obvious as those of good organization. Associations such as professional societies, business associations, and labour unions, which have a guaranteed income from a large and steady membership or from affluent donors, can greatly increase their effectiveness by making substantial contributions to politicians or political parties, by mounting expensive publicity campaigns, and by employing salaried staff, researchers, and lobbyists.

One should also remember that effective political activity may involve individual expenses such as those of dining out, entertaining, attending conventions, paying organizational dues or costs, and even babysitting and housekeeping. These expenses mean that not only the 'lower class,' but young people, the aged, and women generally will be disadvantaged in political action.

Participation requires not only time, but to be most effective the freedom to take time during working hours in order to meet, call, or correspond with others involved in the political process. In small towns, it is not unusual for important community issues to be discussed and resolved in mid-morning coffee hours at local restaurants. In cities, most government officials and many organizational leaders are accessible only during office hours. This gives a great advantage to businessmen, professionals, academics, housewives without heavy family duties, and others who have some discretionary power over their daily schedules. On the other hand, most office workers, manual labourers and women with heavy household duties are not free during much of the time when political and organizational matters are being determined.

With these considerations in mind, it becomes evident that voluntary associations are an instrument which can be more readily and effectively used by the already advantaged groups in society than by those who wish to challenge the status quo. For this reason, the predominant role of existing voluntary associations in the political process is to protect the interests of the already privileged groups and therefore to prevent basic change. I would cite the two-stage watering down of the tax reforms proposed by the Carter Commission as a case in point.

Nevertheless, ameliorative changes are sometimes won through the efforts of reform groups. I would suggest that this usually happens under one of the following conditions:

1 / when an organization succeeds in mobilizing sufficient popular support to make an issue relevant to the electoral success of politicians;

2 / when an organization with widespread support creates such a nuisance by militant tactics that policy-makers consider it less costly to compromise or capitulate than to resort to police and court action;

3 / when an organization succeeds in 'co-opting' leaders who have personal influence with the authorities concerned;

4 / when an organization presses for reforms which have little or no import to established elites, or on which the latter are divided;

5 / when the goals of an organization coincide with the ideals or ulterior motives of top civil servants or politicians.

None of these conditions guarantees success. But even when a movement 'fails' to achieve its goals, it may leave a residue of minor ameliorative change and some small contribution towards the development of revolutionary consciousness. On either count, it may justify the efforts of the radical humanist. The fact that the over-all effect of existing voluntary associations is to support and preserve the *status quo* does not preclude successful initiatives by change-oriented groups.

THE STRATEGY OF COALITIONS

Because of the diversity and complexity of dissatisfactions, motivations, and orientations among Canadian people today, the more goals an association has, the more restricted is its potential membership. For example, when the Radiation Hazards organization decided to take stands on political issues other than nuclear testing, it lost the support of many of its members who favoured the NATO alliance or opposed the recognition of the People's Republic of China. When a coalition of women's groups decided to make abortion one of its four or five key issues, Roman Catholic women withdrew publicly from the organization. Left-wing groups and radical women's organizations have been plagued by the splits and defections of members who could not accept one or another of the many standpoints, dogmas, or goals which they have insisted upon.

On the other hand, groups like Stop Spadina or the Committee for Abolition of the Death Penalty were able to mobilize all people who were willing to support these single issues, whether or not they favoured high-rise development or general penal reform. These temporary coalitions were able to draw support from people who would never have cooperated with one another on other issues. Furthermore, they were able to benefit from the support of business and professional men and women who, as we have seen, can contribute a great deal to the political efficacy of organizations.

The radical humanist is concerned about many issues. He will not find and cannot create one or two organizations through which to work on all of them. He will not find complete agreement even with other humanists within socialist, communist, or other radical groups. For the time being, at least, he must resign himself to working through a variety of organizations with limited goals. This is what I call the strategy of coalitions.

Joining or forming an association means entering into a coalition with its members for certain stated purposes. For some purposes a coalition will be greatly strengthened by the inclusion of businessmen and professionals whose views may otherwise be fairly conservative. For the sake of efficacy towards a limited goal a radical humanist might support the Committee for an Independent Canada, for example, or the World Federalists. Even though his own goals go far beyond theirs, other organized causes such as Pollution Probe or Zero Population may also appeal to him.

The humanist who is also a radical, however, will not lose sight of his goal of basic transformation of society's institutions and values. This raises a dilemma for him with regard to organizations seeking reforms which, if effected, might allay discontent and increase complacency. Unfortunately, it is extremely difficult to forecast the effects of organizational activity. Furthermore, one cannot automatically assume that ameliorative change postpones revolutionary change. Some reform movements create desires for more fundamental changes by revealing the vested interests or intransigence of existing elites. Successful reforms often generate rising expectations which cannot be met by the existing regime. In fact, students of revolution have argued that revolutions usually occur not under stable conditions of mass misery but under improving conditions and accelerated hopes. Thus reformism, whether thwarted or successful, can lead to revolutionary consciousness.

The reverse is also true. Under certain conditions revolutionary agitation may do little to spread revolutionary consciousness but much to win from reluctant regimes the reforms advocated by moderates. A revolutionary group may also diminish popular revolutionary potentialities by taking extremist action at the wrong time or in the wrong measure. The FLQ at different times, has had both of these effects.

The possibility that reformist activity will delay revolutionary change is greatest in times of widespread discontent and frustration. Even in such times, in order to decide to withhold support from reforms which would increase human well-being one would have to be convinced that there was a strong possibility that a worthwhile transformation of consciousness or institutions would arise out of this disaffection. Since revolutionary consciousness does not depend upon the absolute level of well-being of a population, but upon the level of well-being relative to aspirations, and since ameliorative change normally has the effect of raising aspirations as well as benefits, radical humanists will usually find reforms worth supporting or fighting for.

On the other hand, realizing that transformation of the system will only come if aspirations run ahead of realities, the radical humanist must constantly seek opportunities to change values, to convince people that the present system is rotten at its core, to create aspirations for a truly humane society — to generate revolutionary consciousness. Under present circumstances this can be done not by providing utopian dogmas or total ideologies but by encouraging basic criticism and radical dissent. For this reason, the former Waffle strategy of working within a major political party was an effective one. Having been ousted from the party, the Waffle group will find it much more difficult to reach wide audiences and will be tempted to adopt a purist package of radicalism which, for the time at least, might further isolate them from the public.

There is always the danger that radical leaders will isolate themselves from their potential followers by an unrealistic assessment of their readiness for change. This danger is greatest in periods of non-revolutionary complacency such as we find in Canada today. On the other hand liberal intellectuals have often been over-cautious, even timid, in judging change potential. Thus the radical humanist has a double problem: to select his coalitions with as great foresight as possible, aware of, but not immobilized by, the risk of misjudging the consequences; and to gauge his efforts to arouse revolutionary consciousness to the real potentialities of the situation.

There are so many changes worth working for that the radical humanist may choose his causes primarily on the basis of his personal inclinations, abilities, and the potentialities of his particular position. There is one kind of change, however, which seems to me to have high priority today: that which is designed to involve more citizens, particularly people of disadvantaged groups, in decision-making in their places of work, their communities, or their nation.

Earlier I referred to the limited success of ratepayer groups, tenant and resident associations, organizations of the welfare poor, and the like. The recent elections in some cities, such as Toronto, suggest that the demands of these groups will be represented rather than ignored by some of the new municipal councillors. This will give impetus to similar groups throughout the country. But we must expect that conservative business and professional leaders will seek to prevent basic changes not only by mobilizing the established voluntary associations (which, as we have seen, have some formidable advantages in politics), but also by joining and attempting to take over many of the residents and ratepayers associations. They will have the support of most old-line politicians at every level and of major sectors of the mass media across Canada.

Under these conditions, it may well be that newly elected reformers will be severely limited in their efforts to bring about change. Nevertheless, the 'citizen participation' movement is fast establishing the legitimacy of the principle that citizens should be allowed to take part in decisions which vitally affect them. More and more people are coming to feel a right and a desire at least to be consulted, if not to participate in policy formulation. This surely is a necessary step towards forming the rising aspirations and revolutionary consciousness which must come before a period of rapid transformation of society.

NOTES

1 *The Pursuit of Loneliness: American Culture at the Breaking Point* (Boston, 1970), 120-48
2 *Sociology: The Study of Human Relations* (New York, 1965), 420
3 Donald E. Willmott, 'Voluntary Associations in the Political Process,' a paper delivered to the Seminar on Voluntary Associations in the Political Process, sponsored by the Committee on Voluntary Action of the Canadian Association for Adult Education, Toronto, April 1971
4 *Urban Political Systems: A Functional Analysis of Metro Toronto* (New York, 1967), 178, 197
5 See 'Political judgment and the viability of institutions,' pp. 89-104, above.

Joan Williams

Professionalism vs Parkdale

When Parkdale Community Legal Services opened in September 1971, it was greeted with great expectations. It was to be a creative and flexible type of service to local residents, an exciting setting for law students to learn on the job, and a focal point and resource centre for community issues. But most importantly, it was to be a model for social change and a clear demonstration to the legal profession and to the citizenry that community legal services could stand side by side with agents of radical change in the fight for social justice. As staff members, we had many ideas on how to launch our program: ideas on how to provide good service, on how to get involved in community issues, on our roles as 'professionals' in a low-income community, on the role of an office such as ours in a community such as Parkdale. Some of us thought of ourselves as reformist, some as radical; yet we had been unable to come to grips with the essential difference between a reformist stance and a radical stance in a community legal service by the time we began operations in Parkdale.

We knew that to be reformist meant to work for change within a system, and that to be radical meant to challenge the rules of a system, but we seemed unable to formulate a clear and consistent conception of how these theories applied to our situation, which also meant that we were not sure whether reformers and radicals could work together. But the fact that we had both of these elements in the project meant that we were willing to try.

Looking back over the first months of the project, I see that some things have emerged more clearly in relation to the question of reformist and radicalism. For the clinic to be an agent of reform meant that it provided a service to residents of the area. The service consisted of a caseload centring on problems of welfare, unemployment insurance, family court (desertion, separation, child support), and landlord/tenant problems. Most of the people who were able to take advantage of the service available were people who had never before been able to afford a lawyer. Many of them did not even realize that a lawyer could help them with these problems. So our service function quite naturally transformed itself into an educational function as well. Our presence and service made people aware that they could find this kind of help; as well it built up among the students a considerable expertise in areas of law that lawyers rarely specialize in, since of course these are not lucrative areas.

Our Parkdale organization set up a watchdog desk in the local welfare office to improve the functioning of welfare officials. We acted as resource people to local citizens groups such as Single Parents and the Parkdale Tenants Association. We ran seminars for high school students on areas of the law that interested them. We helped obtain funding for three local groups to do community work and renovations to houses in the area. Together with a citizens group we fought off a developer and obtained a new park instead of a high-rise. We joined the Parkdale Coalition (an umbrella group) as resource people and as a local agency. Some of these services were highly innovative, not because lawyers had never done them before, but because they had done them mostly for those who could hire them, namely middle- and upper-class people. By providing these services to people who had been relatively power-less in the past, we forced institutions to fight for what they had been accustomed to taking with ease. Children's Aid, Welfare, the Unemployment Insurance Commission, and other 'social welfare' institutions, were made to justify and often change their course of action in relation to our clients. Often clients not only gained what they were fighting for, but equally impor-tant they had their own perception of right and wrong confirmed, effected a tiny measure of control over their lives and circumstances, and felt that they had allies where they usually fought alone.

These actions benefited the clients, certainly, but they also benefited the office staff. Every victory was gratifying to us, and every fight gave us more of a glimpse into the lives of people that many of us had neither lived with nor socialized with before. We became more and more conscious of different psychological, social, and political realities of different classes of people. This new awareness was a step in the right direction for the office, but it still fell far short of the expectations and aspirations we had for the project.

At this point it would be useful to reiterate the goals of the law office. It was to provide both a service setting through field placement work of student lawyers and a focus for social change. Staff were attracted to the project by either of these goals. However it turned out that the goals were not always consistent with one another.

Some of the reform programs have been described above. The goal of effecting social change led us to try to deal with our own internal structure in a non-traditional way. We spent many of our early office meetings on this issue. Some of us pushed strongly for a structure which was horizontal rather than vertical. This tended to polarize students into those who felt they were in the clinic for 'solid legal training,' and those who felt that genuine educa-tion included personal participation in decision-making. Those of us who pushed for horizontal structure argued strongly that we could not serve the community in any innovative or creative fashion unless we felt ourselves to be a collective of some sort in the office. We felt that we had to change the traditional bureaucratic ways in which office personnel related. We wanted to humanize our internal processes and neutralize the destructive dynamic of a highly competitive law school. We wanted to concentrate on skills rather than on roles, and to nurture collective decision-making as human beings with a stake in what we were doing. We were trying, however inarticulately, to pose the whole question in terms of understanding ourselves as workers who were to work under certain conditions. Some of us were concerned that professionalism and professional independence excluded policy-making. We wanted some control over policy-making in our own office in order to open the doors to community control, our focus was still on a target group 'out there.'

Eventually a shaky consensus was reached around the idea that we ought to make our own policy decisions. However at this point the goals of solid legal training and social change came into conflict.

The code of ethics of the legal profession lays down certain requirements which affected our office very directly. For example the code prohibits advertising. However, in our community many people are not only unable to afford lawyers; they do not even know that lawyers can help them. We needed to tell people that our services were free, and we needed to tell them that our services were different. Most lawyers give their services where they can make the most money. As a consequence the law tends to be elaborate and specialized in areas which serve the wealthy – in tax law, corporation law, etc. There are almost no specialists in welfare law or landlord/tenant law, no lawyers available to people having trouble with the Unemployment Insurance Commission or Workmen's Compensation, few services for deserted welfare mothers, and so on. It would be our task to work in these areas because these are the problems of a community like Parkdale. It was critical that we advertise ourselves to them. In fact the office, after careful calculation of the consequences, did take on the legal profession over the issue of advertising. This was a relatively mild change to ask for, particularly since the Law Society had already broken with tradition and allowed Legal Aid to advertise. A committee of interested community members was formed as the beginnings of an advisory board and a buffer system between the office and legal institutions. (This process is described in more detail on p. 000. The community committee consisted mainly of individual clients plus members of local groups the office had worked with. The office and the community committee jointly held meetings and sent briefs to the Law Society to ask for advertising privileges, obtaining a six-month trial period. Unfortunately, the office allowed the community committee to fall apart shortly after this issue was won.

The Code of Ethics states, as well, that lawyers have an obligation to all who request their services. This caused major conflicts around decisions as to who our clients should be in an agency dedicated to social change. When the office opened it had already negotiated the right to lay down financial and residence guidelines so that it was in fact serving the less-advantaged members of the Parkdale community (the less-advantaged members comprise the great majority of the community). The Tenants Association tried repeatedly to press for a policy decision from the office that the office would not take on landlord cases, and that they would refer tenant problems to the Association. In an area like Parkdale where the great majority of people are tenants – and poor tenants at that – even the poorest landlord is often better off than his tenant, and in any case most landlords were less than generous. Parkdale is a highly exploited area and tenant victims are often powerless in a number of ways. They may be not only poor but old, deserted, on welfare, or powerless in any number of ways. The office was unable to take a firm policy stand on the side of tenants as a class of oppressed people because it consistently put its professionalism above its politics. It always put forth the argument that 'lawyers have a professional obligation to take on whoever needs service.' The staff could debate endlessly about the obligation of the profession – 'what would happen if no lawyer would defend murderers?' and so on, but attendance to this item of the code also allows people to ignore and sidestep collective injustices.

By the same token the code imposes a requirement of confidentiality on lawyers. This means again that class problems such as those of tenants cannot be shared in an organizing effort. In order to build their organization and to confront the housing problems of the community, the Tenants Association needed to reach any persons with problems in these areas. Such persons came in numbers to the law office, and while the office could resolve individual problems, in their reluctance to share information and their eagerness to provide casework for learning students, they tended to undercut the work of the Tenants Association.

In terms of theories for social change, we saw our task as altering the balance of power between classes. What we failed to see, or worse, to connect, was our own function in the system. The major thrust of the office was outward, towards a target group that had to be changed in some way. We were supposed to be the agents of change. In spite of many deliberate and exhausting efforts to be conscious of our own stance, we were never really able to integrate a conception of ourselves as workers into our self-consciousness. As a group we never fully accepted the notion that we were subject to the constraints of institutions and power groups in the same way that our target group was exploited and controlled by power groups. Instead we continued to act as professionals with something to give to people and no problems of our own. Like so many other professionals and others of the middle class, we were corrupted by the illusion of freedom through our independence of judgment in treatment matters.

At this point it might be useful to summarize the discussion. When the clinic opened, it had a number of stated goals. We can separate these into reformist and radical goals. We were able to implement the reformist goals of service to the community and an innovative kind of field training to produce a new breed of lawyer. We attempted to deal with the goal of radical social change (challenging the structure and its rules) by experimenting with a horizontal decision- and policy-making structure. Our involvement with the community forced us to grapple with specific policy decisions, but our professional outlook or mindset effectively blocked the possibility of our making decisions which would take on the system. In fact our professionalism often hampered collective organizing efforts with which we were associated in the community. We were not able to realize our radical goal.

Why did we cling to professionalism? To answer this question it is necessary to examine the function and rationale of professionalism in the larger political and social system. The essence of professionalism is to serve. Behind the service concept lies the assumption that problems tossed up by the system can be solved in casework fashion. It assumes that the basic structures and institutions underlying individual problems are just and rational. It assumes that individuals are equal before the law and that 'lawyering' is a matter of adjusting their relationships in an equitable forum. It assumes that class and power have little or no bearing upon the development or outcome of problems. It also assumes that once the legal problem is solved, the client goes back to a well-regulated life. Perhaps most insidious of all, it assumes that the legal problem a low-income person may present (particularly before civil tribunals) arises from misunderstanding or faulty use of the system rather than bad faith on the part of the institution. Problems seen in this way provide no impetus for the restructuring of institutions. Furthermore, they bog lawyers down in day-to-day casualties so that they have little energy or creative imagination left over to tackle these institutions.

The problems of individuals are not simple isolated aberrations, they are staggeringly complex and interwoven. Poor people's legal problems are usually severely entangled with general social problems. Thus one basic relationship in question concerns the social welfare system. Any question of social change relates not only to the law and the social welfare system it involves a conception of the relation of the social welfare institutions to the over-all political and social system. In effect the social welfare system serves as a buffer and a first-aid station to the people who are the leftovers of political and social policy. Strategies for reform directed at social welfare systems can only result in a change of personnel, or perhaps minor modifications of administrative discretionary power.

Much the same analysis can be applied to legal problems which are brought to the court system. The crucial question again is not who runs the courts and dispenses justice, but what is the function of the court system in relation to the lower classes? Is it really dispensing justice? Or is it locking up those who have never had the material or emotional option of obeying the law?

Had we formulated this analysis clearly, we could have taken another step in questioning the function of our law office. Poor people's problems are not so much individual problems as the common problems of a class. The role or skills a lawyer brings to them must therefore be different from his traditional role or skill. He must in some sense acknowledge in his practice that these are class problems, and that only in organizing themselves can people fight their problems. Solving individual problems alone serves to isolate and pacify people who need to be fighting for basic changes which will prevent their problems from arising in the first place. The lawyer must be prepared to re-examine the rules that prescribe how he practises, and to help people organize around their problems.

However the system is a lockstep one, providing personal rewards for those who play by its rules. These rules permeate the very air we breathe from the day we are born. It may be easy to see that certain groups in society are oppressed but it is enormously difficult for a professional servant of the public interest to see himself as an oppressor – or to see himself as oppressed. Society accords lawyers a good deal of respect. If one is a 'good lawyer' one receives society's rewards – financial success, security, status, and respectability. Most people are taught to strive for these things.

If the clinic was to pursue its goal of social change, then it would be necessary to challenge the rules of professionalism, putting at risk its rewards. It would need to struggle against its own controlling institutions. The legal profession as an institution in society stands for and practises the values of a money-hungry and power-hungry elite, and as long as this group controls an agency like the Parkdale one, the clinic cannot extend itself beyond the function of a buffer.

The clinic never really decided to challenge the legal profession. Not only that, it was never able to formulate an analysis which would lead it to making that choice. The action program consequently bogged down, alienating many of the dedicated workers so that they became unwilling to undertake any kind of theoretical discussion.

To reiterate, behind all the agonized indecision-making ran the threat of professionalism. Much of the uncertainty as to how we should function and what stand we should take was the unresolved dilemma of professional ethics versus radical political action. As long as the students in the clinic gave their major loyalty to professionalism, they could not rid themselves of these dilemmas. As long as professionalism holds out the illusion of freedom it blinds people to their function in the system. It has become another tool in the hands of the powerful. It distracts people from really looking at what they are doing to others, and at what they are doing to themselves. As long as people see themselves as independent professionals rather than as workers in an oppressive institution, they will be bound by the sophistries of this myth: a myth which puts a safe distance between the professionals and the people they serve.

Many good things have happened through the clinic. Its mere existence as a free legal service has altered the balance of power in the Parkdale community to some extent. Fights have been undertaken − and won − that might never have even been undertaken had we not been there to act as a resource and a support. It is the setting for a stimulating and consciousness-raising experience for some law students. It is a model for alternative ways of practising law. But on many issues it has refused to take stands which might have precipitated it into radical action.

It seems that the possibility of radical action was constantly emerging from our reform function. We could provide service in many areas, but it became clear that to provide better service some restructuring was required. To reach the people of Parkdale we needed to advertise, to attack the roots of problems such as landlord/tenant problems we needed to organize, to organize we needed a community group, and so on.

At one point the office did choose to confront the legal profession and make certain demands. A group of interested community people − most of whom were clients of the office − were brought together to discuss mutual needs and problems. This group, together with the office staff decided to tackle the issue of advertising. Both this group of advisers and the office prepared briefs outlining community needs and the rationale for advertising. Law Society members were invited to an open meeting to discuss the issue and to take back the briefs to the Law Society. The over-all tone of this strategy was polite and non-aggressive, although some individuals were quite demanding. In the end the Law Society agreed to allow the office to advertise through its advisory committee and the issue was resolved to the satisfaction of all. At this point, however, the staff member responsible for getting the advisory committee together left the project. No further efforts were made to help this group grow and expand its perspective or function as an agent for change in Parkdale. Indeed, it was allowed to die. The group won the first issue fairly easily, but this does not suggest that it was significant victory. The law students were not overly enthusiastic about confronting the Law Society. The advisory committee consisted largely of a working-class, conservative group whose dedication to the issue was founded on the basis of their gratitude for service rendered. There were a few members who had a more radical and generalized perspective on why they should seek control

over office functions, but among the group as a whole there was little awareness or interest in a power struggle. They were extremely protective of the
lawyers in the office and perhaps more cautious in pushing the issue than was
the staff itself. It is still an open question as to whether the spark of interest
could have been fanned into a greater awareness or desire to take risks. One
thing is certain – it would have taken a great deal of work and energy to test
whether this group could have grown into a significant force. The office chose
not to make that effort. Staff and community people who had been involved
in pushing concepts of worker and community control gradually became discouraged and disillusioned. The staff tended to retreat into casework and
community people simply became disillusioned and somewhat indifferent.
Much valuable energy was lost.

Out of this process at least two things became clear. If reformist and
service actions were desired, lines to the system had to be kept open.
Students could not serve clients if they were alienating themselves from
judges, court workers, and to some extent social agencies. Much success in
legal casework depends upon the cooperation of legal and social networks,
upon keeping good informal lines of communication open. As well, a great
deal of satisfaction comes from being able to achieve this success, both to
clients and to staff. Furthermore, this success encourages people to aim
higher, by playing along with the rules to an even greater extent. Co-opting
occurs at both a professional and a personal level.

The other side of this process is that radical action cannot be directed at
institutions by workers who propose to bring their service problems along at
the same time. To begin with, the load of casework is too great to give proper
attention to organizing efforts. Because organizing is a long term effort without the minute-to-minute pressure of casework, it tends to get lost in the
shuffle. If it is to succeed, it must be the priority of at least some people who
do not have to worry about service functions. Ideally, perhaps, an enthusiastic and politically aware community group can play the role of organizer with
the office as resource staff. If the community board and the office staff can
work together, issues can be carried out through the community group, with
the added advantage that this group also protects the service function of the
office. Furthermore, it is right that organizing issues and strategies be defined
and formulated primarily through the community itself. The biggest problem
with this theory is that a politically aware community board does not spring
forth full blown from the grass roots. It must be actively encouraged and
supported by the office and by other active community groups.

Parkdale Legal Services has moved consistently away from this conception
of its role. It has allowed the beginnings of a community advisory group to
fade away. It has replaced the community worker with lay advocates and

local community people who serve as caseworkers and 'community consultants.' They are used as the voice of the community. It has now established its priorities as law reform in consumer law, unemployment standards, and landlord tenant law; and it has done this by consulting with itself and its own office staff rather than with community people. More time than ever is being devoted to academic seminars and the student staff is on the conservative side. Its priorities are quite clearly law reform and career poverty law.

Perhaps a year and a half of operations in process was necessary for Parkdale's priorities to emerge clearly. On the other hand one is tempted to speculate that they have been there all along, glossed over with talk of community boards, community involvement, radical change, and social action. Because radical social change as a possibility through community groups and community control over the office was never really tested, it is impossible to say whether it could work. It is possible to see that it would be a long and difficult process to undertake, with no certainty that a community group would be radicalized.

Nevertheless, this community legal service does teach some things. It demonstrates the necessity for analysis of goals and consequences. It demonstrates the need to state goals clearly and then stick by that choice. If the project is to be a reform project, let it be clear that no more is intended. There is a good deal of room for law reform and extended service to lower income groups, and in the end more can be accomplished by a group that is what it says it is than by a group which seems to be more than it is. The experience of this project also seems to suggest that if service and action are both to be undertaken, then the service function and the service people should be clearly separated from the action component. It suggests that the action component, while it may have to be given its original impetus from the project, may have to move outside of the project and beyond the reach of funding authorities as quickly as possible.

Put into more general terms, the project suggests that professionalism supports the rules of the system. It can easily absorb and even encourage reformism, but it militates against radical change on two levels. Firstly, it prevents professionals from challenging their own methods of practice and their relationship to their institutions. Secondly, it constrains radical action as much by sins of omission (withholding of information) as by sins of commission (providing individual rather than collective solutions). Professionalism is good practice only for those who are convinced that the system is basically a good one and that they have sufficient control already over their own destinies.

If the project is professional in orientation, then, its strategies will be designed to be educational, to free up lines of communication, to remove abuses, to extend services, and to generally improve the functioning of the system.

Active anti-professionalism (community control) is a radical strategy which attempts to restructure a subsystem – in this case, legal institutions. This re-structuring involves breaking down the monopolistic control of the Law Society over the practice of law. It rejects the traditional code of ethics and opens the door to class-conscious law. Control is transferred from legal institutions to community groups. Some effects beyond the legal profession itself can be predicted as a consequence of this strategy. Because legal institutions are such central institutions in our society, change in them will provide a model and an impetus for parallel change in other social institutions. This new kind of law office may provide more than a model for change. The community group together with the law office may force change in social welfare agencies and institutions such as Unemployment Insurance or Children's Aid. It may also force change in powerful individuals such as slum landlords through strategies such as rent control and rent strikes.

This would indeed be radical change. But as long as central questions such as rejecting professionalism and establishing radicalized community groups are not adequately tested, it remains a dream.

James D. St John

The political cornucopia of participation in a movement-party:
a brief introduction

The day is passing when political parties can get into office and run the
country merely because they are political parties.
BROOKE CLAXTON, 1934

The term 'social change' is in danger of becoming an empty and dulling catch-phrase of the language of politics. Nonetheless, through all the academic analyses and political invocations of social change, one idea has not only survived but remained vibrant. That idea is to increase citizen particpation in political life.

Clearly, participation is a political cornucopia. Compared to the abstract nature of the larger concept of social change, the concept of participation seems concrete and realistic. It enjoys the advantages of association with the democratic idea without the perils of association with academic incomprehensibility and without the odour of association with particular interest groups. Further, participation displays the rare virtue of being both means and end; it is a means to social change while itself being an example and essential part of social change. Yet further, seen from different perspectives, it is desirable or at least acceptable to radicals, moderate reformers, and pragmatic conservatives alike. What better credentials can a political idea have?

Implementation, however, is another and contentious matter. Who participates? How do they participate? And where does participation end and representation begin? Debates over these questions may be found throughout our political history; such debates have taken place in particular within our political parties and social movements, and it is from that context that current discussions usually draw the 'lessons' which, it is asserted, experience has taught us.

These 'lessons' are precisely what I intend to discuss in these pages. I contend that our political parties have deluded themselves with regard to the values and possibilities of participation. Participation is considered workable only in the form of casting or soliciting ballots or, at most, of forming policy. Beyond such limited forms party theorists and anti-parliamentary radicals alike often contend that experience shows an inescapable incompatibility between participatory politics and parliamentary politics. This is an unfortunate conceptual error. Exaggeration of the contradictions between participation in political parties and in social movements leads to a failure to grasp the political potential of parties working for social change while in parliamentary opposition. Parties in opposition unnecessarily deny themselves the opportunity to point at what they have done, most notably at the local level, and content themselves with saying what they will do, if elected. The voters, as it should be needless to say, subscribe to the cliché that 'actions speak louder than words.' When will opposition parties, particularly third parties, rediscover this?

The purpose of this paper, then, is not only to discuss historical 'lessons' about participation, but also to emphasize the political virtues of actions through participatory politics. Such actions, conceptualized as 'movement-party' actions, will be argued and illustrated at length in the body of this paper, but for the present they may be described as representing a synthesis: a synthesis of such participation as is characteristic of contemporary political parties with that which is characteristic of social movements. The argument for this synthesis is presented in several stages. Initially, in order to reveal how the delusion about participation may have arisen within parties, attention is focused upon the concepts of 'social movement' and 'political party' within our history. Next, a clarification of the confusion of these concepts is suggested, a clarification based upon participation. Finally, with the grounds of discussion thus cleared of obstacles, the idea of opposition participatory politics, movement-party politics, is argued out. It is argued through reference to that party with the greatest claims to a participatory nature, namely the New Democratic party.

THE CONFUSION OF 'MOVEMENTS' AND 'PARTIES'

Howsoever social change is conceived and whatever role participatory politics plays in such a conception, attention must eventually be given to the core question of how social change will be realized. What will be its vehicles? Historically, the most frequently projected vehicles have been political parties and social movements. Also historically, however, these terms have been rhetorical facades for conceptual confusion. Are the ideas of movement and party contradictory or supplementary?

Originally the term social movement came into popular use in the nineteenth century as a mechanistic metaphor. Although it appeared in a variety of forms and meanings, it commonly indicated a popular commitment to change directly affecting its advocates and conceived by them as 'progressive.'[1] This now forms the core of what is called the traditional concept of a social movement. This traditional concept, however, has been unacceptable to social analysts who pursue the myth of pure objectivity and 'value-freedom.' Whereas traditional usage only in rare instances assigned the status of social movement to conservative, reactionary, and non-political movements, social scientists in pursuit of objectivity came to so designate them as a matter of course. The 'social' element in the concept of a social movement was reduced as much as possible to a purely quantitative meaning. In practice, however, the attempt at quantification fell prey to a tendency for categorization, a tendency that became a fetish. In the works of specialists, the definition of term social movement was splintered into social movements proper, specific social movements, expressive social movements, and spatial social movements.[2] In categories now more familiar but scarcely more enlightening, a conceptual maze was created wherein social movements were distinguished from (to name a few) social trends, historical trends, voluntary associations, pressure groups, protest movements, religious movements of several varieties, episodic manifestations of discontent such as riots, and, perhaps most contentiously, political parties.[3] The confusing sterility of these terms becomes evident when an attempt is made to apply them to the phenomena of our history. They do not suffice.

The term political party presents similar confusion when we attempt to establish its precise meaning in our social analyses. In itself, the term 'party' has merely meant a detachment from a larger social group, and only in the nineteenth century did a political connotation become widely dominant. The traditional concept of a political party which emerged in that century, as one authority has recently expressed it, 'designated organizations whose goal was the capture of public office in electoral competition with one or more other parties.'[4] Such a concept has proven to be insufficient for social scientific purposes. The term indicates several quite different groups and again a fetish for categorization has been developed, albeit with more beneficial results than in the previous case. In the illustrative terms of V.O. Key, Jr, a dean of American political science at midcentury, these groups are the party-in-the-electorate, the party professionals, the party-in-the-legislature, and the party-in-the-government.[5] Further, the term political party has been used in connection with minor parties whose electoral participation aims more at education than directly at power, revolutionary organizations which disdain electoral politics and, in a somewhat different sense, reference is made not only to competitive parties in party systems but to one-party, quasi-party, and no-party systems.

In general, the only point relevant to this paper which can confidently be asserted on the basis of this confusion of meanings for the terms social movement and political party is that traditionally they were compatible. In the nineteenth century, for example, the term 'movement-party' was common, and in Britain the Radical party was alternately known by that name, the Movement party.[6] In Canada, while such usage has been familiar, it has been so only as qualified by the renowned 'anti-partyism' which initially perceived social movements as distinct alternatives to political parties. In the 'new politics' of the prairies fifty years ago, Henry Wise Wood argued that 'to turn from organized political action (by occupational groups) in which people move systematically, from the bottom up, is to turn from democracy. To turn to the political party, which is guided by an executive committee — guided from the top down — is to turn back to individualism and political autocracy.' Similarly, in what became their founding statement, the 'Ginger Group' proclaimed in 1924 that 'there are two species of political organization — one the political party that aspires to power, and in so doing perpetuates that competitive spirit in matters of legislation and government which has brought the world well nigh to ruin; the other is the democratically organized group ...' For the Ginger Group, as M.N. Campbell wrote at the time, the basic idea was to preserve 'the movement,' the progressive movement.[7]

Yet in each of these instances the movements became parties, albeit parties different in nature from the established parties they had railed against. In Alberta politics, as C.B. Macpherson has written, the result was neither a competitive party system, nor even a one-party system, but rather a 'quasi-party' system. The Ginger Group, similarly, led to the CCF – a political party avoiding even the label of party, preferring to be a 'federation' of 'farmer, labour, socialist' elements.

The Co-operative Commonwealth Federation and its successor, the New Democratic party, have perhaps exemplified the idea of a movement-party as much as any other phenomena in the Canadian political experience. Indeed, Walter Young opens his book *The Anatomy of a Party: The National CCF 1932-61* with the assertion that 'socialists belong to movements, capitalists support parties. From beginning to end, the [CCF] was referred to as a movement by its leaders and members.'[8] Nonetheless, Young also writes of a transition from 'movement into party' in the years from 1933 to 1940. Complicating the situation, the NDP has widely been considered as more of a party and less of a movement than was its predecessor. This view seems to conflict with the nature of the origins of the NDP, which was formed by the merger of the CCF with a substantial portion of the organized labour movement. In other words, a movement-party was invigorated by the addition of a movement and this resulted in a party exhibiting fewer movement characteristics than it had before the addition. Such conceptual looseness has scarcely assisted students of our political history in their search for 'lessons' about parties and movements.

What happened was that the terms party and movement fell prey to similar difficulties in both popular and social scientific usage. In each case the adjectives 'social' and 'political' were dropped. The resultant latitude in usage reduced all that was 'party' to ideas and actions directly concerned with electoral victory. All else – whether it was referred to as cooperative politics, socialist agitation, extra-parliamentary activity, anti-parliamentary opposition, or whatsoever – was relegated to the catch-all category of 'movement.' The uncritical use of these terms in an either-or fashion indicated a conceptual blindness. Certain possibilities were defined away.

A CLARIFICATION OF MOVEMENT
AND PARTY IN CANADA

In order to rescue these possibilities, and, indeed, to make sense of the terms movement and party as they are used in our political history, let us make use of the concept of participation. Considered as pure types, social movements and political parties distinguish themselves through participatory characteristics. An oversimplification, but one which is meaningful and not entirely untenable, would be that social movements are inherently participatory and political parties are inherently non-participatory. This statement will be elaborated and illustrated in the following paragraphs.

The idea of 'party' signifies a detachment from a larger social whole, and, generally, it fits within the wider idea of a division of labour. At least, there is an implication of leadership. The continuing survival of the idea of a 'working party' exemplifies this, and a similar, although contentious, case might be made for the idea of a 'vanguard party.' By restoring the adjective 'political' we signify at least a relation to conflict and social power and, at most, to the profound questions of how to satisfy human needs and wants. This addition, however, purges the idea of any implication of mass participation. In this context the ideas of working party or vanguard party become elitist and, generally, participation transforms itself into the blander idea of 'support.' This becomes vividly evident when attention is switched from definition to practice and the categories suggested by V.O. Key, Jr, are recalled to mind. The party-in-the-electorate participates, clearly, by the act of voting, or, for a relatively small number, by stuffing envelopes, canvassing, and participating in other campaign activities. Participation here refers to a few minutes or a few days a year, and even this participation is simply to choose representatives who will in turn participate in the parliamentary arena. Even in the most internally democratic of our major parties, the NDP, participation by members is extended only to include the submission of resolutions to the conventions which set party policy or the selection of convention delegates. Therefore, if political parties are viewed in terms of participation, that participation may at most be called sporadic and indirect, that is, through representation.

The contrast of this to participation in a social movement is striking. Members of a social movement do not participate through representation, through actions taken on their behalf by individuals whom they elect, but preeminently through actions they themselves perform. The term 'movement' itself indicates actions taken in common by a number of individuals. Whether they know each other or are even aware of each other is of no intrinsic importance to their participation in a movement. This is easily illustrated: Canadian nationalism was recognizable as a social movement long before the arrival of such groups as the Committee for an Independent Canada and the Movement for an Independent Socialist Canada. The movement existed in terms of the conscious participation of its members, participation in terms of such constant and direct actions as 'buying Canadian.' To assert that this is a social movement, further, is to make a qualitative assertion about the nature of the participation in the movement. If one follows traditional usage, this indicates a progressive element and thus, in contemporary usage, a relation to social change.

The above analysis could be continued with further elaboration and valuable results, but it becomes sterile and confusing if made in a void. An illustration is in order. Let us return to the conceptual confusion about the CCF and NDP as described earlier in these pages.

The federation that was the CCF was a merger of social movements and minor political parties. It embodied participation both by members of its constituent movements on a direct, continuing basis and by election workers on a sporadic, representative basis as decreed through the electoral system. It was a 'movement-party.' However, Walter Young was accurate when he wrote of a transition from movement into party. Unfortunately this transition has been described as a decline in the hold of ideological positions upon the flexibility of the party as a political organization. But such a description falls into serious difficulty by implying that the Liberal and Conservative parties were somehow not ideological, that their brokerage nature precluded ideology. This absurdity can be avoided by replacing the conventional wisdom with an interpretation based upon participation. Such an interpretation would perceive the transition of the CCF in terms of a decline in direct and continuing participation, characteristic of social movements, and a relative rise in sporadic and indirect participation, characteristic of political parties. The CCF remained a 'movement-party' only to the extent that the former survived. This survival, moreover, was relative; it could be measured not only by an absolute decline in social movement activities but by an independently absolute rise in the numbers of CCF supporters participating only through casting their ballots or canvassing during elections. Beyond this relative change, it could be argued that the goals which social movements sought to achieve through the participation of their members (especially through such organized movement activities as cooperatives) were slowly transformed into political goals which were seen as realizable solely through political participation resulting in electoral victory. The energies of the one were drained into the other. When the CCF emerged as the NDP the addition of a portion of the organized labour movement, as previously stated, was widely interpreted as strengthening the party characteristics of the movement-party, rather than, as would seem to follow, the movement characteristics. The reasons for this, too, become clear through looking at participation. The participation involved was not the direct and continual participation of the union member in his local, but his participation, and that of his local, in the sporadic and indirect actions of the electoral system. Once again the goals which a social movement had sought to achieve through the direct and continual

participation of the members of the movement were at least partially transformed into political goals seen as realizable only through participation in the
electoral system. The 'movement-party' remained primarily a party for participation in the realm of decision-making rather than in the realm of action.

THE MOVEMENT-PARTY AS A SYNTHESIS:
THE CASE OF THE NDP

It should now be clear that to discuss increasing political participation within
a political party is to discuss increasing the level of the participation that is
characteristic of a social movement, participation that is direct and continuous rather than indirect and sporadic. Such participation is characteristic of
a 'movement-party' and thus this discussion will continue through centring
upon the movement-party which is the NDP.

Conceptual problems aside, a proposal to increase participation faces two
problems of particular note. The first of these problems is that such a proposal may be overly idealistic – the participants are simply not potentially
available. Unless this objection is overcome, further discussion is futile. The
second of these problems is to make clear that the proposal is the creature of
neither the 'left' or the 'right' of a party's membership. In the case of the NDP
this is particularly important and difficult. It must be made clear that the
proposal is a synthesis of modes of participation proposed by each. In the
context of factional arguments this may be all too easily obscured.

The objection of an overly idealistic vision being implicit in a proposal to
increase direct and constant participation appears more serious than it is.
Proponents of this pessimism assert that the general movement for social
change which resurged in Canada in recent years, particularly in the form of a
youth movement, has already fragmented and declined much as did the
general movement for social change in the early years of the CCF. In each case
it is argued that there has been a decline in commitment. For the youth
movement of the 1960s total commitment was referred to as 'living the
revolution.'[9] Similarly, for many participants in the early years of the CCF
there was 'no clear distinction between politics, sociability, entertainment,
and even work.'[10] In each case it is hardly tenable to assert that the situation
has not changed. The crux of the argument, however, rests upon the interpretation of a decline in the extent of active involvement as indicating an
equivalent lessening of commitment. Implicit in this, also, is that active involvement remains, when present, constantly public and measurable. A youth
who 'lived the revolution' during his student years, for example, is implicitly
asserted to have been co-opted and to have lessened his desire for social
change – or at least his willingness to assist in it – simply because as he grew

older his life may have become adjusted to the time-demanding realities of job and family. The argument is plausible, and undoubtedly true in isolated instances, but it is less than convincing as a generalization.

Furthermore, this argument deals with, and is limited to, symptoms and interpretations of current conditions. As such, it does not inherently define potentials. The issue of potentials, however, is precisely what is at stake in the participation debate.

Indeed, the argument of potentials is normally posed within the NDP in the context of the debate between 'left' and 'right,' the second problem of particular note. In what are now quite familiar debates, the right wing of the party (or at least the group commonly designated as such) focuses upon electoral victory while the left wing (similarly more designated than real) focuses upon the social-movement aspect of the party. It replies to the electoral enthusiasm of the right wing by stating that, at times, as in Saskatchewan in 1964, the NDP has appeared ideologically to the right of the Liberal party. Significantly, the social movement aspect of the party is frequently represented by both sides in the debate, as 'anti-parliamentary politics' designed to put 'parliamentary politics' in a proper perspective. This representation, however, obscures the issue of participatory politics which are *not* anti-parliamentary, but which have a potentially positive electoral impact as a secondary effect.

Let us first consider the view from the right wing of the party. The parliamentary strategies which some have identified with that wing have recently borne fruit in three of the four western provinces. In terms of success in achieving power, these strategies has thus been proven. Or have they? That the centres of power are not in governmental hands or that in each province there has scarcely been a mandate of extensive, structural change are arguments with a substantial degree of truth. The voters have as much been 'throwing the rascals out' as 'giving the NDP a chance.' The parliamentary strategy may offer definite appeals in situations where the NDP is the official opposition but, the example of Manitoba notwithstanding, it has neither been validated nor vitiated for situations where the NDP has not achieved such standing. Nationally, in Alberta, in Quebec, in the Maritimes, and, to a lesser extent, in Ontario, the NDP, if it depends solely upon the parliamentary strategy, is in the position of awaiting the collapse of established parties.

If this description is accurate, then the parliamentary strategy may essentially be called a negative one, and the question arises of whether there is any positive strategy open to the NDP other than the 'left' one of 'building the movement' without regard to short-term electoral effect. The reply of that part of the party identified as the right wing lies pre-eminently in what has been called a 'demonstration effect.' In this theory the NDP suffers less from voters' fears of wasting their votes upon a third party than from their distrust. Socialism as term and as symbol is often misconceived and remains emotionally significant. Many voters, moreover, are less than enthusiastic about the union movement; they evidence concern about its influence upon the NDP. The chance to demonstrate in the three NDP-governed provinces that such fears are groundless will, it is argued, lead to an increase in the popular vote for the NDP throughout the nation.

Whatever the virtues of this argument, however, it does little to answer the question of what is to be done in a positive sense. It is a negative strategy for party members in provinces not governed by the NDP. A participatory, movement-party element remains to be added. But if participatory strategies are not to be rejected out of hand by those who favour electoral strategies, they must be as much supplementary as alternative. Actions in this grey area, for example, might function with a demonstration effect of their own.

Let us, therefore, now consider the view from the left wing of the party. The movement strategy identified with the left wing of the NDP – and, indeed, with former and potential members of the NDP now to the left of it – appears under the designations of extra-parliamentary politics, anti-parliamentary politics, extra-parliamentary opposition, etc. This strategy, recently embraced in part by the Waffle and now by the Movement For An Independent Socialist Canada, bases itself upon the following interconnected points: the NDP is not socialist enough in its program and where it obtains power it will fail to implement a substantially socialist program due to a fear of being rejected by the voters at the next election and due to the real centres of power in our society being, in any event, beyond parliament, in the world of business and capital. A revolution 'from above' is thus unlikely and a revolution 'from below' is a necessity. The path to this goal is through building a social movement. This process, in itself, is 'building the revolution.'

Outside the NDP this strategy has undeniable appeals and significant difficulties which are beyond the scope of this paper. But within the NDP this strategy is one of education, persuasion, and slow growth. Although the right-wing strategy of the demonstration effect is essentially negative, the left strategy may also be called a negative one, for it too is a long-range strategy. Consequently, the right wing of the party has often referred to supporters of this strategy as 'the real reactionaries' who would return the party to the position it held during its early years. This uncharitable assertion has a grain of truth in it to the extent that proponents of the left strategy seek to build the movement even at the expense of risking or denying short-term benefits in electoral contests. The party, it is asserted, is only a means to an end and must be prevented from becoming an end in itself.

But what, then, is the strategy of building the movement that the left advocates? Besides tactics of promise and persuasion, the left implicitly argues its own 'demonstration effect.' If 'workers' control' or 'community control' is implemented in one area, it is argued, the virtues of such control will become evident and imitated. People will act. They will demand similar rights to participate in their own areas. In a reform although not exclusively left-wing example this has happened, at least to a limited extent, at the municipal level in Toronto, and other cities, in the formation of resident and ratepayer organizations.

Clearly, there is no inherent necessity for the strategy of the demonstration effect, as envisaged by the left, to be contrary to the parliamentary, electoral, goals of a political party. If the party is means and not end, this does not negate the possibility of 'movement-party' actions which, to the delight of the left wing of the party, build the movement, and which, to the delight of the right wing of the party, increase the party's electoral prospects.

Perhaps the most familiar variety of what *can be* movement-party actions arises in the area of 'tending the grass roots' as undertaken by MPs and MLAs, regardless of whether they are members of the governing party. Functioning primarily in an ombudsman role, the MPs and MLAs build political trust and accumulate political support among their constituents. The citizen who has received help from his parliamentary representative remembers this at election time. This is common but essential political wisdom. The representative has not just promised, he has delivered upon a promise. In this ombudsman function, however, there is rarely any movement element, rarely any participation. The process is almost wholly paternalistic, yet this need not be the case. Party organizations which participated in these activities could, to some extent, convert this paternalism into an expression of community concern and cooperation.

Yet such activities as fulfilling an ombudsman role would function as movement-party actions in only a minor way. On the whole, they would promise little likelihood of the beneficiaries coming to participate themselves, for the paternalistic element would inevitably remain, albeit reduced. We must look elsewhere for illustration of participatory, movement-party activities. A variety of these is apparent in the old CCF connection with co-operatives. More specifically, relevant potentials exist in the whole range of activities which often now pass under the anaemic title of community services. In day-care centres, food cooperatives, community improvement associations, and even in such 'service club' activities as care for youth and the aged, the potential exists for party organizations to 'become involved,' to perform services, and to build the trust and solicit the participation of members of the communities in which these activities take place. A temptation exists to dismiss these activities as trivial. To do so, however, would be an expression of the distances which frequently yawn between party theorists and party activists, and the communities to which they appeal. Through such activities the 'spectres' of socialism and unionism may be diminished in minds which have fallen prey to anti-socialist and anti-unionist propaganda, and, simultaneously, the peoples' social movement be built.

To illustrate this, let us consider the issue of day-care centres. Few would deny the crying need for more and better day-care centres, yet the political parties are in the position of promising rather than performing. Model day-care centres under NDP auspices would say much more to the mother who needs day-care facilities than do mere promises. Certainly a party in opposition is denied possibilities to 'deliver' that are open to a governing party. But while the party clearly could not take on the burden of day-care on a wide scale, model day-care centres are a real possibility. I would contend that the primary obstacle to the cooperative formation of more day-care centres than currently exist is the lack of organizers for them — organizers with an institutional basis for continuity and for the exchange of information of techniques and legal difficulties. The NDP riding associations in many cities are strong enough to provide precisely such an organizational and institutional basis. Part of the necessary 'price' of families taking advantage of such a centre, moreover, could be the devotion of a few hours each week to the centre, of participation in its activities. This would be a small — but significant — step towards both building a movement and increasing electoral prospects. In the latter sense the NDP would benefit not only among those who participate, but among those who become aware of this 'demonstration' of the policies of the party.

The electoral advantages of such movement-party actions would also be present in regard to the perennial NDP problem of co-optation. Other opposition parties, and even the party in power, would find it less easy to co-opt NDP actions than they currently find it easy to co-opt NDP promises. The NDP could point to records of action even in constituencies where there is no NDP representative to the provincial or federal legislature. Individuals who have such 'records of action' in their communities are precisely the most sought after by political parties as candidates, so it is doubly surprising that party units do not currently establish such records for themselves as groups.

Since the development of only one example in many is fraught with the dangers of objections to the specific action rather than to the idea behind it, let us develop a second example, namely that of general community improvement organizations. To invoke such associations may seem dreary and trivial — yet the social and political potential is significant, perhaps enormous.

If a portion of the 'army' of canvassers for which the NDP is justly famous at election time were to knock on doors to seek assistance in cleaning up the banks of the local river, tracking down sources of pollution, or even, in actions productive in a far different sense, to invite residents on a community tour, the response would, I suggest, not be insignificant. Small groups would be willing to participate in such actions as both a community centred and a social activity. Non-partisan organizations would undoubtedly 'spin-off' from such actions, but would remember their origins. The NDP co-participants in these activities would not be seen as dangerous members of 'the socialist hordes' but as fellow, community-spirited citizens. The perception would, of necessity, be correct.

While this type of action would, by its very nature, be an option for each of the political parties, it is particularly suited to the NDP. This is not solely due to the progressive nature and social-change orientation of NDP members. What old NDP campaigner does not recall election campaigns in which the canvassers have talked loudly and at length of trying to continue to 'do something' between elections. Nonetheless, when the election is over, such enthusiasm is quickly – usually immediately – extinguished by long and dreary meetings, seemingly productive of nothing except verbiage. Those individuals who have canvassed, I suggest, are far more willing to act than to sit through meetings.

Since such movement-party strategies are not already a continuing reality of Canadian politics, it would seem that there must be either insurmountable obstacles or solid arguments in opposition to them. Although, in my opinion, the root reasons lie in conceptual blindness about the natures of movements and parties as much as in anything else, the arguments in opposition must nonetheless be seriously examined.

On a purely technical level there are undoubted difficulties. These vary with each possible movement-party action. As an illustration, let us return to the idea of a party constituency organization functioning in an ombudsman role. If the party offers advice and assistance to individuals caught within a maze of red rape, these individuals may have to declare the constituency organization to be their formal agent. In discomforting contrast, a sitting member of a legislature does not face this problem in carrying out the same actions.

On a level more substantive than the technical one, the idea of participation in a movement-party faces arguments such as the question of feasibility – in terms of manpower – raised earlier in this paper and dismissed as an argument over potential. It might be argued that canvassers who participate during election campaigns would not participate in non-electoral activities. Such an argument would imagine each canvasser asking 'what's in it for me?'

As well, such an argument would assert that non-electoral participation would lack the sense of drama and moral satisfaction that elections involve. These arguments, I assert, are overly pessimistic as to the nature of the commitment of electoral workers and as to the satisfactions attendant upon individual participation in organized activites. The pessimistic position, drawn from observation of the sporadic and disjointed nature of electoral participation, implicitly assumes that participants generally fail to form social bonds. However, with continuing rather than sporadic activities, the social bonds that currently hold together service organizations would function within party constituency organizations as well. If word play upon clichés may be excused in order to make a point, the citizens who volunteer together, play together.

This latter point, the word play aside, is far from trivial. It is important enough that it , in itself, would undoubtedly be subject to objection. It could be argued that this implies an unacceptable 'politicization of everyday life.' Yet this is not new. It may be well to recall the summation of an author of a sociological study of the CCF published in 1964: 'many others ... found the movement so close to the centre of their lives that no clear distinction existed between politics, sociability, entertainment, and even work. The CCF membership card was a low cost ticket of admission to all four.'[11] It might be argued that to return to this situation, overstated as it perhaps is, would be a reactionary resurrection of the past. But in today's world of increasing leisure time, increasing social isolation and alienation, is it not possible that a step in this direction would be desirable?

In the final analysis, however, the argument of this paper is based upon a qualitative rather than a quantitative conception of social change. Implicit in that position is the idea that to work for social change is to work for anything that serves to meet real human needs and wants. In the first book the Research Committee of the League for Social Reconstruction produced for the CCF, *Social Planning for Canada* (1935), the comment was made that 'politics in Canada has never risen above the level of being our major national sport.'[12] If those who have worked for the NDP in elections – canvassing, with impressive commitment – have risen above such a level, as I think they have, then their commitment to social change is not merely a phenomenon of election years. This commitment will assure enough participation to make movement-party strategies worth trying, and in the process, they will decrease their own subjection to inter-election paternalism. It may be appropriate to repeat the quotation from Brooke Claxton which prefaces this essay: 'The day is passing when political parties can get into office and run the country merely because they are political parties.'[13]

NOTES

1 Paul Wilkinson, *Social Movement* (London, 1971), chap. I, and Rudolf Herberle, *Social Movements* (New York, 1951)
2 See Herbert Blumer, 'Collective Behaviour,' in H.M. Lee, ed., *Principles of Sociology,* 3rd ed. (New York, 1969).
3 Herberle, *Social Movements,* or see Joseph Gusfield, 'Introduction,' *Protest, Reform, and Revolt* (New York, 1970).
4 Joseph Schlesinger, 'Party Units' in *The International Encyclopedia of the Social Sciences* (New York, 1968)
5 *Politics, Parties and Pressure Groups,* 5th ed. (New York, 1964), 163-5
6 Wilkinson, *Social Movement,* 11
7 W.L. Morton, *The Progressive Party in Canada* (Toronto, 1950), 169, 195, 199
8 (Toronto, 1969), 3
9 See David L. Stein, *Living the Revolution* (Indianapolis, 1969).
10 Leo Zakuta, *A Protest Movement Becalmed* (Toronto, 1964), 53
11 Ibid., 53
12 (Toronto, 1935), 464
13 In the *Canadian Historical Review* in 1935, quoted in R.M. Hamilton, ed., *Canadian Quotations and Phrases* (Toronto, 1952)

Gerry Hunnius

Participation vs Parliament

An editorial in *Our Generation* provides a useful starting point for this article:

It is extremely important to remember that the terms parliamentary and extra-parliamentary not only refer to strategies for social change but also suggest differing goals (i.e. a different pattern of social relationships). Parliamentary action leads logically to the seizure of state power. The goal of extra-parliamentary action on the other hand is less clearly defined but, in our view, is essentially directed *not* at the seizure of state power but at its transformation, from its present capitalist and elitist nature to one based on the social ownership of the means of production *coupled with* the introduction of self government by collectivities in the work-place and the community. To replace the present power holders by a new group of individuals will not *by itself* change the nature of elitist and oppressive institutions. People will still be *ruled* and self-government will be denied to the majority of Canadians.[1]

I shall proceed with an elaboration of this argument starting with a discussion of the 'elitist and oppressive institutions' of the Canadian political system and the theoretical positions on which they are based, followed by a discussion of the possibilities and limitations of parliamentary and extra-parliamentary politics in the struggle for socialist democracy.

REPRESENTATIVE INSTITUTIONS AND THE ELECTORAL SYSTEM

There is an unfortunate credibility gap between the realities of representative institutions and politics in Canada and the material often presented to students in political studies. For over twenty years, the standard text on the government of Canada has been the work by Dawson. This is how Dawson sees the reality of Canadian representative democracy: 'The House of Commons is the great democratic agency in the government of Canada: the "grand inquest of the nation"; the organized medium through which the public will finds expression and exercizes its ultimate political power. It forms the indispensible part of the legislature; and it is the body to which at all times the executive must turn for justification and approval.' Dawson goes on to argue that the House of Commons speaks, 'as no other body in the democracy can pretend to speak, for the people. It presents in condensed form the different interests, races, religions, classes, and occupations, whose ideas and wishes it embodies with approximate exactness.'[2] The reality of parliamentary politics, however, bears little resemblance to this theoretical formulation.

The theory of representative government presents a depressing picture. There is no agreement on what representation is or means. The range of opinions covers the entire spectrum from those such as Dawson who maintain that every government represents the people it governs to the view that no government can be truly representative.[3]

Political scientists agree on very few principles but one of their time-tested arguments concerns the obsolescence of direct democracy. Since our academic mentors are all democrats, this belief in the impossibility of direct democracy in today's complex societies leads them to the belief that we must be governed by popularly elected representative institutions backed up by a competent and non-political bureaucracy. Since representation is seen as essential to democracy, two schools of thought have emerged. There are those who believe that representative democracy is a necessary but unsatisfactory system of government. Advocates of this school attempt to democratize representative government with devices such as the referendum, recall, and initiative. The second group, and this is by far the more influential in Canada, believes that democracy can only work through representation. Thus, this elitist school of democracy tends to fear the 'rule of the mob' and puts its trust in the leaders to prevent the degeneration of democratic rule into the tyranny of the masses.[4] Coupled with this almost paranoid fear of popular participation is the present stress of theorists and politicians alike on law, order, and stability.

Carole Pateman has recently drawn attention to two assumptions that provide much of the basis for the elitist theory of democracy. The first assumption is associated with the development of modern political sociology through the writings of Mosca and Michels and involves a belief that all social organizations tend towards oligarchy. The second assumption involves an interpretation whereby participation of the 'masses' in the politics of the state leads to totalitarian regimes.[5] Studies which purport to show that the 'low socio-economic status groups' (the masses) exhibit widespread apathy and authoritarian attitudes rarely enquire why people are alienated, why they do not want to participate, and why authoritarian attitudes prevail among these groups. This political misuse of psychological and sociological data is inexcusable particularly since the more serious studies in this field clearly indicate that these 'antidemocratic attitudes' are directly related to the environment of the community or the workplace.[6]

These arguments for the necessity of elite rule which now pass for democratic theory are little more than the theoretical formulations of the status-quo in the Anglo-American democracies. Democracy is no longer an ideal to be striven for, and constantly in need of creation; it has been reduced to a justification of what is.

What is the nature of elite rule in Canada? John Porter's analysis of class and power in Canada was the first major study to come to grips with the realities of the elitist institutional orders of Canadian society.[7] His general conclusion shatters the liberal notion of Canada as a citizen-participating democracy. Democracy is absent and elites are, by and large, not open to recruitment from outside their own ranks. The ruling classes in Canada are basically the parties of 'corporations, the real estate lobbies, and the rich,'[8] in short, those parties that control what George Grant calls the 'private governments (that is, the corporations) and those that control the public government which co-ordinates the activities of these corporations.'[9]

While one of the major political myths of our age is the elitist argument that democracy is safeguarded by competition among elites, an equally influential assumption is the assertion that vigorous local associations, professional bodies, and other voluntary associations provide the opportunity for ordinary men and women to participate in their self-government.[10] As Porter and others have pointed out, such associations and organizations are no more democratic than our national and provincial parliaments. They are effectively governed by elites which are in most cases indistinguishable in their make-up and their policies from the larger national elites.[11] The argument of the pluralists that the bargaining among such voluntary organizations culminates 'roughly' in the public interest, is open to another criticism, namely that all interests are not equally represented in the bargaining arena. Real competition takes place between a relatively small number of powerful groups and associations. The bargaining power of consumers, welfare recipients, Indians and Eskimos, and most workers and employees is no match for that of big business, private developers, and government bureaucracies.

These 'democratic' processes reflect the relations between income, wealth, and power in capitalist Canada. Porter has pointed out that these relations are based on the existence of class divisions, which not only exist in Canada 'but stand in the way of implementating one of the most important values of western society, that is, equality ... The structure of power reflects the structure of class, for class determines the routes and barriers to advancement up our institutional hierarchies. Power is used to perpetuate a given structure of class.'[12]

Class relationships in a capitalist society are based upon the existence of private property and it is clearly absurd to even think in terms of real democracy, accountability, and equality in a society based on institutions and political processes which are dominated by private property. As C.B. Macpherson has remarked, 'the market ... does not maximize utilities equitably according to work. Nor does it maximize equitably according to need ...'[13] As long as access to the means of life and labour is determined by the institutions of private property, no social or economic reforms can be expected to alter the fundamentally unequal distribution of wealth and power in Canada.[14]

In the light of these considerations, we must reject Dawson's praise for the parliamentary system of representation. A critical appreciation of the representative system must recognize the fact that it leads to the rule of the few over the many, the former having greater political power than those they represent. The influence of the voter is restricted to passing judgment, 'at fairly long intervals, upon the activities of the minority.'[15] Universal suffrage coupled with the representative system allows at best for an assessment of popular opinion on a number of issues. The very fragmentation and lack of permanent organization of the electors means that they cannot impose their will on their representatives.

The form and structures of representative democracy are being maintained to 'stabilize power.' One influential critic of parliamentary democracy has pointed out what would seem to be the main political purpose of maintaining the institutions of representative democracy. He argues that the people, who believe in genuine democracy, 'are neutralized through an institution which gives the illusion of participation.'[16]

Canadians are asked to view the House of Commons as the organized medium through which the public exercises its ultimate political power. It has in the meantime become part of the conventional wisdom that decisions are made by the cabinet and then, with the aid of the party whip, rubber-stamped by a majority in the House of Commons. An indication of the acceptance of this view is the fact that it is no longer restricted to critical academics but has found its place in the more serious columns of our daily press. Anthony Westell says that it is in the cabinet, 'where the executive decisions are made, and the caucus room where the members of the majority party review those decisions and pledge their support.' He continues by stating that 'what goes on in the House of Commons is mostly play-acting. The chamber is a political theatre rather than a forum for debate and decisions.' Westell goes on to point out some of the undemocratic realities of our parliamentary system. The daily question period, he argues, is a 'performance by actors on both sides, simulating alarm, anger and outrage, between knowing smiles, to win the applause of the public.' Conclusions to debates are predetermined by the fact that the government can count on the support of the majority in the House. He concludes that 'in effect, we elect a dictatorship at each general election, a prime minister and his cabinet commanding enough support to impose their will on Parliament and the public.'[17]

The elitist character of the representative system is clearly visible in the recruitment and background of MPs. Recruitment of candidates is controlled by political parties. These individuals who are supposed to 'represent' the

Canadian voter are essentially drawn from the upper social strata of Canadian society. Canadian MPs tend to be members of a profession, usually law. A study of the 25th Parliament shows that although lawyers constitute only a fraction of 1 per cent of the population, they made up 33 per cent of MPs.[18] Porter, in his study of the *political elite* in Canada (federal cabinet ministers, provincial premiers, and senior judiciary) concludes that 64 per cent of this group were lawyers. Even if we remove the judiciary, who must be lawyers, the percentage remains very high, which leads Porter to state the obvious: 'the political elite in Canada is not representative of the population which it leads.'[19]

Businessmen, both self-employed and corporate executives, are also over-represented. In Kornberg's sample of the 25th Parliament 76 per cent were in business or were members of the professions, 'while only 18 per cent of the Canadian population (ages 25-64) of 1961 were so employed.'[20]

We have travelled a long way from the time when *representation* was a concept worth fighting for. Today, in Canada, it has become a thinly veiled, routinized rule by the capitalist elite of North America. The entire complex of liberal institutions, the ostensible purpose of which was to safeguard the democratic tradition, has become a gigantic hoax. The practical application of the elitist theory of democracy is the rule by an elite – the democratic element turns out to be of peripheral significance in the actual decision-making process.

POLITICAL PARTIES AND DEMOCRATIC ELITISM

A political party is founded to insure not freedom in general, only its own freedom to attain power. To attain this goal the party has to be organized. The political apparatus which is developed and the professional politicians who come to dominate political parties are tied up with the economic elite, with the result that the fragmented citizenry is left without any real influence in the functioning of the state. The only legitimate channel for political participation by an individual is the political party, which is dominated by a professional clique and firmly anchored to the economic elite.

The elitist nature of political parties as well as other unpleasant by-products of the party system, are sometimes explained away in terms that are identical with the attitudes of the elitist theorists. This is what J.A. Corry has to say:

It is true that a small group of leaders tries to control the party, but that is a general feature of all human organization, not limited to political parties ... The parties do not frustrate the will of the people, because it is only rarely that even a transient majority of the people is genuinely of one mind about a specific political problem. The parties deceive the public, but so do propagandists of every kind. The deception does not often arise from cynicism but rather from zest for the game itself, a general human trait. It may be said generally in conclusion that the evils in the party system are not peculiar to it but are the outcome of general human frailties. Indeed, it is hard to see how the parties that must woo the electorate with success can do other than reflect its virtues and its vices. Perhaps it is people as much as institutions that need to be reformed.[21]

Corry justifies the existence of political parties by arguing that they are essential, 'as long as we adhere to the rule that ultimate power rests with a diffused electorate.' Political parties, he continues, make peaceful change of government possible, 'and thus eliminate the necessity for the armed coup d'etat as a means of changing government, and the counter necessity of ruling by force and terror to prevent such a coup d'etat.'[22] Nazi Germany and the Soviet Union are cited by Corry to illustrate what is in store for us if we abandon our cherished party system. In short, Corry, when focusing on political parties, emphasizes those very traits and techniques of argument that Carol Pateman exposed as characteristic of the elitist theory of democracy.

Anthony Downs has pointed out in his *An Economic Theory of Democracy* that '... parties in democratic politics are analogous to entrepreneurs in a profit-seeking economy. So as to attain their private ends, they formulate whatever policies they believe will gain the more votes, just as entrepreneurs produce whatever products they believe will gain the most profits for the same reason.'[23] The comparison is, of course, no coincidence. Since the Canadian party system serves the economic elite rather well, it is, we may say, its political arm. It has been said many times before but needs repeating: *the modern party system is a direct consequence of the requirements of capitalist democracy.*[24] The attempt to rationalize the shocking behaviour of our political parties by putting all the blame on general human traits and frailties of people is an idiotic statement which confuses human nature with human behaviour, the latter being very much influenced, if not determined, by the institutions, including political parties, of a given society.

Given the nature of our political parties and the power of the local and national party organization in the nomination of candidates, as well as the power of the parties to discipline their MPs, the lack of choice available to the voter should not surprise us. As one critic has pointed out: 'the difference between candidates can only be as significant as the difference between those who *select* the candidates. The interests to which candidates owe allegiance cannot extend beyond the range of interests of their benefactors.'[25]

Both major political parties in Canada are wedded to corporate interests. Elections are not the mechanism by which people impose their will on the rulers; they are, on the contrary, confirmations of the power of the ruling elite. Elections are not autonomous elements to decide on policies; they only ratify the existing power relationships in Canada which are the result of a political game which has been played outside the parliamentary process.

The real centres of power are located outside of parliament and are not subject to the voter's influence at elections. They remain constant whatever party is in power. If we were allowed to vote for those who actually control Canada (for example, the directors of corporations, financial institutions, and those who own and control the multinational, largely American, corporations) the phony nature of parliamentary politics would be more easily exposed for all to see. As it is, the voter is left with no choice but to support one of the competing parties. Since the difference between the parties is largely one of management rather than policy it is little wonder that we witness a crisis of confidence in the parliamentary system. This does not mean that these differences that characterize our political parties are meaningless or not worth voting for, but it does mean that the political system has no legitimized avenues for bringing about fundamental social change in Canada.

Agnoli sums up the function of the parliamentary system as follows: 'The Parliament is neither master of the people nor law-maker representing the people. It functions more as an acceptable and constitutional instrument for the publication of resolutions which have come about through the cooperation of the state apparatus and social power groupings. It functions as a transmission belt for the decisions of oligarchic groups. These (the oligarchies of both economic and cultural groups, the churches, for example) find themselves *well* represented. In this sense Parliament works and functions as representation of the power structure, and only as such, is it acceptable to bourgeois-capitalist society. Elsewhere, where a drive for emancipation breaks in, the ruling class makes use of stronger means, as, for example, in Greece.'[26]

The fundamental justification of the multiparty system is the argument that it ensures political freedom. We are told that the very existence of an opposition party defines our political system as a democracy. Since it has become increasingly difficult to prove that our governments are in any real sense accountable to the electorate, the accent of the defenders of our elitist system now rests on the existence of an opposition. We are told that we have a choice – we can vote for this party or that, and we can replace one government by another if we are dissatisfied with its performance. Thus one of the cornerstones of democracy – the principle of accountability – has been replaced by the more-or-less meaningless slogan that the existence of an opposition party guarantees the maintenance of the democratic system.

The implementation of consensus politics so necessary for the functioning of our political system does not rest solely on the close ties between the professional politicians of our political parties and the economic elite; it is further strengthened by internal organizational mechanisms which have become an important part of our party system. A characteristic common to bureaucratic systems, but particularly prevelant within our political parties, is the development of mechanisms for reducing internal conflict. Cleavages within a bureaucratic system impair its effectiveness in competition with other systems. Conflicts, particularly those originating from competing ideas and policies, are met basically by compromises and mutual concessions, and by 'not permitting all of the dissident voices representation in decision-making.' This process applies not only to national bureaucracies but also to local governmental and private ones. Daniel Katz describes this process convincingly. 'The general pattern for conflict reduction is the narrowing of channels for their expression so that many divergent views are reconciled or silenced at lower levels in the structure. A small unit has to resolve differences among members so that it speaks with one voice in its own subsystem, the unit differences have to be compromised so that the subsystem represents but one position to the higher levels in the structure. This pattern means that many conflicts are handled at lower levels ... The example par excellence of this pattern is the two-party system. By the time the wishes of the many interest and factional groups have been filtered up through the hierarchical structure, the party line is not far from dead center.'[27]

Many citizen groups have experienced the conflict reduction mechanism at one time or another in political parties at the local level, with service agencies, social planning councils, or other governmental and non-governmental bureaucracies. It is important to remember in this context that leadership of low-income protest groups is largely composed of people outside the basic power structure of the society. This factor further weakens their influence in the kind of process described above. Katz concludes by stating that the 'structure is built to accommodate conflict, to mute its expression and to redefine clashing positions on clearcut issues as moderate stands on ambiguous generalities.'[28]

Consensus politics, administered through parliamentary institutions, is an essential part of capitalist rule in Canada. Political socialization to this end pervades our entire social order. The liberal ethic of middle-of-the-road 'objectivity' is illustrated in a school textbook authorized for use in the province of Ontario under the caption, 'Moderates who stand near the centre are usually those who think over a problem calmly and carefully.' The middle-of-the-road position is taught as the ideal position on *all* controversial matters, including such issues as prejudice, discrimination, persecution, and human rights. The following textbook lesson, under the above-mentioned caption, illustrates this point. 'In most school debates you can divide your class into two camps very clearly. Try it on one of these topics: (*a*) Children should have homework; (*b*) Mixed classes make the best classes. Did you find that some students gave a quick, loud, decided "Yes," and others voted a quick, firm decided "No"? We call people like those "Extremists"; if you were trying to place them on a blackboard chart, they would go at the *extreme* opposite ends. Do you find that some of your classmates see points on both sides? We call them "Moderates." '[29]

What needs to be said in relation to the entire process and purpose of political socialization in Western political systems has been stated very clearly by Ralph Miliband who argues that '... the process is intended, in these regimes, to foster acceptance of a *capitalist* social order and of its values, an adaptation to its requirements, a rejection of alternatives to it; in short, that what is involved here is very largely a process of massive *indoctrination.*'[30]

Another significant weapon in the armory of the ruling elite is the use of their power in preventing the raising of issues which might challenge the status quo. In other words, power can be reflected in so called *nondecisions.* This particular method of manipulation of the democratic process is described by two social scientists in the following words: 'a nondecision, as we define it, is a decision that results in suppression or thwarting of a latent or manifest challenge to the values or interests of the decision maker. To be more nearly explicit, nondecision-making is a means by which demands for change in the existing allocation of benefits and privileges in the community can be suffocated before they are even voiced; or kept covert; or killed before they gain access to the relevant decision-making arena; or, failing all these things, maimed or destroyed in the decision-implementing stage of the political process.'[31]

What the Canadian party system, as it now operates, has accomplished is to fragment and to emasculate existent or latent class opposition and to incorporate this opposition into parliamentary party channels.

PARLIAMENTARY SOCIAL DEMOCRATIC PARTIES:
POSSIBILITIES AND LIMITATIONS

Given the nature of the institutions of representative government, particularly Parliament, elections, and political parties, what are the possibilities and limitations of political action for a parliamentary social democratic party such as the NDP in Canadian politics? Perhaps the most relevant criticisms of involvement in parliamentary politics were made by Georg Lukacs in 1920 when he criticized the German Communist party (KPD) for advocating participation in elections.[32] A number of points relevant to the function of the NDP in Canadian politics emerge from the position stated by Lukacs. We may summarize them briefly as follows:

1 / The German Communist party (in 1919-20) could still be considered a revolutionary party, a claim which is admittedly difficult to apply to the NDP.

2 / In referring to parliamentary politics as a question of tactics, Lukacs points out that, 'tactics are the practical application of theoretically established principles.'[33] They form the link between the final goal and the immediate given reality and are therefore determined by both.

3 / In a non-revolutionary situation, the proletariat often finds itself on the defensive vis-à-vis the bourgeoisie. Parliament, which must be viewed as an instrument of the bourgeoisie, can only be used as a defensive weapon in the class struggle. To take up parliamentary activity implies 'the realization and admission that revolution is unthinkable in the foreseeable future.'[34]

4 / The twin dangers of losing sight of one's revolutionary goal and of being co-opted by the system of bourgeois parliamentary politics are always present.

5 / Since, however, parliamentary activity is necessary in given historical situations, it must at all times be completely and absolutely subject to extra-parliamentary leadership.

6 / Theoretically and practically, whenever extra-parliamentary action is possible (for example, workers' councils) parliamentarianism is redundant.

The history of communist and socialist parties in the capitalist West provides ample proof that the dangers Lukacs refers to are indeed real. If we now turn to social democratic parties that are not in power – such as the NDP – we are confronted with political manoeuvring without any clear theoretical formulation of goals, without a revolutionary strategy and with tactics which are dominated largely by the given framework of capitalist politics. The likelihood that such a party will ever be able to transcend the elitist system of bourgeoisie democracy is, I would argue, extremely slim.[35]

The record of socialist or social-democratic parties in power is no less disturbing and has rarely gone beyond piecemeal reform compatible with the maintenance of capitalist rule.[36] The function of social-democratic governments, like that of all elected governments, is to guarantee and defend the existing socio-economic system including its constitutional super-structure. The contradiction between the desire for revolutionary change (if it is present) and the maintenance of 'law and order' is in practice always resolved in favour of the latter. It must also be recognized that the separation between the party and the masses as well as between party membership and its leaders perpetuates some of the worst manifestations of bourgeois democracy. It is elitist and undemocratic (that is, the people are 'represented' by leaders); it maintains the alienation of both the masses and the party members; and it facilitates the process of co-optation of the leadership into the bourgeois parliamentary system.

We must therefore view social democratic parties as weapons for immediate and realizable reforms (within the limits set by the capitalist system) and as defensive tools for the protection of the underprivileged. These are essential and important tasks but they are severely limited. To look at social democratic parties as agents of fundamental social change leading to a democratic socialist society based on self-government is not only unsound, it is also dangerous. It directs any emerging class struggle into 'safe' and reformist parliamentary channels.

Gad Horowitz has recently advocated 'the democratic class struggle' as an answer to the present dilemma of social democratic parties in the capitalist West.[37] His proposal is of direct relevance to the subject under discussion here. It is based on the following assumptions:

1 / Some form of elite rule is probably inevitable in a modern industrial society. Rule by politicians comes closest to democracy since politicians are most sensitive to the needs of the people.

2 / Thus a satisfactory approximation to 'utopian' democracy (that is, rule by the people) is a system where the people act through their elected political leaders (representative democracy).

3 / Apart from the question of whether people do act through their elected representatives (Horowitz is not at all certain of that) he realizes that most of the important political decisions (decisions pertaining to policy) are not in fact made by our political leaders. We therefore have not even achieved a 'satisfactory approximation of rule by politicians.'

The *democratic class struggle* will be lead, according to Horowitz, by a powerful party of the 'left.' This party will be responsive to the needs of the underprivileged and it will be successful in mobilizing popular support for programs of social change. The role of such a left party will be, 'to agitate – to train the masses to be discontented with their lot, to maximize their demands, to get what they want.'[38]

One can criticize this proposal on many grounds. At this point I shall simply discuss briefly some of the contradictions and weaknesses of the approach taken by Horowitz. Horowitz sees the democratic class struggle being waged by a party of the left which would agitate and maximize the demands of the underprivileged to get what they want. At the same time he sees the democratic class struggle as being carried on 'within the framework of a broad integrating consensus; it is not a class war.'[39] I find this proposal to be highly disturbing. Translated into practice the scenario would likely run as follows: The left party would agitate and maximize essentially anti-capitalist demands. In order not to endanger the underlying consensus these demands must not be pressed 'past the point of obvious impracticability.' What else can that mean other than that these anti-capitalist demands would be directed into reformist channels within the limits set by the capitalist system. The difference between the proposal and the present role of the NDP would seem to be largely one of degree. We cannot envisage how one can conduct a class struggle within the limits proposed by Horowitz.

There is another assumption made by Horowitz which must not be left unchallenged. He assumes that, 'the masses are seldom capable of expressing autonomously their need for power ...'[40] Hence the necessity of a party of the left. The recent history of mass action by workers and students in Italy, the spread of plant occupations in Britain, the emerging direct action by workers and citizen groups in Quebec and the uprising in France in 1968 – these and many more are indications which refute the pessimism displayed by Horowitz. Clearly the lesson for radicals is that the antagonisms inherent in our capitalist class system should never be institutionalized. Given the current and past performance of political parties of the left within the capitalist West, we would argue that the proposal by Horowitz would soon lead to an institutionalization and subsequent emasculation of class conflict.

PARLIAMENTARY OR EXTRA-PARLIAMENTARY POLITICS AND SOCIALIST DEMOCRACY

Supporters of the parliamentary system (including liberals as well as social democrats) would agree substantially with advocates of a participatory socialist democracy in the desirability of freedom, equality and fraternity as paramount values of a democratic system. One should, however, be aware that these principles can be taken in different directions. While liberals and social democrats regard freedom as the choice between candidates, jobs and schools; advocates of socialist democracy would generally argue 'that the essence of freedom is inextricably linked to the ability to democratically control not only candidates, but also jobs, schools, and other major areas of choice.'[41] For liberals and social democrats, discussion of freedom is focused not on democracy but on the concept of pluralism.

While liberals, and to a lesser extent social democrats, emphasize equality of opportunity, socialists are concerned with *de facto* equality, insisting that the political system must redistribute wealth and power between classes, regions, and by other relevant criteria. Equality of opportunity within a capitalist framework is an empty slogan voiced by liberal humanists who oppose 'inequality' but refuse to locate its sources in the social structure. In contrast to a stress on the inadequacies of the individual, socialists seek the source of personal troubles in the social system.

The principles of socialist democracy lead naturally to a participative political structure based on self-managing and self-governing local units. While there is little clarity as to how such units in the workplace and the neighbourhood would be linked to the political superstructure of the society, the principle of direct representation of micro groups on regional and national levels of the political process is an essential element of a participative socialist democracy. Representativeness would thus be achieved through multiple, direct representation.[42]

Functional representation, albeit within a capitalist framework, as a means of correcting some of the undemocratic features of the parliamentary system based on party politics, was practised with some initial success by the United Farmers of Alberta (UFA) during the early part of this century. The UFA critique of the party system is summarized by C.B. Macpherson as follows: 'the worth of any method of political organization is to be tested by its efficiency as an instrument for hastening the destruction of the competitive social order; the old party system is a method of maintaining that order by dividing, confusing, and ruling the masses, the old parties being subservient to the moneyed interests; no new party, however democratically begun, can be an adequate instrument for social change, since a party as such is conglomerate, unstable, lacking in principle, and undemocratic. The farmers as an organized democratic force seeking a new social order must therefore reject party organization.'[43]

The UFA saw our party structure to be inconsistent with democratic control of elected members. In having to appeal to the 'general interest' of the entire population, parties necessarily cease to be guided by any principle other than the drive for power (that is, the full control of the state). The UFA advocated the replacement of the party system by the political mobilization of economic classes (that is, functional representation by occupation or industrial groups). The theory of group government which they developed was seen to solve the problems of accountability of the elected member to his or her constituents, which the UFA viewed as the essence of the democratic process.[44]

One of the much neglected lessons of history was stated succinctly by Martin Buber in his *Paths in Utopia* where he wrote that 'the hour of revolution is not an hour of begetting but an hour of birth – provided there was a begetting beforehand.' This message applies as much to the need to clarify and test the theoretical foundations of a socialist union of the future as it does to the practical task of preparing ourselves to meet the challenge of the future socialist democracy based on self-government and self-management. While it is possible, although difficult, to imagine a situation in which a socialist political party would win power within our present bourgeois parliamentary system, it is impossible to visualize how such a process would prepare us to undertake the difficult task of 'governing ourselves.' We would argue that 'socialism from below' cannot be achieved through political parties as they now exist.

The recent crisis in Italy, erupting during 1968 in a series of industrial conflicts and culminating in what has been called 'the hot autumn of 1969,' provides an illustration of extra-parliamentary action *involving* workers in an anti-capitalist struggle in a manner political parties would find difficult to duplicate. One of the issues which originated with the rank-and-file and which saw unions and managements locked in a long conflict was the issue centring around job qualifications and categories. This struggle — which went on most notably at Fiat and Italsider — aimed not only at reducing the wide spectrum of job classifications, but also at radically questioning management's criteria for such classifications as well as the criteria for promotion from one category to another. In the various plants where this struggle went on, the workers undertook to narrow the range of existing categories and to prevent the introduction of new technology from affecting the content of their jobs. At Italsider, in particular, the workers succeeded in narrowing the range of categories for workers and clerical employees from thirty-one categories to eight. The tactics pursued by the workers in this conflict, coupled with their degree of militancy, has led many observers to suggest that the underlying implication of this struggle was the workers sharp rejection of the capitalist criteria of division and organization of work. As one of the leaders of the FIOM-CGIL metal workers union put it: the workers struggle 'for a new policy of job classification — which must link directly the struggle against wage disparity to the struggle for a different organization of work — is the first step towards the goal of workers social control over the production process.'[45]

This reinforces certain lessons drawn from the May 1968 events in France. The most important perhaps is that these and similar less spectacular events elsewhere refute the notion about the integration of the working class in capitalist countries. The events in France show that it was not the working class which was integrated but the political and trade-union organizations which speak in the name of the working class. The events in France, Italy, and elsewhere thus demand a fresh look at the relation between spontaneity and organization in the revolutionary process. These events have shown that small, almost unorganized groups, drawing their support from work-place, university, and community, can play the role of revolutionary catalysts.

The possibility and importance of developing workplace-based political consciousness, which allied with politically conscious elements within citizen groups can turn militancy into politically radical action for change, has been recently advocated in Canada by a number of activists. Rick Deaton, an official of the Canadian Union of Public Employees has described the revolt of the public employees which derives at least in part from a distaste for the kind of duties they have to perform. They have become 'dirty workers,' engaged in clearing up or controlling society's problems. 'The public employee who is a dirty worker has become a zoo keeper and is engaged in a social control function. Social workers, prison guards, garbagemen, teachers and employees in Homes for the Aged are employed to keep our social misfits, inconveniences and undesirables off the streets and out of sight. We have created an entirely new type of worker — one whose job it is to hide and control our society's failures.'[46]

He concludes his analysis of the fiscal crisis and the position of public employees by arguing that the latter will be pushed into action 'not because they want to but because they will have to. Building *political* alliances between workers in the public sector and users of social public services is a necessity. Putting forward *qualitative* collective bargaining demands which affect both groups — workers and users — is a necessary prerequisite to building these alliances. These political alliances are critically necessary to strengthen trade union action in the public sector ...'[47]

In Quebec, politicization of trade union action, frequently in cooperation with citizen groups, has developed further than anywhere else in Canada. Quebec represents one of the rare instances where nationalism and socialism have merged within important sections of the labour movement to produce an emerging mass movement based to a significant extent on libertarian socialist values and strategies.

The manifestoes of the major trade union federations, originally published as study papers in 1971, constitute a milestone in the development of Marxist working class thinking in Quebec. The Confederation of National Trade Unions (CNTU), which has been in the forefront of this struggle, has been involved in political action since as early as 1962. In 1966, the CNTU published a document entitled, 'A Society built for Man,' which called for industrial democracy at the workplace. This was followed in 1968 with a new policy statement on 'The Second Front' which situated the worker both as a producer and consumer and linked the membership of the CNTU with the growing number of citizen committees in Quebec. Part three of the 1971 CNTU manifesto defines socialism clearly in terms of workers' control by demanding that, 'workers participate directly and collectively in the management of industry and the economy and in setting economic priorities ...'[48]

It is of considerable importance to note that the growing demand for a participatory democracy has been understood by at least one prominent social scientist in North America. Robert Dahl, until recently one of the staunchest defenders of the elitist theory of democracy, has now put forward what at first glance appears to be a blueprint for revolutionary change in the United States. Dahl now admits that power can only be legitimate, 'if it issues from fully democratic processes.' This compels us, he argues, 'to reconsider the foundations of authority.' Dahl, in a sense, reaches back to the notion that democracy, which has never been fully achieved, 'has always been and is now potentially a revolutionary doctrine.'[49]

In order to change the present uneven distribution of political influence, Dahl proposes a system of self-management which would encompass all institutions in society such as political parties, economic institutions, universities, trade unions, etc.

The political genius of the author lies in the fact that he argues for the introduction of full self-management without upsetting the capitalist economic system (that is, the private ownership of capital). Using the example of a large corporation, Dahl isolates three broad categories of control. Internal controls exercised by those who manage the enterprise, economic controls of the market, and governmental controls. The latter two categories of controls would remain while the internal control would pass into the hands of those working in a given enterprise. Employees would simply elect a board of directors which in turn would appoint competent managers. Management, after all, has become increasingly professional and is 'therefore available for hire.' Dahl sees no difficulties in this transformation and argues that it would effectively put power into the hands of employees (ownership, according to the author, is already now effectively split off from management).

We need not be concerned with the details of Dahl's proposal. He has borrowed freely from some of the classical democratic theorists, from the Swedish model of 'functional democracy,' as well as from the Yugoslav experience. In developing his theoretical rescue operation of bourgeois democracy he has been careful to leave the private ownership of capital intact. We are thus confronted by what could be termed the most far-reaching extension of management's human relations approach, which the author extends to the macro level of the political process.

One can thus readily envisage a socio-economic system which would maintain present inequalities in wealth, income, and political power while *permitting* an increased degree of participatory democracy at the micro levels of the system. Dahl simply accepts the notion without any attempt at proof that government and management are neither influenced nor controlled by the owners of capital.

CONCLUSION

Returning to Canada, we are faced with the following situation. John Porter
is probably correct when he argues that the elite, as well as the mass of the
population in Canada, is characterised by conservatism to a greater degree
than in the United States.[50] We should add to this the statistical fact that
most Canadians know perfectly well that the real power is located in the
boardrooms of corporations and not in Parliament.[51] Also, a recent study
conducted in 1968 has shown that 75 per cent of the respondents perceived
voting as the only way people can have any influence on the way the government runs the country.[52]

The paradox is of course not unexpected. The parliamentary route to
social change is the only one we know from experience. It might be useful to
remember that political parties and the representative system as we know it
today have not always existed. Political parties, to all practical purposes,
appeared parallel to the rise of the bourgeoisie, which organized its parties in
the struggle to defeat feudalism. Parties will end in time just as they began.

It is not my purpose to offer blueprints on strategy; nor is it my intention
to build a model of a future socialist society. It would seem, however, that
the critique of existing institutions and politics permits us to eliminate certain
strategies and policies as unworkable or undemocratic.

If the parliamentary system has certain inherent qualities which divide the
people into rulers and ruled, we should look to different methods of representation and accountability.

If geographical representation fragments the electorate and thus lends
itself to the rule of organized elites over the unorganized mass, we should
begin to think in terms of an organizational and electoral base which unites
the people without the need of geographically based political parties.

If emancipation from above is recognized for what it is — namely permanent promise held out by the ruling elite 'to keep the people looking
upward for protection, instead of to themselves for liberation from the need
for protection,' then we must seek ways and means of strengthening the
experiences of direct democracy. Freedom and equality cannot be legislated,
and cannot be administered by 'representatives.' Freedom and equality must
be taken.

If socialist self-government can only exist if it embraces all parts of society, then the 'politics of self-government' must permeate every institution
and organization in society. We would particularly stress the importance of
breaking down the authoritarian decision-making structures in the workplace.
As G.D.H. Cole once said: 'A servile system in industry inevitably reflects
itself in political servility.'

The point made by Cole would seem to be obvious and struggles for workers' control and self-management have been central to many socialist and anarchist struggles of the past. Demands for participatory democracy today fall essentially within this tradition. It is only recently, however that social scientists have begun to be concerned with the effects of the job on the activities of the workers in their leisure time. A recently completed study by Martin Meissner of the University of British Columbia comes to conclusions which are of crucial importance to anyone concerned with radical social change.[53]

Meissner has attempted to discover what effect work in a factory has on an employee's life away from work? The data for his analysis is drawn from a sample of 206 industrial workers in an industrial community on Vancouver Island. The sample was restricted to workers of a large wood-products manufacturing company with a number of integrated operations in the community. The sample was further restricted to male union members below the level of foreman. Three possible relations betwen work and leisure are considered: (1) workers *compensate* for the constraints[54] or lack of discretion and social isolation of the job in their free time; (2) the experience of constraint and isolation *carries over* into free time; (3) life away from work is unaffected by the job.

Meissner was particularly interested in studying the effects of technical constraints on participation in voluntary organizations. The findings clearly favour a 'carry-over' hypothesis. The study shows that workers who have a chance for social interaction on the job participate more in voluntary organizations. Similarly, work with little discretionary potential results in reduced workers participation in formally organized activities.

The importance of Meissner's conclusion would seem to be obvious. He states: 'The design of industrial work creates or prevents opportunities for the development or maintenance of discretionary and social skills. When choice of action is suppressed by the spatial, temporal, and functional constraints of the work process worker capacity for meeting the demands of spare-time activities which require discretion is reduced. They engage less in those activities which necessitate planning, coordination, and purposeful action, but increase the time spent in sociable and expressive activities.'[55]

Management has frequently argued that workers will (and should) compensate for alienating and frustrating work by enriching their leisure activities. Unions, by concentrating on financial rewards, have until recently encouraged this trend. The above evidence by Meissner confirms what socialists have long argued. To quote C.B. Macpherson' 'This kind of calculation ... overlooks the unreality of dividing a single human being's activities into two separate parts as if they had no effect on each other. Such a calculation not only separates analytically, productive and extra-productive uses of capacities, but treats them as independent variables. It sets up two profit-and-loss accounts, one for each of the two departments, into which the operations of the maximizing individual (now dividual) are separated, and adds them together to get a net profit and loss.'[56]

It has been noted above that the core of the prevailing elitist theory of democracy is the presumption of the average citizen's incapacity to govern himself. Apathy and political 'incompetence' are seen to be essential ingredients for the maintenance of our stable democratic system. One should not therefore be too surprised if the struggle of workers for democracy and ultimately self-management within the workplace meets with the solid opposition of the owners and managers of corporations and institutions in our society.

The artificial separation of politics from everyday life is one of the means of perpetuating the political emasculation of citizens. The stress on political parties as the only legitimate avenue for political participation ignores, as we have pointed out, so-called 'non-political' areas of life such as the corporations and institutions within which most Canadians spend the bulk of their waking hours. It also ignores the entire voluntary sector with its thousands of organizations and associations. Our elitist system functions best if all the various competing organizations and institutions are hierarchically structured and led by 'responsible' elites. Elite accommodation thus becomes the dynamic by which we are ruled and governed. If elite rule in one of the important links in the system, such as industry were to be broken (that is, if the workers were to demand and achieve control and self-management of their workplace) the entire system of elite accommodation would begin to crumble.[57]

As long as 'legitimate' political participation is restricted to political parties and the electoral process and political power is shared by the interlocking elites of parties and corporate interests, politics will remain an 'alienated force.'

Since bourgeois democracy excludes democracy from the basic cells of everyday life, the workplace and the community, and since nationalization, state socialism, does not by itself bring about social self-government, it would seem to follow that demands by the left for nationalization must be coupled with massive attempts to introduce self-government at the *micro and macro level*. Social self-government which is restricted to the micro-level will not only leave ultimate power in the hands of national elites and their bureaucracies, it may, furthermore, degenerate into a system based on autonomous, competitive groups which could exploit and threaten each other as well as society as a whole.

Attempts to overcome the elitist characteristics of the representative model of democracy have frequently led to experiments with some form of functional or occupational representation. The advantages of this form of representation in comparison to the representative model can be summarized as follows:

The unorganized and fragmented electorate under the representative model is replaced by an electorate which is drawn from occupational and other functional or interest groups which can be expected to have greater social cohesiveness as constituencies.

The members of such functional constituencies are directly represented by elected and recallable delegates, thus eliminating the brokerage function of political parties. Representative bodies thus elected would be composed of a majority of delegates who retain their firm links (that is, their jobs) within their self-managing structures. They would leave jobs only when the assembly sits. The number, function, and power of professional politicians would thus be sharply curbed and politics as a separate and professionalized sphere of social decision-making would be partly overcome through the 'socialization of politics.'[58]

Elected and recallable delegates may actually begin to represent the interests of their constituents in a more meaningful way than presently possible within the representative parliamentary model.

The necessity (of political parties) to appeal to a wide variety of frequently conflicting interests leads to the dilution of party programs (see the discussion on the conflict-absorption mechanism above) so that their stated goals become ambiguous and devoid of any political substance. The functional model would allow the formulation of clear-cut policies. Conflicting policies of diverse functional groups would, instead of being suppressed, emerge in the open.

To the extent that it is possible in complex industrial societies, decision-making power will be brought down to the level of the individual within functionally or occupationally oriented collectives.

In terms of developing an effective strategy we are convinced that, whatever the mix of parliamentary and extra-parliamentary action may be, the struggle within the workplace would seem to be of crucial importance for at least three reasons: (1) it attacks capitalist power at its source (the parliamentary struggle does not); (2) if successful, it will avoid the worst manifestations of state socialism; (3) since individual self-fulfilment depends (at least partly) on the elimination of traditional authoritarian hierarchies within the corporations and institutions of our society, the struggle within these structures is of concern to every working individual, regardless of his or her political affiliation.

Participation in politics in any country has two aspects. One refers to the channels through which citizens exert real influence or control over decisions affecting them. In the second, participation is an instrument through which a regime enlists support for itself and its policies and attempts to create social solidarity through a sense of involvement. The first is real participation from below, the second, manipulative participation from above. All existing systems exhibit both forms of participation. My argument is simply that the manipulative aspects of parliamentary electoral politics render this particular form of participation useless as means for real participation (control) from below.

NOTES

1 *Our Generation,* 8, no. 3, Part 2 (June 1972), editorial, 1
2 Robert MacGregor Dawson, *The Government of Canada* (Toronto, 2nd ed.), 357
3 Hanna F. Pitken, 'The Concept of Representation,' *Representation* ed. H.F. Pitken (New York, 1969), 7
4 Harold F. Gosnell, 'Pleasing the Constituents: Representative Democracy,' ibid., 116
5 *Participation and Democratic Theory,* Cambridge: Cambridge University Press, 1970, pp. 1-2.
6 See, for instance, Arthur Kornhauser, *Mental Health of the Industrial Worker: A Detroit Study,* New York: John Wiley & Sons, 1965. Charles Hampden-Turner, 'The Factory as an Oppressive and Non-Emancipating Environment,' Gerry Hunnius et al (eds.), *Workers' Control: A Reader on Labor and Social Change,* New York: Random House, 1973, pp. 30-45.
7 *The Vertical Mosaic* (Toronto, 1965)
8 Ian Adams et al., 'The Renegade Report on Poverty,' *The Last Post,* 1, no. 8 (1971), 3
9 *Lament for a Nation: The Defeat of Canadian Nationalism* (Toronto, 1965), 8
10 On this topic see the articles in this volume by Willmott and Hill.
11 See, for example, John McCready, 'Lucky Who? The United Community Fund of Great Toronto,' *Praxis Notes,* 1, no. 1 (1971), 14-20
12 *Vertical Mosaic,* 6. The situation in Canada is of course more complex since a very large proportion of our productive resources are owned by individuals and corporations in the United States. In a very real sense, American corporate capitalism is the major force shaping our society.
13 *Democratic Theory: Essays in Retrieval* (Oxford, 1973), 7
14 ibid., 120-1
15 T.B. Bottomore, *Elites and Society* (Harmondsworth, Eng. 1966), 116
16 Johannes Agnoli, 'Theses for the Transformation of Democracy,' *Our Generation,* 6, no. 4 (1969), 91
17 'Public Never Sees The Real Work of Government – MP,' *Toronto Daily Star,* 20 February 1971

18 Allan Kornberg, *Canadian Legislative Behaviour: A Study of the 25th Parliament* (New York, 1967), 43. Kornberg. concluded his study with the remark that, 'once a cohesion norm has been internalized completely, the Canadian M.P., with a few improvisions of his own plays the roles ascribed to him by his party' (p. 149).
19 *Vertical Mosaic*, 388
20 *Canadian Legislative Behaviour*, 44
21 *Democratic Government and Politics* (Toronto, 2nd ed. 1955), 230
22 Ibid., 231
23 (New York, 1957), 295
24 C.B. Macpherson, 'Address to the Third Congress of the International Political Science Association,' Stockholm, 1955, quoted by John Wilson, *The Meaning of Socialism; a Community of Friends* (Toronto, 1971), 18n
25 W. Fisher, 'Democracy and Social Change' Toronto, September 1969, 2 (mimeo)
26 Agnoli, 'Theses for the Transformation of Democracy,' 93
27 'Group Process and Social Integration: A Systems Analysis of Two Movements of Social Protest,' *The Journal of Social Issues,* XXIII, no. 1 (1967), 8
28 Ibid., 9
29 Garnet McDairmid and David Pratt, *Teaching Prejudice: A Content Analysis of Social Studies Textbooks Authorized for Use in Ontario,* The Ontario Institute for Studies in Education, Curriculum Series 12, Toronto 1971, p. 100.
30 *The State in Capitalist Society: an Analysis of the Western System of Power* (London, 1969), 182
31 Peter Bachrach and Morton S. Baratz, *Power and Poverty: Theory and Practice* (New York, 1970), 44. The various possible forms of nondecision-making are discussed by the authors on pp. 44-6.
32 *Political Writings 1919-1929: The Question of Parliamentarianism and Other Essays* (London, 1972), 53-63
33 Ibid., 54
34 Ibid., 55
35 See, for instance, Miliband, *The State in Capitalist Society,* 53. Miliband describes the dilemma of left opposition parties in parliament which are forced to cooperate to a certain extent with the government and are compelled to play according to rules which are not of their own choosing.
36 Miliband discusses in some detail of performance of social democratic leaders: ibid., 70-1 and 273-4.
37 'Toward the Democratic Class Struggle,' *Agenda 1970: Proposals for a Creative Politics,* ed. Trevor Lloyd and Jack McLeod (Toronto, 1968), 241-55.
38 Ibid., 244
39 Ibid.,
40 Ibid., 243
41 G. David Garson, 'On the Political Theory of Decentralized Socialism,' *Participation and Self-Management: First International Sociological Conference on Participation and Self-Management* (Zagreb, 1972), 84
42 Ibid., 85
43 *Democracy in Alberta: Social Credit and the Party System* (Toronto, 1970), 44
44 Ibid., 49
45 Excerpted from Bruno Ramirez, 'The Struggle for Workers' Control in Italy,' *Our Generation,* 8, no. 3, part 3, 13-19. See also *Italy: New Tactics and Organization,* I, no. 1 (Community Resource Centre, 3210 Sandwich Street, Windsor, Ontario)
46 'The Fiscal Crisis and the Public Employee,' *CUPE Journal* (June-July 1972), 7
47 Ibid., 8
48 Black Rose Editorial Collective, *Quebec Labour: The Confederation of National Trade Unions Yesterday and Today* (Montreal, 1972), 167. See also Daniel Drache, ed., *Quebec – Only the Beginning: The Manifestoes of the Common Front* (Toronto, 1972).

49 *After the Revolution? Authority in a Good Society* (New Haven, 1970), 4, 7
50 'The Canadian National Character in the Twentieth Century,' *Cultural Affairs* (Spring 1969), 50
51 Donald E. Willmott, 'Voluntary Associations in the Political Process,' prepared for the *Seminar on Voluntary Associations in the Political Process,* sponsored by the Canadian Association for Adult Education, Nov. 19-20, 1971, (mimeo), 22-4
52 George J. Szablowski, 'Policy Making, Bureaucracy and Social Change in the Ontario Government,' Toronto, 1972 (mimeo)
53 'The Long Arm of the Job: A Study of Work and Leisure,' *Industrial Relations,* 10, no. 3 (October 1971), 239-60
54 Three constraints are considered: time (work pacing); space (confinement to work location); function (task dependence and work type).
55 Meissner, 'The Long Arm of the Job,' 260
56 C.B. Macpherson, *Democratic Theory,* 68
57 See, for instance, R. Presthus, *Elite Accommodation in Canadian Politics* (Toronto, 1973).
58 See, for example, Zagorska Pesic-Golubovic, 'Socialist Ideas and Reality,' *Praxis* (International Edition), no. 3-4 (1971), 413.

Contributors

HOWARD ADELMAN teaches in the department of philosophy, Atkinson College, York University

MILDRED BAKAN teaches in the department of philosophy and the division of social science, York University

BARRY COOPER teaches in the department of political science, York University

MELVYN HILL teaches in the division of social science and the division of humanities, York University

GERRY HUNNIUS teaches in the department of social science, and the faculty of environmental studies, York University

ALKIS KONTOS teaches in the department of political economy, University of Toronto

BENTLEY LE BARON teaches in the department of political science, Brock University

WILLIAM LEISS teaches in the faculty of environmental studies, York University

JAMES D. ST JOHN is completing a doctoral dissertation in the department of political economy, University of Toronto, and is an administrative consultant

DAVID P. SHUGARMAN is a member of Bethune College and teaches in the department of political science, York University

JOAN WILLIAMS is a social worker and teaches philosophy at Centennial College

DONALD E. WILLMOTT teaches sociology at Glendon College, York University

Books by the University League for Social Reform

The Prospect of Change
Edited by Abraham Rotstein

Nationalism in Canada
Edited by Peter Russell

An Independent Foreign Policy for Canada?
Edited by Stephen Clarkson

Agenda 1970: proposals for a creative politics
Edited by Trevor Lloyd and Jack McLeod

Close the 49th Parallel etc: the Americanization of Canada
Edited by Ian Lumsden

The City: attacking modern myths
Edited by Alan Powell

Thinking about Change
Edited by David P. Shugarman

Domination
Edited by Alkis Kontos (forthcoming)